# CONTENTS

# CONTENTS

# Introduction

The demand for Farmhouse Kitchen recipes continues to grow. This omnibus edition contains over 400 recipes which we have produced since the series first began.

You will find we have grouped the recipes under the various chapter headings and also every recipe is in alphabetical order in the index at the back of the book. I hope you find as much pleasure and enjoyment from them as I have had in preparing them for you.

Best wishes

*Dorothy Sleightholme*

Dorothy Sleightholme is the Presenter of the Farmhouse Kitchen television programmes and has prepared all the dishes mentioned in this book, which are derived from her own and viewers' recommendations. The Publishers thank her for her help in the compilation of this publication.

# CHAPTER 1

# SOUPS, SAVOURIES, SALADS AND COLD MEATS

## DOROTHY SOUP

*2 lb. onions*
*1 lb. tomatoes or a 14 oz. tin of tomatoes*
*2 oz. butter*
*1½ pints water*
*1 good tablespoon medium oatmeal*
*Salt and pepper*
*1 level teaspoon sugar*

1. Chop onions finely.
2. Melt butter in saucepan, add onion and cook about 5 minutes until soft but not brown.
3. Wash and slice tomatoes and add to pan. Cook until both tomatoes and onions are very soft, stirring occasionally.
4. Pour on half of the water, bring to boil and put through a sieve. Or you can liquidise it and then sieve.
5. Meanwhile, rinse pan and boil oatmeal with remaining water for 10 minutes.
6. Add vegetable purée to oatmeal, season with salt, pepper and sugar. Simmer 20 minutes. Add more water if it is too thick. Taste and season again if necessary. Also good with a tablespoon of cream added, but do not let it boil again or it may curdle.

## MUSHROOM SOUP

*1 oz. butter*
*1 large onion, finely-chopped*
*1 oz. green pepper, finely-sliced and chopped*
*1 small clove of garlic, crushed*
*4 oz. mushrooms, chopped small*
*Salt and black pepper*
*2 dessertspoons flour*
*¾ pint chicken stock*
*¾ pint milk*
*Chopped parsley*

1. Melt butter in a heavy-based pan which has a lid. Fry onion, green pepper and garlic until beginning to soften but not going brown.
2. Add mushrooms and toss together over low heat. Add salt and pepper taking care not to over-salt if stock is well-seasoned.
3. Put lid on pan and leave on very low heat for 5 to 10 minutes so that vegetables "sweat". If using old mushrooms 5 minutes is enough. Do not let them catch. An asbestos mat under the pan will help.
4. Stir in flour, add stock and bring to boil. Simmer 2 or 3 minutes.
5. Add milk and reheat. Sprinkle on chopped parsley, stir and serve.

## MINESTRONE

*½ oz. margarine, butter or good bacon dripping*
*2 oz. streaky bacon, diced*
*1 large onion*
*1 stalk celery*
*2 oz. swede*
*2 oz. carrot*
*4 oz. potato*
*2½ pints light stock*
*2 tablespoons tomato purée*
*1 oz. macaroni or spaghetti*
*1 teaspoon sugar*
*4 to 6 oz. cabbage*
*Pepper and salt, seasoned salt gives more piquancy*
**To serve**
*Parmesan cheese*

1. Melt fat in large pan, add bacon and diced onion, cook 1 minute.
2. Add celery, swede, carrot and potato, all finely-diced and fry gently for 3 to 4 minutes.
3. Heat stock, mix in tomato purée and stir into pan of bacon and vegetables.
4. Add macaroni or spaghetti broken into small pieces. Cover and simmer for 30 minutes. Add sugar.
5. Shred cabbage finely, cut into 1-inch lengths, add to pan and simmer 12 to 15 minutes until tender. Add salt and pepper to taste. Serve with grated Parmesan cheese on top.

## ONION SOUP

*2 oz. margarine or butter*
*1½ lb. finely-chopped onion*
*1 level tablespoon flour*
*1 teaspoon Salt and Pepper Mix**
*2 pints stock, chicken is excellent but a light bone stock is adequate*

*See page 9.

**To serve**
*Thick slices of French bread, one
for each serving of soup
Grated cheese*
1. Melt fat in large pan, add onions, cook gently until soft.
2. Add flour and seasonings and cook for 2 minutes, stirring.
3. Stir in the stock, bring to boil and simmer for 30 minutes. Check for seasoning.
4. Toast the slices of French bread on one side only.
5. Cover untoasted side of bread thickly with cheese. Place under grill just to melt.
6. Place a slice in each soup bowl, ladle soup over and serve at once.

**\*Dorothy Sleightholme's Salt and Pepper Mix**
For seasoning: 3 teaspoons of salt to 1 teaspoon of pepper. Mix well together. Keep in screw-top jar.

## CARROT SOUP
*1 oz. butter, bacon fat or pork fat;
1 lb. carrots, cleaned and grated;
1 grated onion; 1 chopped stick
of celery; 1½ pints of stock; ½
teaspoon of sugar; 2 tablespoons
top of milk or thin cream.*
1. Melt butter in large saucepan, add carrot, onion and celery, cook gently for 10 minutes to soften vegetables.
2. Add 1 pint of stock and the sugar, simmer gently for 15 mins.
3. Sieve or liquidize.
4. Add rest of stock, test for seasoning, (if stock is well flavoured, extra seasoning may not be necssary).
5. Boil up. Stir in cream. Heat, but do not boil again.
Serve, sprinkled with chopped parsley.

## GOLDEN VEGETABLE SOUP
*1½ lb. of diced vegetables—
onion, carrot, swede, celery
2 oz. butter
1 oz. flour
2 pt. well seasoned stock,*
*preferably a light one, e.g.
chicken or bacon
4 oz. cooked peas*
1. Fry vegetables in butter until lightly golden, but do not brown.
2. Stir in flour, sizzle 1 minute.
3. Gradually add stock, bring to boil and simmer with lid on pan until vegetables are tender. Test for seasoning.
4. Add peas and boil up. If frozen peas are used add and cook for time advised on packet.

## CARROT AND LEEK SOUP
*2 carrots
2 large leeks
1 oz. butter
1 teaspoon horseradish sauce
1 oz. medium oatmeal
Salt and pepper
Mace (or bay leaf)
1 pt. stock
¼ pt. milk*
1. Slice carrots and leeks.
2. Sauté in butter for seven minutes. Add horseradish sauce, oatmeal, salt, pepper and mace (or bay leaf).
3. Pour on stock and milk.
4. Bring to the boil, simmer for 25 minutes.

## CAWL CENNIN
**Leek Broth**
This cawl or soup would be made when a piece of bacon was being boiled and would either be served as a first course or kept for another meal. It was made with whatever vegetables were available and the quantities also just depended upon what there was. So the following may be regarded simply as a guide and altered to suit what vegetables you have.
*1½ pt. stock from boiling a joint
of bacon
8 oz. potatoes, peeled and diced
8 oz. carrots, diced
2 leeks, sliced
½ small cabbage, shredded
2 tablespoons oatmeal
Salt and pepper
Chopped parsley*
The addition of oatmeal is op-

tional and may be omitted if a thinner broth is preferred.
1. Put potatoes and carrots in the stock, bring to the boil and cook for 10 minutes.
2. Add the leeks and cabbage.
3. Mix oatmeal with a little cold water and add.
4. Bring to boil again and simmer 10 to 15 minutes until the vegetables are cooked. Check for seasoning.
5. Serve sprinkled with chopped parsley.

**Mrs. Wesley Evans,
Denbighshire.**

## CHEESE AND ONION SAVOURY

*1 lb. onions*
*A little salt*
*½ pt. milk*
*8 to 10 oz. Cheshire cheese*
*2 tablespoons fresh breadcrumbs*
*Pepper*
*2 tomatoes, to garnish*
*A little butter*
*Thick slices of bread*
1. Peel and thinly slice the onions.
2. Place them in a pan with half a teaspoon salt and just enough of the milk to cover. Cook gently until onions are soft.
3. Place in a greased shallow casserole or small oven tin. Cover with the thinly-sliced cheese. Sprinkle over the crumbs shaking on a little pepper.
4. Arrange thickly-sliced tomatoes down centre of dish.
5. Dot with butter.
6. Place in oven heated to Gas 4, 350°F. and leave until the cheese "melts"—about 15 to 20 minutes. Usually served with a thick slice of bread to mop up the juice.

**Miss G. S. Davies,
Flintshire.**

## COLD STUFFED TOMATOES

*4 to 6 tomatoes depending on size. Choose firm ones.*
*1 tin sardines in oil*
*2 hard-boiled eggs*
*2 oz. butter, softened*
*1 teaspoon made mustard*
*1 teaspoon chopped parsley*
*Seasoning to taste*
1. Stand tomatoes stalk end down, cut a lid from rounded end which is uppermost, remove pulp, sprinkle lightly with salt and invert on a plate to drain.
2. Drain sardines, remove tails and backbones, and mash.
3. Remove yolks from eggs, work into softened butter. Add mustard, parsley, sardines and chopped egg whites. Season to taste.
4. Fill into tomato shells, replace lids at an angle.
Serve very cold with green salad.

## FRENCH DRESSING

*1 clove of garlic optional*
*¼ level teaspoon salt*
*¼ level teaspoon dry mustard*
*A grating of black pepper*
*¼ level teaspoon sugar*
*1 tablespoon vinegar*
*2 tablespoons oil*
Put seasonings and sugar in a small basin, add vinegar and oil, mix well.
This dressing can be made in advance but should not be used until the last minute before serving the salad. As oil and vinegar naturally separate mix again immediately before using.
If not to be used at once, keep in screw-topped jar and shake before using.

## MAYONNAISE

*1 egg yolk*
*½ level teaspoon dry mustard*
*½ level teaspoon salt*
*½ level teaspoon sugar*
*¼ level teaspoon pepper*
*¼ pint salad oil*
*1 tablespoon white vinegar or lemon juice*
1. Put egg yolk and seasonings in a basin. Mix really well using a wooden spoon.
2. Add oil, drop by drop at first, stirring briskly with a wooden spoon.
3. When very thick add a teaspoon of vinegar, then remaining oil a little more quickly, then beat in

rest of vinegar as required.
It should be thick enough to hold the impression of the spoon.

**A milder mayonnaise**
Beat into the finished mayonnaise 2 teaspoons of lemon juice or 2 teaspoons of cream.

## MUSHROOM SALAD

*8 oz. small, cultivated mushrooms*
*1 small, red pepper*
*1 small, green pepper*
*1 to 2 tablespoons French dressing*
*(see page 10)*
*Leaves of crisp lettuce*
1. Wash mushrooms in tepid, lightly-salted water. Drain and pat very dry. Slice.
2. Remove core and seeds from peppers. Cut flesh into strips, or dice. Blanch as follows: Drop the strips or dice into a pan of boiling water and bring back to the boil. Drain, refresh in cold water, drain again and pat dry. If you like the full flavour of peppers blanching is not necessary.
3. Place dressing in bowl, add mushrooms and peppers, toss together lightly. Spoon on to lettuce leaves just before serving. Serve with brown bread and butter, rye bread or crispbreads.

## DUCK AND ORANGE MAYONNAISE
**Quite as good with Pork**
**For 4 persons**
Have ready both French dressing and mayonnaise. Try the French dressing suggested for Royal Slaw on this page. A bought mayonnaise will do provided it is a good brand.
*¾ pint chopped, cold, cooked duck or pork*
*½ cup French dressing*
*Celery salt to taste*
*1 tablespoon chopped cashew nuts*
*¼ pint chopped seedless orange*
*½ pint cooked green peas*
*4 to 5 tablespoons mayonnaise*
*Salt and pepper*
**To garnish and serve**
*4 small sprigs of parsley*

*Chopped mint*
*Lettuce heart or curly endive*
*A little more French dressing*
*A bowl of mayonnaise*
1. Sprinkle meat with the half cup of French dressing. Cover and leave to stand for 2 hours.
2. Drain well. Add celery salt, nuts, orange and green peas.
3. Mix in mayonnaise to coat. Season if necessary with salt and pepper.
4. Divide equally among 4 individual salad plates.
5. Place a sprig of parsley in the centre of each portion. Sprinkle chopped mint around parsley. Fringe with one or two lettuce leaves or sprigs of curly endive, coated with French dressing.
Serve with additional mayonnaise in a bowl.
**Note.** When required for a party, cut large oranges in half. Carefully scoop out the flesh and all the membrane. Zig-zag round the edges with scissors. Fill oranges with salad. Place each on an individual plate, and arrange the lettuce or endive round the base. Garnish with parsley and mint as described.

**Mrs. Sybil Norcott,**
**Irlam, Manchester.**

## ROYAL SLAW
**First make a French dressing**
*1 cup salad oil*
*⅓ cup vinegar*
*1½ teaspoons salt*
*2 tablespoons sugar (more if a sweet dressing is preferred)*
*1½ teaspoons dry mustard*
*1 teaspoon paprika*
*a little pepper*
1. Combine all ingredients and beat together with a whisk until really well-mixed and the colour of salad cream. Most easily done in a liquidiser.
2. Put into a tightly-covered jar and chill. If not using at once mix well, whisk again or shake up thoroughly before using.

Use as required. Keeps well for at least a month.

**The Salad**

¼ cup of the dressing
½ cup of sliced peeled apple
1 banana
2 cups red cabbage, finely-shredded
½ cup diced celery
½ onion, chopped

1. Combine the dressing and apple slices.
2. Slice banana and add. Make sure it is well coated with dressing to prevent discolouration.
3. Gently combine with cabbage, celery and onion.

Keeps in refrigerator for 2 or 3 days.

**Mrs. Sybil Norcott,
Irlam, Manchester.**

## COLESLAW
### A Cabbage Salad

1. Wash, dry and shred finely some firm white cabbage.
2. Chop finely a small onion.
3. Toss cabbage and onion in a dressing of your choice (see page 10).

Try also adding chopped celery, grated carrot, a few sultanas, walnuts, chopped parsley.

## POTATO SALAD

1 lb. large potatoes
French dressing (see page 10)
1 or 2 tablespoons mayonnaise (see page 10)
Salt and pepper
Parsley or chives

1. Peel and dice potatoes. Put into boiling, salted water. Cook until tender but not broken, 5 to 10 minutes.
2. Drain well and while still hot trickle over a little French dressing.
3. When cool drain away any surplus dressing and then gently mix in the mayonnaise and seasoning to taste.
4. Sprinkle on chopped parsley or chives.

Try also adding cooked peas, diced carrot, sweetcorn.

## TOMATO AND CUCUMBER SALAD

Tomatoes
Cucumber
French dressing (see page 10)
Chives

1. Wash and thinly slice tomatoes and cucumber.
2. Arrange overlapping alternate slices.
3. Pour over a few spoonfuls French dressing.
4. Sprinkle with chopped chives.

Serve with cold ham or bacon.

## WATERCRESS AND ORANGE SALAD WITH SOUSED HERRINGS

Watercress
Oranges
Soused herrings
*French dressing

1. Wash watercress thoroughly, pat dry.
2. Remove peel and pith from 1 to 2 small oranges, cut them into thin slices and remove pips.
3. Arrange herrings down centre of dish, sliced oranges overlapping down each side.
4. Just before serving, dip sprigs of watercress in French dressing and arrange attractively at ends of dish and on orange slices.

## YORKSHIRE SALAD

Lettuce
Onions or spring onions
Mint
Sugar
Vinegar

1. Wash and finely shred some lettuce—the good outer leaves can be used.
2. Finely slice 1 to 2 onions or use spring onions when available.
3. Finely chop a little mint.
4. Add sugar to taste to a cup of vinegar and stir to dissolve. Pour over salad.

Serve with hot roast meats.

## POTTED BEEF

1 lb. shin beef
¼ level teaspoon mixed spice

*See page 10

1 level teaspoon salt
Grating of black pepper
1 teaspoon vinegar
2 teaspoons Worcester sauce
4 tablespoons water
4 oz. soft table margarine
A little melted butter

1. Trim excess fat and gristle from meat. Cut meat into one-inch cubes.
2. Put in a 1½ pint basin with spice, salt, pepper, vinegar, Worcester sauce and water. Cover tightly with foil.
3. Stand basin on a trivet or upturned saucer in a large pan. Pour into the pan sufficient boiling water to come halfway up sides of basin.
4. Cover pan, simmer 2½ hours, checking level of water from time to time.
5. Cool a little, drain meat, reserving the liquor.
6. Mince meat finely, stir in liquor and beat in margarine. Re-season if necessary.
7. Place in small pots, cover with a little melted butter.
Use for sandwiches.
This will freeze successfully for 1 month.

## MOCK GOOSE

1 lb. sausage meat
1 beaten egg
1 teaspoon Salt and Pepper Mix*
1 teaspoon made mustard
1 to 2 oz. fresh breadcrumbs
2 tablespoons dried breadcrumbs

**Stuffing**
1 oz. dripping
2 large sliced onions
1 teaspoon Salt and Pepper Mix*
1 teaspoon sage
1 to 2 oz. fresh breadcrumbs

1. Mix together sausage meat, egg, Salt and Pepper Mix and mustard using fresh breadcrumbs to make a firm mixture.
2. **Stuffing.** Melt dripping, fry onions to soften a little. Mix in seasonings and sufficient of the fresh breadcrumbs to bind, but do not make too dry.

3. Grease a 1 lb. loaf tin, coat generously with dried breadcrumbs.
4. Spread half of the sausage meat mixture in tin, then stuffing mixture and the rest of the sausage meat on top.
5. Cover with foil.
6. Cook for 1 hour at Gas 5, 375°F.
Serve with salads. Can be served hot with apple sauce.

*See page 9.

# CHAPTER 2

# CHEESE AND EGG DISHES RICE, PASTA

## FLUFFY CHEESE PUDDING

*1 pint milk; 2 oz. margarine;*
*4 oz. fresh white breadcrumbs;*
*1 teaspoon grated onion; 1 level*
*teaspoon made mustard;*
*½ teaspoon Salt and Pepper Mix\*;*
*2 eggs (separated); 6 oz. grated*
*cheese.*

1. Heat the milk and margarine, add the onion and crumbs, leave at least ½ hour (or overnight).
2. Beat mustard, salt and pepper into egg yolks, add these and cheese to crumb mixture.
3. Fold in firmly whisked egg whites.
4. Pour into a 2½ pint lightly greased pie dish, and cook at Gas 6, 400°F. for 40 minutes, lowering heat if necessary as top may brown before centre of pudding is cooked. Eat hot.

If you add a further ounce of breadcrumbs the pudding will hold together quite well when cool and is good for picnics.

## CHEESE CROQUETTES

*1 oz. margarine; 1 tablespoon*
*grated onion; 1 oz. plain flour;*
*½ level teaspoon dry mustard;*
*½ teaspoon Salt and Pepper Mix\*;*
*¼ pt. milk; 6 oz. grated*
*Cheddar cheese; 1 large egg*
*(separated); 1 teaspoon chopped*
*parsley; 1 teaspoon Worcester*
*sauce; 4 oz. fresh white bread*
*crumbs; dried crumbs for coating;*
*beef or pork dripping for frying.*

1. Melt margarine in pan, add onion, stir in flour, mustard and salt and pepper. Cook together for 1 minute.
2. Add milk, stir until boiling, cook one minute, remove from heat.
3. Add cheese, beat in. Then drop in egg yolk, parsley, Worcester sauce and fresh crumbs. Mix to a firm paste.
4. Divide into 12, roll out with floured hands into cork-shaped pieces about 2½ inches long. Leave 10 to 15 minutes (or overnight) in cool place for crumbs to swell and croquettes to firm up.
5. Beat egg white lightly, brush croquettes with this and roll in dried crumbs.
6. Deep fry for 2 to 3 minutes until golden.

## CHEESE SOUFFLÉ

To start with you need:
A 5 inch soufflé dish
Greaseproof paper, 21 x 14 inches
String
*Cooking oil*
*Dried breadcrumbs*
*1 oz. butter*
*1 oz. flour*
*¼ pint milk*
*½ teaspoon salt*
*½ teaspoon made mustard*
*¼ teaspoon cayenne pepper*
*3 eggs*
*3 oz. cheese, either all cheddar*
*or ½ cheddar, ½ parmesan*

1. Pre-heat oven to Gas 5, 375°F. as it must be up to heat when soufflé is ready to go in.
2. Grease soufflé dish with cooking oil.
3. Prepare a piece of greaseproof paper 21 x 14 inches.
(a) Fold it in half so that doubled sheet measures 21 x 7 inches.
(b) Turn up folded edge 2 inches (it now measures 21 x 5 inches).
(c) Grease the top 3 inches of the paper above the fold.
(d) Wrap the paper folded side inwards and greased section uppermost, around the dish. To contain the risen soufflé there must be 3 inches of paper above the top of the dish.
(e) Tie securely with string.
4. Shake in breadcrumbs so that both dish and greased paper are coated. This will stop the soufflé sticking.
5. Now start the soufflé. Make a

panada (which is a thick glossy sauce) as follows: Melt butter, add flour, cook gently. Add the milk gradually, stirring as it thickens.

6. Remove from heat, stir in seasonings: salt, cayenne pepper, mustard.

7. Add egg yolks and stir.

8. Stir in the grated cheese.

9. Beat egg whites up stiffly so they will stand in a peak. (This could be done in advance but make sure you have them really stiff before folding into soufflé mixture).

10. Fold egg whites gently into soufflé mixture.

11. Pour into prepared dish. Make deep cuts in the soufflé mixture, both across and in a circle. This cuts the egg white and allows the soufflé to rise, if not, the whites would set and not rise very well.

12. Put straight into the oven at Gas 5, 375°F. and cook exactly $\frac{1}{2}$ hour.

Serve immediately.

# WELSH RAREBIT

1 oz. butter
1 teaspoon made mustard
$\frac{1}{2}$ teaspoon Salt and Pepper Mix*
2 tablespoons fresh white breadcrumbs
1 egg yolk
4 oz. strong Cheddar Cheese, grated
3 tablespoons beer

**To serve:**
3 slices hot buttered toast

**NOTE:**
This mixture must **never** boil or it will go stringy.

1. Melt butter in saucepan.

2. Add mustard, Salt and Pepper Mix and breadcrumbs. Stir over gentle heat.

3. Add egg yolk, mix in, then cheese and stir to melt.

4. Add beer, mix in.

5. Spread on to hot buttered toast.

# COTTAGE CHEESE CAKE

**Flan Case**
4 oz. plain flour
Bare $\frac{1}{4}$ teaspoon salt
2 oz. softened butter
1 egg yolk
1 oz. castor sugar
1 teaspoon water (no more)

**Filling**
2 oz. sultanas
4 oz. cottage cheese
1 egg (separated)
2 oz. castor sugar
1 level tablespoon cornflour
Grated rind and juice of
1 small lemon
3 tablespoons thick cream (or evaporated milk)

1. Start with the flan case. Place flour and salt in a bowl, make a well in centre.

2. Add butter, egg yolk, sugar and water.

3. Work these together with a fork, drawing in flour gradually. Finish combining these ingredients with finger tips. Leave 15 minutes to relax.

4. Roll out on floured board to 9 inches diameter.

5. Fit into an ungreased 7 inch flan ring placed on a lightly greased tray. Roll off surplus pastry with rolling pin.

6. Prick base well with a fork. Cut a round of greaseproof paper approx. 9 inches in diameter, grease lightly, fit into case, greased side down, and weight with dried peas or beans.

7. Bake at Gas 6, 400°F. for .15 minutes until set, but only very lightly baked. Remove from oven and remove beans and paper. Reduce oven to Gas 3, 325°F.

8. For the filling. Sprinkle sultanas on base of hot flan.

9. Mix together cheese, egg yolk, sugar, cornflour, lemon rind and juice and cream.

10. Whisk egg white until firm but not dry, and fold in.

11. Pour mixture into flan case.

12. Bake on centre shelf of oven, Gas 3, 325°F. for approximately

*See page 9.

40-45 minutes until set. It should not be allowed to get too brown.
13. Turn off oven, if electric open door also 1 to 2 inches. Leave flan in oven a further 15 minutes.
14. Cool on wire tray, removing ring.
Serve cold, first sifting on a little icing sugar.

## COTTAGE CHEESE WITH HERBS
*2 pints milk; 1 teaspoon rennet; salt and freshly milled black pepper to taste; 1 teaspoon chopped fresh thyme; 1 teaspoon chopped chives; 2 teaspoons chopped parsley; ½ clove garlic, crushed (or a little chopped onion if preferred); 2½ oz. carton double cream (optional).*
1. Pour the milk into a pan and heat gently to blood temperature.
2. Stir in the rennet, pour the mixture into a jug and leave it for about four hours at room temperature. The milk will set like junket.
3. Place a double layer of muslin over a colander in a bowl.
4. Turn set milk on to the muslin. Tie up the corners with string and hang up to drain overnight.
5. The next day place the cheese (still in the muslin) into a seive with a weight on top so that the remaining moisture can be squeezed out – about two hours.
6. Take the cheese out of the muslin and put it in a bowl. Mix in the remaining ingredients adding the cream if liked or even a little 'top of the milk'.
7. Leave the mixture for a few hours so that the herbs can flavour the cheese.
8. This cheese will keep five days in the refrigerator.

## COTSWOLD DUMPLINGS
Makes 36.
*2 oz. butter*
*4 oz. grated cheese*
*Salt and pepper*
*3 small beaten eggs*
*5 oz. fresh white breadcrumbs*
*2 to 3 tablespoons dried bread-crumbs*
*Fat for frying*
1. Cream together butter and cheese. Add salt and pepper.
2. Beat in all but 2 tablespoons of the beaten eggs, add 1 to 2 table-spoons crumbs.
3. Work in remaining crumbs to make a stiff paste.
4. With floured hands, roll mixture into small balls. It will make about 36. Leave for about 1 hour. This allows the crumbs to absorb the moisture, and swell a little—prevents bursting on cooking.
5. Using a skewer, dip each ball in remaining beaten egg, then roll in dried crumbs.
6. Heat fat—it should be 3 inches deep. A chip basket is an advantage.
**To test heat of fat:** Drop in a 1-inch cube of dry bread—it should sizzle at once and gradually go golden in 1 minute.
7. Place dumplings in basket, only 1 layer, and fry for 1½ to 2 minutes until golden. Do not overcook. Drain on kitchen paper.
Eat hot with home-made tomato sauce (see page 24). Try also serving the tomato sauce cold as a. dip for the hot dumplings.

## OMELETTES
**Basic method:**
*2 large eggs*
*2 teaspoons water*
*Salt and pepper*
*Large nut of butter*
1. Beat eggs lightly with water, salt and pepper. Do not whisk.
2. Using a small frying pan (a 6-inch is ideal) heat butter until frothy, but not browning, tilting pan so that bottom and sides are well-coated.
3. Pour in eggs. After a few seconds move edges with a fork or spatula to allow uncooked egg

to flow underneath.

4. Continue for about 2 minutes until set underneath and turning slightly golden but still a little moist on top.

5. Fold in half, tilt on to a warm plate and eat at once.

**Variations:**

Add 1 tablespoon finely-chopped fresh parsley or 1 tablespoon grated cheese when beating eggs. Or make a filling of fried mushrooms, or crisp chopped bacon or shredded pieces of poultry, well seasoned and heated in butter, or skinned and sliced fried tomato, or thinly sliced kidney or chicken liver fried lightly in butter. Put the hot fillings on to one half of the omelette, fold the other half over.

## VEGETABLE OMELETTE

*2 large eggs*
*2 teaspoons water*
*Salt and pepper*
*1 oz. butter*
*1 teaspoon oil*
*1 small onion cut into fine rings*
*1 small potato, cooked and cut into small dice*
*1 large tomato, skinned and chopped*
*1 or 2 finely-sliced mushrooms, optional*

1. Lightly beat eggs, water and salt and pepper.

2. Melt butter and oil in small frying pan. Fry onions until soft, add potato, tomato and mushrooms, mix together and heat.

3. Pour in eggs and stir lightly. Cook until base is firm.

4. Place under pre-heated medium grill until just set.

Serve flat on warm dish.

## APPLE WINE OMELETTE
**Omelette:**

*3 eggs*
*1 tablespoon water*
*1½ dessertspoons vanilla sugar**
*¾ oz. butter*

**Filling:**

*1 cooking apple*
*¾ oz. butter*
*1 dessertspoon vanilla sugar**
*1½ tablespoons double cream*
*1 dessertspoon apple wine*

1. Make the filling first. Peel, core and slice apple thinly. Cook gently in the butter. Add sugar, cream and wine and keep warm.

2. Separate yolks from whites, remove cords.

3. Add water and sugar to yolks, blend together.

4. Put butter on to melt in omelette or heavy frying pan.

5. Whisk egg whites until stiff and fold into yolks.

6. Pour into omelette pan and smooth out. Cook the omelette slowly until golden brown.

7. Put under the grill to cook the top.

8. When golden brown on top put on to plate, put filling on, fold over.

9. Dust with icing sugar, mark with hot skewers.

Serve at once with thick cream.

## SYLLABUB - an old English sweet

*¼ pt. double cream*
*1 small teaspoon lemon juice*
*½ teaspoon finely grated lemon rind*
*1 - 2 teaspoons sugar to taste*
*Approx. 3 tablespoons sherry*
*or more depending on taste.*
*Chopped almonds*

1. Whip the cream until quite thick.

2. Add the other ingredients slowly and whip until thick again.

3. Serve in small glasses, sprinkled with chopped nuts.

If you add a lot more sherry the liquid may separate from the cream, but it is still delicious.

## CARAMEL CUSTARD
**Caramel:**

*3 oz. granulated sugar dissolved in*

1 tablespoon of hot water.

1. Dissolve sugar in water in small heavy pan and then boil, without stirring, until golden.
2. Have ready heated an ungreased, 6 inch, heatproof soufflé dish or similar, or 6 inch cake tin. Pour in the caramel, tilting to coat the bottom.
3. Allow to cool and set.

**Custard:**

3 eggs and 1 egg yolk; 1 tablespoon vanilla sugar*; ¾ pt. milk.

1. Beat eggs and sugar together lightly, but not frothy.
2. Pour on the milk.
3. Strain into caramel dish.
4. Place the dish inside a small dripping tin or container with enough cold water to come halfway up sides of dish.
5. Cook at Gas 3, 325°F. for about 1 hour until firm. To test, slip knife in diagonally, taking care not to touch the caramel. Knife will come out clean if custard is cooked.
6. Leave until cold. Turn on to a plate to serve.

Keep the spare egg white for your Yorkshire Puddings.

## POURING CUSTARD

½ pt. milk; 1 dessertspoon vanilla sugar*; 2 eggs.

1. Heat the milk and vanilla sugar, but do not boil.
2. Pour on to the lightly beaten eggs.
3. Strain into a heat-proof basin.
4. Stand this over a pan of simmering water, not touching the water. Stir from time to time with a wooden spoon. It is cooked when there is a thin coating of custard on spoon — about 10 minutes.

Serve hot or cold with pies, puddings, etc.

## CLOTTED CREAM

Clotted cream is a traditional product of South West England and the traditional farmhouse method of manufacture is as follows:

1. Channel Island milk is placed in shallow pans or bowls and left until the cream rises to the top.
2. The milk is then scalded for about one hour by placing the pan or bowl over a pan of water maintained at a temperature of about 180°F (82°C).
3. The cream is ready when it is straw coloured and wrinkled in appearance. It is then cooled overnight or for about twelve hours.
4. When cool the cream should be skimmed off the surface using a perforated skimmer or a shallow spoon.
5. If the skimmed cream is left in the refrigerator for a few hours it will thicken further.

Alternatively, clotted cream can be made using the direct scald method. Double cream is placed in shallow pans or bowls and scalded as for the traditional method. After scalding and cooling the whole contents of the pan are used as clotted cream.

## BREAD AND BUTTER PUDDING

5 oz. stale bread (without crusts)
Butter
2 oz. sultanas
A little candied peel
2 tablespoons demerara or
plain white sugar
1 large egg
½ pint milk
Nutmeg

This is delicious made from stale Hot Cross Buns, Bun Loaf, or Sally Lunn. Where fruit is already incorporated in loaf or buns, extra sultanas and candied peel are not needed, nor is it necessary to remove crusts.

1. Butter a pie dish of approximately 1½ pint capacity.
2. Slice bread, butter it and cut into small pieces.

20     *See page 89.

3. Place half the bread in pie dish, sprinkle on fruit and half the sugar. Cover with remaining bread.
4. Beat the egg and milk, pour over, leave 30 minutes to soak.
5. Sprinkle top with remaining sugar, grate on a little nutmeg.
6. Bake at Gas 4, 350°F about 1 hour.

## ORANGE SEMOLINA

*1 pint milk*
*Rind 1 orange*
*1½ oz. (or 2 level tablespoons) semolina*
*1½ oz. castor sugar*
*Pinch salt*
*1 oz. butter*
*1 egg (separated)*
1. Heat the milk with thinly peeled strips of orange rind, bring slowly to boil. Leave 5 minutes to infuse.
2. Remove orange rind, sprinkle semolina into milk. Stir over gentle heat until mixture thickens.
3. Remove from heat. Add 1 oz. of the sugar, salt, ½ oz. of the butter, and the egg yolk. Mix, cool a little, then fold in the stiffly-whisked egg white.
4. Turn into a buttered 1½ pint to 2 pint dish. Dot with rest of butter, and sprinkle on remaining sugar. Bake at Gas 4, 350°F. 35 minutes.

## PANCAKES

*4 oz. plain flour*
*½ teaspoon salt*
*Lard*
*1 large egg*
*½ pint milk*
Use a small frying pan. This quantity of batter will make about 14 pancakes 6 inches across.
1. Place flour and salt in basin. Make a well in centre.
2. Drop in egg and begin to mix gradually adding ¼ pint of the milk as the flour is drawn in.
3. Beat well until bubbles are visible.

4. Gradually beat in remaining milk.
5. Put into a jug for easier pouring into the pan.
6. Heat pan, place in a piece of lard (size of hazel nut). Allow to spread over pan and become fairly hot.
7. Pour in a little batter, tilting pan to cover. When nicely golden toss or turn over to cook the other side. Repeat to use batter.
To serve traditionally: sprinkle with lemon juice and sugar and roll up—but there are many other ways.
To freeze. Lay pancakes as they are cooked on a clean cloth placed on a large cooling wire. When cool, pack flat, with greaseproof paper or polythene film in between, into a bag and seal. To use: allow to thaw and reheat with a stuffing or in a sauce.

## CHICKEN AND MUSHROOM PANCAKES

Make pancakes from recipe given on this page.
**Filling**
*3 oz. butter*
*2 oz. flour*
*½ teaspoon Salt and Pepper Mix**
*½ pint milk*
*6 oz. cooked and chopped chicken*
*4 oz. mushrooms, sliced*
1. Melt 2 oz. of the butter in a saucepan.
2. Add flour, salt and pepper, cook 1 minute.
3. Gradually stir in milk, cook 2 minutes.
4. Add chicken.
5. Fry mushrooms in remaining 1 oz. butter for 2 minutes. Add to sauce.
6. Divide filling between pancakes, roll up and place in a shallow casserole. Heat through in oven, Gas 5, 375°F. about 10 minutes.

*See page 9.

Pancakes can be kept hot, as they are made, on a plate over a pan of simmering water. Cover with foil. They should not then need to be warmed in oven.

To freeze: Allow to become cold after filling, pack into containers, seal. Heat in oven when required.

## ORANGE PANCAKES
Pancakes from recipe on page 21.
**Orange Sauce**
*2 oz. butter*
*Grated rind and juice of*
*1 large orange*
*2 oz. castor sugar*
*4 tablespoons sherry or*
*sweet white wine.*
1. Lay pancakes, as they are cooked, on a clean cloth placed on a large cake wire.
2. Fold in quarters to heat through in sauce.
3. For the sauce. Melt butter in large frying pan, add orange rind and juice, then sugar, and allow it to dissolve. Add 3 tablespoons of the sherry.
4. Place folded pancakes in sauce and heat through.
5. Pile on to hot serving dish, pour sauce over.
6. Add the remaining tablespoon of sherry to pan, swirl round, pour over pancakes.

To freeze: Put pancakes and sauce in a rigid container, allow to become quite cold, cover. To use: Heat through, still frozen if necessary, in frying pan. Takes about 15 minutes.

## LAGER PANCAKES
Pancakes made with lager turn out especially light and may be served traditionally with lemon and sugar or with sweet or savoury fillings. For example, banana or other fruit may be heated through in a little lager, sweetened with syrup and the finished pancake sprinkled with castor or soft brown sugar. Savoury fillings may be fried first if necessary, for example, bacon,

onions and mushrooms, the fat drained away, then the ingredients cooked over a good heat for about 5 minutes in a little lager—or cooked meats may be chopped or minced, flavoured with tomato puree or chutney then heated thoroughly over a good heat in a little lager, ready to fill the pancakes.

**For Four 10 inch pancakes**
*4 oz. plain flour*
*2 eggs*
*Pinch salt*
*2 teaspoons oil, olive oil*
*preferably*
*½ pint (10 fluid ozs.) lager*
1. Beat the eggs into the flour, add salt, oil and lager and beat well or whisk into a smooth batter.
2. Leave for 30 minutes if possible.
3. Fry in very hot lard or oil on both sides.

Best served immediately but may be prepared in advance, staying fresh for up to 48 hours if stacked on top of one another, interleaved with greaseproof paper, wrapped in a teacloth and put in refrigerator.

**To reheat:**
1. Spoon filling on pancakes and roll up. Place in fireproof dish.
2. Sprinkle lightly with lager or coat with any remaining filling and bake in a hot oven, Gas 7, 425°F, for 10 minutes or so until heated thoroughly.

## STUFFED EGGS
*4 large eggs*
*1 oz. butter softened,*
*1 oz. Parmesan or finely-grated*
*Cheddar cheese*
*1 to 2 teaspoons mayonnaise or*
*salad cream*
*Salt and pepper*
**To garnish:**
*Paprika pepper or parsley*
1. Boil the eggs for 12 minutes and then plunge them into cold water.
2. Shell when cold and cut in half lengthways. Remove yolks.
3. Sieve the yolks or mash well with a fork.

4. Add softened butter, cheese, enough mayonnaise or salad cream to soften mixture and salt and pepper to taste.
5. Pile or pipe mixture into whites. Sprinkle lightly with paprika pepper or garnish with tiny sprigs of parsley.

## LONG-GRAIN RICE FOR SAVOURY DISHES

Rice
Salt
Lemon juice
1. Allow $1\frac{1}{2}$ to 2 oz. of uncooked rice per person.
2. Put the rice in a sieve and wash it under running cold water.
3. Use a large saucepan about $\frac{2}{3}$ full of water, bring to the boil, add 1 teaspoon of salt and 1 teaspoon of lemon juice, shower in the rice. Stir until boiling again and boil fairly rapidly, uncovered, for 12 minutes.
4. Leave off heat for 2 or 3 minutes, testing if rice is cooked— it should not be too soft.
5. Drain through a large sieve and pour over boiling water. Stir lightly with a fork to drain well.
6. Place a knob of butter in pan to melt, add rice and shake pan gently over low heat for 1 to 2 minutes. It is now ready for use.

## SAVOURY RICE

To serve with chops, steak gammon etc.
1 tablespoon cooking oil
8 oz. uncooked rice
$\frac{3}{4}$ pint hot, well-flavoured stock
1. Heat oil in large pan, add rice, stir gently until oil is absorbed. Do not allow rice to colour.
2. Add stock, test seasoning and bring to boil.
3. Transfer to a $2\frac{1}{2}$ pint casserole, cover tightly. Cook in the oven Gas 6, 400°F. until stock is absorbed and rice is cooked adding extra water or stock if becoming too dry. Time, approximately 45 minutes.

**To serve**
Add cooked peas, cooked diced carrot (or a packet of frozen mixed vegetables, cooked), or lightly-fried, sliced mushrooms.

## PILAFF OF LAMB WITH COURGETTES

2 oz. butter or margarine
8 oz. cold, cooked lamb, cut in $\frac{1}{2}$-inch cubes
6 oz. uncooked rice
1 medium-sized onion, chopped
2 tablespoons diced celery
2 tablespoons diced green pepper
1 small clove of garlic, crushed
$\frac{1}{3}$ pint stock
1 tablespoon Worcestershire sauce
$\frac{1}{2}$ teaspoon salt
A dash of pepper
4 oz. unpeeled courgettes, sliced in $\frac{1}{2}$-inch discs
1 oz. grated Parmesan cheese
1. Melt butter in a large heavy saucepan.
2. Add lamb, rice, onion, celery, green pepper and garlic. Cook, stirring until rice is transparent.
3. Stir in stock, Worcestershire sauce, salt and pepper. Bring to boil.
4. Lower heat, cover pan and cook for 10 minutes.
5. Stir in courgettes and cook covered for 10 minutes longer.
Serve sprinkled with Parmesan.

## MACARONI CHEESE

6 oz. macaroni
$1\frac{1}{2}$ oz. margarine
$1\frac{1}{2}$ oz. flour
$\frac{1}{2}$ level teaspoon made mustard
$\frac{1}{2}$ teaspoon Salt and Pepper Mix*
$\frac{3}{4}$ pint milk
6 oz. grated cheese
1. Cook macaroni in fast-boiling, salted water for 15 minutes. Drain well.
2. Melt margarine, stir in the flour and cook 2 minutes. Add mustard and Salt and Pepper Mix. Stir in milk gradually. Bring to boil and stir over heat for 2 minutes as it thickens. Remove from heat and beat in 4 oz. of the grated cheese.

*See page 9.

3. Add macaroni, pour into a greased, oven-proof dish, sprinkle on remaining cheese.

4. Bake centre oven at Gas 5, 375°F. for 15 to 20 minutes until beginning to bubble and turning golden.

### Variations

Add 2 tablespoons of fresh white breadcrumbs to last 2 oz. cheese before sprinkling on top. Makes it crisp.

Or, as a garnish, for the last 10 minutes of cooking time, put slices of skinned tomato on top brushed with a little oil or melted fat.

Or, add with the macaroni (paragraph 3) 4 oz. cooked, cubed ham or lean bacon, and small tin of sweet corn with peppers.

## SPAGHETTI IN CREAM SAUCE

### For 2 persons

*4 oz. spaghetti rings. Try also pasta shells, spirals or shortcut macaroni*
*1 teaspoon cooking oil*
*4 oz. chopped streaky bacon*
*2 oz. sliced mushrooms or 2 skinned and chopped tomatoes*
*2 tablespoons cider or dry white wine*
*A good grating of black pepper*
*2 beaten eggs*
*4 tablespoons single cream or good top-of-milk*
*2 oz. grated cheese*

### To serve

*Extra grated cheese or grated Parmesan*

1. Use a large pan and half fill it with water. Bring water to the boil and add oil. Drop in the spaghetti rings, keep water boiling and cook for 10 to 14 minutes until soft but still firm. Exact cooking time depends on type of pasta. Do not overcook or it may disintegrate when sauce is added. Drain well and return to pan.

2. Meanwhile, fry chopped bacon gently until lightly crisp.

3. Add prepared mushrooms and cook 1 minute.

4. Pour in cider, turn off heat and grate on pepper.

5. Mix eggs and cream or top-of-milk and add to spaghetti.

6. Place over low heat, stir in cheese. Add tomatoes here if used. Add bacon mixture and stir until sauce thickens but do not let it boil.

7. Pour into hot dish. Serve on hot plates with extra grated cheese, Parmesan if you have it, to sprinkle on top.

## TOMATO SAUCE

This is a good sauce or dip for Cotswold Dumplings (page 18).

*1 oz. butter*
*1 medium-sized grated onion*
*1 small grated apple*
*2 level teaspoons cornflour*
*2 teaspoons sugar*
*A 2¼ oz. tin tomato purée*
*Water*
*Seasoning—salt, black pepper, garlic salt, seasoned salt—use as desired*

1. Melt butter in small saucepan, add onion, soften a little, add apple, cook about 15 minutes until quite soft but not brown.

2. Place cornflour, sugar and purée in a half-pint measuring jug. Mix in water to make half a pint.

3. Add to pan, stir until simmering and cook 15 to 20 minutes stirring occasionally.

4. Sieve or preferably liquidize, return to rinsed pan, season to taste (it should be piquant) and bring to boil.

This makes a thick sauce which can be thinned as required using water, stock or milk.

Makes an excellent soup if thinned to correct consistency and seasonings adjusted. If adding milk do not actually boil again or it will curdle.

Not long-keeping but will keep in refrigerator for a week to 10 days.

# CHAPTER 3

# PIES AND PASTRIES

## SWEET FLAN PASTRY
*4 oz. soft plain flour*
*Bare ¼ teaspoon salt*
*1 oz. castor sugar*
*1 egg yolk*
*1 teaspoon water*
*2 oz. butter*

1. Place flour and salt in mixing bowl, make a well in centre.
2. Add sugar, egg yolk, water and butter—which should be soft, but not warm.
3. Mix these together with a fork, drawing flour in gradually. Finish mixing by hand until dough is smooth and pliable.
4. Wrap in foil, leave to rest 15 minutes.
5. Place an ungreased 7 inch flan ring on a lightly greased baking tray.
6. Using gentle strokes, roll out pastry on floured board to circular shape 9 inches across.
7. Fit into ring, floured side uppermost, pressing pastry gently round sides to make an even thickness. Roll off surplus pastry with rolling pin.
8. To bake blind, that is, without a filling. Prick base of pastry well with fork. Cut a circle of grease-proof paper, approximately 9 inches in diameter, lightly grease one side, and crumple paper into a ball. (This will make fitting easier). Fit, greased side down, into pastry case. Fill with dried peas or haricot beans. (Save your baked peas and beans in a jar for the next flan you make—they cannot be eaten.)
9. Bake, centre oven, at Gas 6, 400°F. about 10 minutes to set pastry. If browning too quickly, reduce to Gas 5, 375°F. and bake a further 15 minutes until golden and firm.
10. Remove beans and paper, slide on to a cooling wire and remove ring. When cold, can be used for fruit flans, etc.

Flan cases freeze well before or after baking.

### Fruit Flan
1. Spread a little sieved apricot jam on base of flan case. This prevents any moisture soaking in.
2. Fill with pieces of fruit arranged in pattern. If using tinned fruit drain off juice and save it for the glaze.

### To Glaze a Fruit Flan
Using fresh fruits:
*2 tablespoons sugar*
*¼ pt. water*
*2 squares from a jelly tablet*
1. Dissolve sugar in water.
2. Boil 2 to 3 minutes.
3. Add jelly, allow to dissolve.
4. When cool, spoon over fruit in flan.

Using tinned fruit:
*1 teaspoon arrowroot*
*2 squares from a jelly tablet*
1. Mix arrowroot into ¼ pint of the fruit juice.
2. Boil until clear.
3. Add jelly, allow to dissolve.
4. When cool spoon over fruit in flan.

### APPLE MERINGUE FLAN
*1 baked 7 inch pastry case.*
**Filling:**
*1 lb. cooking apples*
*½ oz. butter*
*Sugar to taste*
*Rind of ½ a lemon*
*1 egg yolk*
**Meringue:**
*2 egg whites*
*(1 will be left from flan case)*
*4 oz. castor sugar*
1. Peel and finely slice apples.
2. Cook in butter until quite soft.
3. Sieve or liquidize.
4. Add lemon rind, egg yolk and sugar to taste.
5. Whisk egg whites stiffly, whisk in 2 oz. of the sugar until shiny. Fold in 2 oz. sugar.
6. Spread base of flan case with raspberry jam, orange marmalade or apricot jam.
7. Place apple in case.
8. Spread meringue on top, being sure that this touches edges of

pastry. Sift on a little castor sugar —not too much.
9. Place in cool oven, Gas 2, 300°F. for about 20 minutes to set.


## CHEESE PASTRY

Makes an 8-inch flan case and a batch of 12 small biscuits.

*8 oz. plain flour*
*½ level teaspoon salt*
*½ level teaspoon dry mustard*
*Pinch of cayenne pepper*
*3 oz. firm margarine*
*3 oz. finely-grated cheese*
*1 egg-yolk*
*2 tablespoons water (use a measure)*

1. Sieve flour, salt, mustard and cayenne pepper into a bowl and rub in margarine.
2. Mix in cheese.
3. Mix egg-yolk with water and bind all together.
4. Knead until smooth. Wrap in foil, leave half an hour.
5. Place an 8-inch flan ring on a baking tray.
6. Using a floured board, roll out three quarters of the pastry and fit into flan ring. Press in firmly and roll off surplus pastry with rolling pin.

Can now be used uncooked or partly cooked for savoury fillings, Creamy Onion Pie, Chicken and Sweetcorn Flan, see page 28.
For savoury biscuits made from the surplus pastry, see this page.


### To bake the flan case blind

1. Prick base of pastry.
2. Lightly grease a round of grease-proof paper 11 to 12 inches in diameter, crumple it up and then spread it out, greased side down in flan.
3. Put in a layer of dried peas or haricot beans, a quarter to half an inch deep. (Save your baked peas and beans in a jar for the next flan you make—they cannot be eaten.)
4. Bake at Gas 6, 400°F. for about 20 minutes until set. Remove

beans and paper. Bake another 5 to 6 minutes.


### To make savoury biscuits from the surplus pastry

1. Roll out thinly, less than a quarter of an inch thick, on floured board. Prick all over with a fork. Cut into desired shapes.
2. Place on lightly-greased baking tray.
3. Bake at Gas 6, 400°F. for 8 to 10 minutes until crisp and lightly golden.
4. Turn on to rack to cool.
Serve with butter or cream cheese. Decorate with sliced, stuffed olives, gherkin, shrimps etc. Can also be used for savoury dips.


## CREAMY ONION PIE

*Cheese pastry made up as on this page, but not baked.*
*⅜ pint (7½ fluid oz.) milk*
*1 small bay leaf*
*6 to 8 peppercorns*
*1½ oz. butter*
*2 large thinly-sliced onions*
*2½ oz. fresh white breadcrumbs*
*2 beaten eggs*
*1 teaspoon Salt and Pepper Mix\**
*1 teaspoon Worcester sauce*
*2 tablespoons thick cream*
*A little grated cheese, optional*

1. Make up the pastry as above and line an 8-inch flan ring placed on a baking tray.
2. Place milk, bay leaf and peppercorns in a pan, heat to nearly boiling. Remove from heat and leave 5 minutes to infuse.
3. Meanwhile, melt butter in pan, add onions, cook a few minutes so that they soften and become lightly-golden.
4. Have breadcrumbs in a large basin, strain the milk and pour it over.
5. Add onions and butter from pan, eggs, Salt and Pepper Mix and Worcester sauce. Stir in cream.
6. Taste for seasoning, add extra if necessary.

*\*See page 9.*

7. Pour into pastry case and bake at Gas 6, 400°F. for about 25 minutes until the pastry is golden and the filling is set.

8. Place under medium grill to finish if a little pale on top. 1 to 2 minutes is enough. If using grated cheese sprinkle it on top before grilling.

Can be eaten hot or cold. To reheat replace flan ring and cover with foil, put in oven Gas 5, 375°F. for 12 to 15 minutes.

## CHICKEN AND SWEETCORN FLAN

*Cheese pastry made up as on previous page*
*1 small onion, finely-chopped*
*1 oz. butter*
*1 oz. flour*
*½ teaspoon dry mustard*
*½ teaspoon Salt and Pepper Mix\**
*¼ pint milk*
*A 7 oz. tin of sweetcorn with peppers*
*4 oz. diced cooked chicken*
*2 tablespoons cream*
*1 to 2 oz. grated cheese*

1. Bake the flan case blind for 20 minutes only. See instructions on previous page.

2. Meanwhile, fry onion in butter until soft, but not coloured.

3. Stir in flour, mustard, Salt and Pepper Mix and cook for one minute.

4. Drain corn, add liquid to milk. Stir this into onion mixture in pan, bring to boil and cook for 2 minutes.

5. Remove from heat, mix in corn and chicken, cream and extra seasoning to taste.

6. Pour into partly-cooked, hot flan case, cover top with cheese.

7. Return to oven, Gas 6, 400°F. and cook 12 to 15 minutes until cheese is melted and turning golden.

Can be eaten hot or cold. To reheat, replace flan ring, cover with foil and put in oven Gas 5, 375°F. for 12 to 15 minutes.

## CHEESE PASTRY—FOR CHEESE STRAWS

*6 oz. plain flour*
*¼ teaspoon salt*
*¼ teaspoon dry mustard*
*A pinch of cayenne pepper*
*3 oz. firm margarine*
*3 oz. finely grated strong Cheddar cheese*
*1 egg-yolk*
*3 teaspoons water*

1. Sieve dry ingredients.

2. Rub in margarine.

3. Stir in cheese.

4. Mix to a firm dough with egg-yolk and water. Leave to rest about 15 minutes.

5. Roll out approx. ⅜ inch thick on floured board. Cut into fingers ⅜ inch by 3 inches. Place on lightly greased baking tray.

6. Bake at Gas 7, 425°F. about 12 to 15 minutes until crisp and lightly golden.

7. Turn on to rack to cool. When cold, ends can be lightly dipped in paprika pepper as garnish.

## CHEESE PASTRY SAVOURIES

*6 oz. plain flour*
*¼ teaspoon salt*
*¼ teaspoon dry mustard*
*A pinch of cayenne pepper*
*3 oz. firm margarine*
*3 oz. finely grated strong Cheddar cheese*
*1 egg-yolk*
*3 teaspoons water*
**Filling:**
*4 oz. cream cheese*
*A good teaspoon salad cream or mayonnaise*
*Seasoned salt*
*Garlic salt*
*Pepper*
**Garnish:**
*Stuffed olives, gherkins, shrimps, etc.*

1. Sieve dry ingredients.

2. Rub in margarine.

3. Stir in cheese.

4. Mix to a firm dough with egg-yolk and water. Leave to rest about 15 minutes.

*\*See page 9.*

5. Roll out approximately $\frac{1}{4}$ inch thick on floured board. Using 1 inch to $1\frac{1}{2}$ inch cutter, cut into rounds. Cut half of the rounds into halves.

6. Place on lightly greased baking tray and prick each biscuit with a fork.

7. Bake at Gas 7, 425°F. for 8 to 10 minutes until crisp and lightly golden.

8. Turn on to rack to cool.

9. Meanwhile, for the filling, mix salad cream or mayonnaise into cheese adding seasonings to taste.

10. Pipe with small star nozzle on to whole biscuits. Place two halves like wings on top.

11. Pipe a little more cheese mixture down centre.

13. Garnish with half stuffed olive, pieces of gherkin or a shrimp. They are delicious.

## FLAKY PASTRY

Makes $1\frac{1}{4}$ lb. of pastry.
*8 oz. plain flour (preferably strong plain flour)*
*Pinch of salt*
*3 oz. butter or firm margarine*
*3 oz. lard*
*$\frac{1}{2}$ teaspoon lemon juice*
*Approximately $\frac{1}{4}$ pint cold water*

1. Place flour and salt in bowl.

2. Cut up butter (or margarine) and lard and mix well together. Chill a little and then divide into quarters.

3. Rub one of the quarters into flour and salt and mix to a pliable but not sticky dough with lemon juice and water. Allow to rest 10 to 15 minutes in a cool place, covered.

4. Using a floured board, roll out pastry 3 times as long as wide— about a quarter inch in thickness.

5. Using a second quarter of fat, place in dabs over the top two-thirds of pastry.

6. Fold bottom third up, and top third down. Seal edges lightly with rolling pin. Turn, leaving pressed edges at top and bottom and at right-hand side. Wrap in grease-proof paper and let it rest in the refrigerator or a cold place for 10 minutes.

7. Repeat rollings with third and then fourth quarter of fat, then wrap and leave in a cold place for 1 hour, or overnight.

8. Roll out and use as required, rolling out quite thinly unless recipe states otherwise.

Keeps in refrigerator for 2 or 3 days. Freezes well.

## ROUGH PUFF PASTRY

Makes $1\frac{1}{4}$ lb. of pastry.
*8 oz. self-raising or strong plain flour*
*Pinch of salt*
*3 oz. firm margarine*
*3 oz. firm lard*
*Approximately $\frac{1}{4}$ pint water*
*$\frac{1}{2}$ teaspoon lemon juice*

1. Place flour and salt in a bowl.

2. Cut fats into half-inch cubes. Mix lightly into flour but do not break up.

3. Mix to a dough with water and lemon juice, it usually requires full amount. Allow to rest 5 to 10 minutes in refrigerator or a cold place.

4. Using a well-floured board, roll out a quarter-inch thick, 3 times as long as wide, rolling lightly at this stage.

5. Fold bottom third up, and top third down. Seal edges lightly with rolling pin. Turn, leaving pressed edges at top and bottom and at right-hand side. Wrap in grease-proof paper and let it rest in the refrigerator or a cold place for 10 minutes.

6. Repeat rolling, folding and resting 3 times more.

Use for meat pies, sausage rolls, etc.

Best eaten fresh.

## SWEET SHORTCRUST PASTRY

Makes a good 1 lb. of pastry, enough for two 7-inch flan rings.
*1 egg yolk*
*1 oz. castor sugar*

*3 teaspoons water*
*8 oz. soft plain flour*
*½ level teaspoon salt*
*5 oz. firm margarine*
1. Mix together egg-yolk, sugar and water.
2. Place flour and salt in a bowl, rub in margarine.
3. Mix to a firm dough with egg, sugar and water mixture. Leave in a cool place for 15 minutes.
4. Using a floured board roll out a quarter of an inch thick to shape required.

**For two 7-inch flan cases:**
1. Stand flan rings on baking tray.
2. Cut pastry in half and on a floured board roll out 2 rounds 9 inches across and a quarter of an inch thick.
3. Fit into the flan rings, floured side uppermost, pressing pastry gently around sides to make an even thickness. Trim off surplus pastry. Prick base well with a fork.
4. Cut a circle of greaseproof paper 9 inches in diameter, lightly grease one side and fit it greased side down into the flan. Fill with baking beans. (Use dried peas or haricot beans and save them in a jar for another baking day—they cannot be eaten.)
5. Bake Gas 5, 375°F. for 10 minutes. Then remove beans and paper and bake a further 10 to 15 minutes till just golden and firm.
6. Slide off baking tray on to a cooling wire and then remove flan ring. Allow to cool.
If filling with fruit spread a little apricot jam on first to stop flan going soggy.
Will keep in a cake tin for 2 weeks. Freeze well, but pack them carefully.

**SHORT CRUST PASTRY**
*2 oz. firm margarine,*
*the cheaper variety*
*2 oz. lard*
*8 oz. plain flour*
*½ teaspoon salt*
*2 full tablespoons water*

Rub fats into flour and salt until like fine bread crumbs. Mix to a firm dough with the water. Do not be tempted to add more water. Knead lightly until smooth and basin comes clean.
Makes approx. 12 oz. short crust pastry.

**Cornish Pasties**
Pastry as above (roughly 12 oz. short crust). Will make seven or eight.
**Filling:**
*½ lb. roughly minced beef*
*Chopped onion, diced potato*
*and carrot to weigh about ½ lb.*
*1 teaspoon Salt and Pepper Mix * *
1. Combine filling ingredients
2. Roll out pastry and cut into 6 to 7 inch rounds. A sauce pan lid can be a good cutter.
3. Place filling down centre of pastry, damp edges with water and bring sides to centre. Join on top.
4. Seal, fluting edges with fingers and thumb.
5. Brush with beaten egg.
6. Place on lightly greased baking tray and bake at Gas 6, 400°F. for 40 minutes, lowering heat if browning too much.

**Raisin Cider Pie**
*12 oz. short crust pastry*

**Filling**
*8 oz. seedless raisins*
*¼ pt. cider*
*Grated rind and juice of*
*1 lemon*
*2 oz. castor sugar*
*1 tablespoon cornflour*
*2 oz. chopped walnuts*
1. Soak raisins, cider and lemon rind for a few hours, or overnight.
2. Place in pan. Mix sugar and cornflour with lemon juice and stir in. Bring to boil, stir until mixture thickens. Add chopped walnuts. Leave to become quite cold.
3. Use half the above pastry to line

*See page 9.*

an 8 inch pie plate. Place filling to within a half inch of edge. Damp edges of pastry with water.

4. Cover with remainder of pastry rolled to size. Take care not to stretch it when laying it on.

5. Seal, fluting edges with fingers and thumbs, make slits in top and decorate.

6. Brush top lightly with water and sprinkle with castor sugar.

7. Bake at Gas 7, 425°F. for 15 minutes. Then reduce heat to Gas 5, 375°F. for a further 15-20 minutes. Serve warm with cream.

## Treacle Tart

*6 oz. short crust pastry*
**Filling**
*4 oz. golden syrup (4 level tablespoons)*
*1 tablespoon lemon juice*
*3 to 4 oz. fresh white breadcrumbs*

1. Using ¾ of the pastry, line a 7 inch pie plate, lightly damp round edge.

2. Add lemon juice to golden syrup and mix in breadcrumbs.

3. Pour filling on to pastry.

4. Roll out remaining pastry to an oblong 7 inches long, cut into ¼ inch strips - you should get 10 - twist and place, lattice-fashion, without stretching, across tart. Seal strips on to dampened edge. Flute edges of tart to neaten.

5. Bake at Gas 6, 400°F. for approximately 30 minutes.

## Yorkshire Cheesecake or Curd Tart

**Pastry:**
*6-oz. short crust pastry*
**Filling:**
*½ lb. curd*
*1 oz. softened butter*
*1 large beaten egg*
*1 tablespoon castor sugar*
*1 tablespoon golden syrup*
*1 oz. currants*
*½ oz. candied peel*
*1 tablespoon rum*

1. Roll out the pastry and line a 7 inch flan ring placed on a baking sheet.

2. Combine the filling ingredients. Spoon into pastry case.

3. Bake above centre of oven at 400°F, Gas 6, for about 30 minutes until pastry is cooked and filling just firm and golden. Best eaten while just warm.

## CHOUX PASTRY

*2½ oz. plain flour*
*Pinch of salt*
*1½ oz. butter (or margarine)*
*¼ pt. water*
*2 eggs*

1. Sieve flour and salt on to a piece greaseproof paper, place on stove to warm through (away from naked flame).

2. Heat butter and water in pan, bring to boil. Shoot in flour all at once, removing pan from heat immediately.

3. Lightly beat together until mixture forms a ball and leaves pan clean. Allow to cool.

4. Whisk eggs really well. Add a little at a time, beating well, checking consistency of paste as it may not require all the beaten egg. The mixture should be smooth and shiny, but still hold it's shape.

**Eclairs**

(i) Using a piping bag and a half inch plain nozzle, pipe in required lengths, approximately 2½ inches, on to a greased baking tray, cutting mixture clear of nozzle with a knife.

(ii) Bake at Gas 6, 400°F. for approximately 40 minutes, reducing heat if browning too quickly before they are crisp and dry. As soon as they are out of oven, split down side to allow steam to escape.

(iii) When cold, pipe in whipped cream. Ice with flavoured glacé icing.

### Choux rings
Pipe on tray in rings and proceed as for eclairs.

### Profiteroles
(i) Pipe or spoon in small blobs on to a greased baking tray and bake for approximately 25 minutes as for eclairs.

(ii) Fill with cream, arrange in pyramid on serving dish, dribble chocolate sauce lightly over top.

### Chocolate Sauce:
Melt together 4 ozs. plain cooking chocolate, ½ oz. butter and 1 tablespoon water in a basin over hot water - do not over-heat. Mix in a good teaspoon of cream.

Choux pastries may be served with sweet or savoury fillings.

### PUFF PASTRY
*8 oz. butter*
*8 oz. strong plain flour*
*Pinch of salt*
*1 teaspoon lemon juice*
*¼ pt. water*

1. Place butter, as it comes from the packet, between two pieces of greaseproof paper. It should be fairly cool. Beat lightly with rolling pin until about ¾ inch thick and pliable.
2. Sieve flour and salt into bowl.
3. Add lemon juice to water.
4. Cut edges of butter into a neat shape and rub trimmings into flour. Mix to a pliable dough with water and lemon juice. Knead smooth and into a neat oblong.
5. Roll out dough into a piece twice the size of the butter plus a half inch all round. Place butter, which should at this stage be of the same consistency as the dough, on one half of the rolled out dough, and cover with second half. Press lightly with rolling pin, leave about 10 minutes to relax, covered.
6. Lightly roll out pastry, three times as long as width, fold into three, bottom end up first and top end over. Position pastry on your board like a book with folded edge to the left and the three cut edges at top, bottom and right side. Always keep this sequence for future foldings.
7. Roll again to three times as long as width, fold again and leave to relax 15 to 20 minutes. Repeat until seven rollings are completed, relaxing pastry between each two rollings.
8. Leave a few hours or overnight in fridge, well wrapped. It will keep for 3 to 4 days in the fridge, or in the freezer for 3 to 4 months.

### Sausage Plait
Half the above quantity of puff pastry (roughly 8 oz.) A little beaten egg.

### Filling:
*½ lb. sausage meat*
*Pinch mixed herbs*
*Shake of salt and pepper*
*2 skinned and chopped tomatoes*
Mix all together.

1. Roll out pastry about 10 by 8 inches. Cut all edges clean and brush all round with beaten egg.
2. Place filling down centre third of pastry leaving a half inch at top and bottom.
3. Slash sides diagonally at 1 inch intervals and bring to centre alternately, sealing top and bottom. Leave in cool place for half an hour if possible.
4. Brush with beaten egg.
5. Bake on an ungreased baking tray at Gas 8, 450°F. for 15 minutes, reduce to Gas 6, 400°F. for a further 25 to 30 minutes.

### Bakewell Pudding
*13 oz. made puff pastry*

### Filling
*4 egg yolks*

2 egg whites
4 oz. melted butter
4 oz. castor sugar
5 drops almond essence
4 tablespoons strawberry jam
1. Well butter an 8 inch pie plate or flan tin, then line with pastry.
2. Blend together egg yolks and whites until well mixed.
3. Add butter, sugar and essence.
4. Spread base of pricked pastry with strawberry jam.
5. Pour in egg mixture.
6. Bake at 400°F, Gas 6, for about 30 minutes until pastry is pale brown round edges and filling is set. Serves 6.

## SUET CRUST FOR A RABBIT AND BACON PUDDING
**Suet Crust**
8 oz. self-raising flour
½ teaspoon salt
4 oz. shredded suet
7 tablespoons water
**Filling**
Approx. 1 lb. rabbit, in joints
1 bay leaf
1 small chopped onion
6 to 8 peppercorns
½ lb. bacon pieces
1 level tablespoon plain flour
1 pint stock (from cooking rabbit)
Salt and pepper
A little brown gravy colouring
1. Prepare filling first. Put rabbit in pan of water with bay leaf, onion and peppercorns. Bring to boil and simmer until tender.
2. Remove joints on to a plate and pick out the bones. Strain stock.
3. Cut up bacon removing rinds and any bones but do not remove the fat. Fry gently for about 10 minutes. Drain and mix with rabbit.
4. Stir flour into fat in pan (if less than 1 tablespoon add a little more bacon dripping). Stir to form a roux, sizzle one minute.
5. Gradually blend in 1 pint of the rabbit stock, bring to boil and

boil 1 minute. Taste for seasoning. Add a little colouring to make the gravy light brown.
6. Now make the suet crust mixing flour, salt, suet and water to a soft but not sticky dough.
7. Lightly grease a 2 pint heatproof basin. Line with ¾ of pastry.
8. Add the rabbit and bacon mixture and 3 tablespoonfuls of the gravy. The basin should not be full to the top to allow for rising.
9. Roll out remaining pastry, damp edges, fit on top.
10. Cover with a layer of greaseproof paper, lightly greased with a 1 inch pleat in top. Cover loosely with foil and press in round rim of basin to seal.
**Either Pressure Cook**
(a) Place pudding on trivet in pressure cooker with 1¼ pints of water.
(b) Place on lid—allow to steam 15 minutes.
(c) Add control at 5 lb. pressure—cook 25 minutes. Reduce at room temperature (7 to 8 minutes). Turn out pudding.
**Or Steam**
Place in top of steamer, cook 1¼ hours keeping water boiling. Serve with gravy and green vegetables.

## PORK PIE
**Hot Water Crust:**
4 fl. oz. water
4 oz. lard
10 oz. strong plain flour
½ level teaspoon salt
1 small beaten egg
**Filling:**
1 lb. pork from the shoulder, which should give roughly
¾ lb. lean and ¼ lb. fat
2 level teaspoons Salt and Pepper Mix*
¼ level teaspoon powdered mace if available.
**Jelly:**
1 pigs trotter
1 bay leaf
6 peppercorns

*See page 9.

1. Prepare jelly a day in advance. Boil trotter with bay leaf and peppercorns in 1 pint water until quite soft and leaving the bone (about 3 hours).
2. Strain liquid into basin, $\frac{1}{4}$ pt. is enough for 1 pie, and leave overnight.
3. Remove any fat from top. If jelly has not set, simmer gently to reduce amount. Discard trotter.
4. Now make the pastry. Boil water and lard, pour on to flour and salt. Mix with a knife (it will be hot) then knead with hands until quite smooth. Allow to cool a little before rolling out.
5. Now mix the filling. Trim gristle from pork which will reduce it to 14 or 15 oz. Cut it into very small pieces and mix in seasonings. Or, using coarse cutters, put the pork and seasonings through mincer.
6. Roll out $\frac{3}{4}$ of pastry to fit a loose-bottomed tin, 6 inches across and 3 inches deep, pressing pastry round sides to make an even thickness.
7. Pack filling in loosely.
8. Roll out lid to fit, brushing edges with beaten egg. Seal firmly. Cut away surplus pastry.
9. Roll this out thinly and cut into leaves. Brush these with beaten egg and arrange on top.
10. Flute edges of pie and brush all over top of pie with beaten egg.
11. Make a hole in centre with skewer.
12. Bake at Gas 6, 400°F. for 30 minutes, reduce heat if browning too quickly to Gas 5, 375°F., and bake for a further 1 hour.
13. Remove from tin on to wire.
14. Boil up jelly.
15. Allow pie and jelly to cool 15 minutes. Using a small funnel, gently pour jelly through hole in centre, as much as it will hold. When jelly has settled into meat, add a little more for extra moistness.
For best flavour leave it 24 hours before eating.

Freezes satisfactorily but not longer than one month.

## EGG AND BACON PIE
**Pastry**
*6 oz. plain flour*
*$\frac{1}{4}$ teaspoon salt*
*$1\frac{1}{2}$ oz. lard*
*$1\frac{1}{2}$ oz. margarine*
*3 brimming dessertspoons water*
**Filling**
*6 oz. bacon, pieces will do, not too fat*
*2 large eggs*
*A good shake of pepper*
*$\frac{1}{2}$ pint, less 2 tablespoons, of creamy milk*
1. Place flour and salt in bowl, rub in fats, bind to a firm dough with the water. Leave to rest 5 to 10 minutes.
2. Roll out a good 10 inches in diameter on floured board, fit into an 8-inch flan ring placed on a baking tray. Roll off surplus pastry with rolling pin.
3. Now make the filling. Cut bacon into 1-inch squares, fry lightly for 5 minutes over gentle heat, do not crisp. Drain from the fat.
4. Place eggs in a basin, add a good shake of pepper. Add the milk and whisk gently together without getting it frothy. This ensures a smooth texture.
5. Cover base of flan with bacon, strain on egg and milk mixture.
6. Bake at Gas 6, 400°F. for 20 minutes. Reduce heat to Gas 4, 350°F. for a further 10 to 12 minutes until filling is set.

## SAUSAGE PIE
**Good for a picnic**
**Pastry**
*8 oz. plain flour*
*$\frac{1}{2}$ teaspoon salt*
*2 oz. firm margarine*
*2 oz. lard*
*2 tablespoons water*
**Filling**
*8 oz. sausage-meat*
*2 tablespoons chutney*
*2 large tomatoes, skinned and*

*thickly-sliced*
*2 hard-boiled eggs, sliced*
*A pinch of mixed herbs*
*Salt and pepper*
**To finish pie**
*A little beaten egg or a teaspoon of top of the milk*
1. First make the pastry. Mix flour and salt, rub in fats and bind to a dough with the water.
2. Cut into 2 portions, one slightly larger than the other. Use larger piece to line a 9-inch foil plate. Roll remainder plus trimmings for the lid.
3. Mix together sausage-meat and chutney, divide into 2 equal portions, spread one portion over pastry in plate.
4. Arrange tomatoes and egg on top, sprinkle on herbs and salt and pepper, spread remaining sausage-meat on top.
5. Damp edges of pastry, place on lid, press to seal. Trim off surplus pastry and use it for pastry leaves.
6. Flute edges of pie and make 8 small slits in top. Brush with a little beaten egg if available, or use a teaspoon of top of the milk.
7. Arrange pastry leaves on top between slits and brush with egg or top of milk.
8. Bake at Gas 7, 425°F. for 15 minutes. Reduce to Gas 4, 350°F. for a further 45 minutes. Cover top with foil towards end of cooking if browning too quickly.

**FRUIT PIE**
**Shortcrust Pastry**
*6 oz. flour*
*¼ teaspoon salt*
*1½ oz. lard*
*1½ oz. margarine*
*1½ tablespoons water*
**Filling**
*1½ lb. fruit—*
*plums (stoned), gooseberries, rhubarb, apples, or half apples and half blackberries*
*2 tablespoons sugar*
*1 tablespoon cornflour*
**To finish**
*A little castor sugar*

A pie plate, 7-inch diameter and about 1¼ inches deep, or a pie dish, 1¼ to 1½-pint size, is suitable for this quantity.
1. Mix flour and salt, rub in fats, mix to a firm dough with water. Allow to rest for 15 minutes. This will prevent shrinkage during cooking.
2. Arrange half the fruit in pie dish. Mix sugar and cornflour, sprinkle over and cover with rest of fruit.
3. Using a floured board, roll out pastry half an inch larger than top of pie dish.
4. Cut a half inch strip away all round, damp edges of pie dish with water, press pastry strip on firmly.
5. Damp this strip, place pastry lid on top, press to seal, trim level.
6. Flute edges, make 4 small slits on top, brush lightly with water and sprinkle with castor sugar.
7. Bake at Gas 6, 400°F. for 30 minutes, reduce heat to Gas 4, 350°F. and bake a little longer until fruit is cooked. To test fruit, put a skewer through slit in pastry.

**SHERRY CHIFFON PIE**
For this you need a 7-inch flan case of short or sweet shortcrust pastry, baked blind.
**A Shortcrust Flan Case**
*4 oz. flour*
*¼ teaspoon salt*
*1 oz. margarine*
*1 oz. lard*
*1 tablespoon water*
1. Mix flour and salt, rub in fats, mix to a firm dough with water. Allow to rest 15 minutes. This will prevent shrinkage during cooking.
2. Place an ungreased 7-inch flan ring on a lightly-greased baking tray.
3. Roll out pastry on floured board to circular shape 9 inches across.

4. Fit into ring, floured side uppermost, pressing pastry gently round sides to make an even thickness. Roll off surplus pastry with rolling pin.

5. To bake blind, that is, without a filling. Prick base of pastry well with fork. Cut a circle of grease-proof paper, approximately 9 inches in diameter, lightly grease one side, and crumple paper into a ball. (This will make fitting easier). Fit, greased side down, into pastry case. Fill with dried peas or haricot beans. (Save your baked peas and beans in a jar for the next flan you make—they cannot be eaten.)

6. Bake, centre oven, at Gas 6, 400°F. about 10 minutes to set pastry. If browning too quickly, reduce to Gas 5, 375°F. and bake a further 15 minutes until golden and firm.

7. Remove beans and paper, slide flan on to a cooling wire and remove ring. Leave to cool.

**Filling**

*2 tablespoons sherry*
*1 dessertspoon gelatine*
*1 large egg, separated*
*3 oz. castor sugar*
*$\frac{3}{8}$ pint (7$\frac{1}{2}$ fluid oz.) hot milk*
*$\frac{1}{4}$ teaspoon almond essence*
*Nutmeg*

1. Measure 1 tablespoon sherry into a cup, sprinkle on gelatine, stir once to combine. Leave to soften.

2. Beat egg yolk and 2 oz. of the castor sugar in a large basin. Stir in the hot milk, strain back into milk pan. Cook over gentle heat, stirring gently, until mixture clings to spoon—do not boil.

3. Remove from heat, stir in the gelatine mixture and almond essence. Beat to dissolve gelatine. Add the remaining tablespoon of sherry. Cool until thickening.

4. Whisk egg white stiffly then whisk in remaining 1 oz. castor sugar. Fold into mixture.

5. Pour into cold baked flan case, grate a little nutmeg on top.

## BUCKINGHAMSHIRE LITTLE MUTTON PIES

To make about 8 to 12 pies.

*8 oz. cold cooked mutton or lamb*
*4 oz. cold potatoes*
*1 small onion*
*1 tablespoon chopped parsley*
*Sage or rosemary, to flavour,*
*(or mixed herbs)*
*Salt and pepper*
*Gravy or stock, to moisten*
*Beaten egg, to glaze*

**Short Crust Pastry:**

*8 oz. plain flour*
*2 oz. firm margarine*
*2 oz. lard*
*$\frac{1}{2}$ teaspoon salt*
*2 full tablespoons water*

Rub fats into flour and salt until like fine breadcrumbs. Mix to a firm dough with the water. Do not be tempted to add more water. Knead lightly until smooth and basin becomes clean.

**The Pies:**

1. Cut up into small squares the mutton and potatoes. Chop the onion finely.

2. Mix together meat, potato, onion, herbs and seasoning adding gravy or stock to moisten.

3. Roll out pastry thinly. Cut rounds to fit patty tins.

4. Spoon in meat mixture. Dampen edges and cover with pastry tops, pressing to seal. Brush with beaten egg.

5. Bake at Gas 7, 425°F. for 15 to 20 minutes.

## QUORN BACON ROLL

This is a dish for a cold day, very popular in the Quorn country.

*6 oz. self-raising flour*
*4 oz. grated suet*
*$\frac{1}{4}$ teaspoon salt*
*Approx. 6 tablespoons water*
*$\frac{1}{2}$ lb. lean bacon rashers, collar is best*
*1 large onion, chopped*
*$\frac{1}{2}$ teaspoon dried sage*
*Pepper*

1. Mix suet into flour and salt adding enough water to make a softish dough which is still firm enough to roll out.

2. Roll out on a floured board to about 12 by 7 inches.

3. Lay bacon rashers across pastry leaving ½ inch around edges. Sprinkle on chopped onion, sage and pepper.

4. Roll up loosely to make roll 7 inches wide. Nip the ends firmly to seal.

5. Scald a strong close-woven cotton cloth at least 12 inches square and sprinkle it with flour. Lay it on a sheet of foil large enough to enclose the roll.

6. Roll pudding in foil, then in cloth. Tie ends securely with string and pin the join with safety pins.

7. Have a saucepan ¾ full of boiling water. Put pudding in, lid on pan and bring back quickly to boil. Simmer for 2 hours. Don't allow water to go off the boil.

8. Serve on a hot dish, sprinkled with chopped parsley surrounded with vegetables.

**Miss Peggy Mills,
Leicestershire.**

## STAFFORDSHIRE RABBIT PIE

*1 rabbit*
*Water*
*Salt*
*Pepper*
*Seasoning—such as bay leaf, mace, parsley and peppercorns made into a bouquet garni*
**Forcemeat Balls:**
*6 oz. fresh breadcrumbs*
*3 oz. butter or grated suet*
*Thyme*
*Parsley*
*Salt and pepper*
*Juice of 1 lemon*
*A lightly beaten egg*
**Short Crust Pastry:**
*8 oz. plain flour*
*2 oz. firm margarine*
*2 oz. lard*
*½ teaspoon salt*
*2 full tablespoons water*
Rub fats into flour and salt until like fine breadcrumbs. Mix to a firm dough with the water. Do not be tempted to add more water. Knead lightly until smooth and basin becomes clean.

**The Pie**

1. Joint the rabbit and leave the pieces to soak about ½ hour in cold, salted water.

2. Put them in a pan with 1 pint of water, salt, pepper and other seasoning at pleasure. Cover and simmer for 1 hour.

3. Meanwhile make forcemeat balls by mixing the breadcrumbs with the butter or grated suet. Add thyme, parsley and seasoning and mix well together. Make it into a paste by adding the lemon juice and lightly beaten egg. Form into balls.

4. Drop these into pan in which rabbit is boiling. Simmer very gently for half an hour.

5. When cooked, place rabbit in a pie dish with forcemeat balls on top and pour in ⅓ to ½ pt. of the liquid.

6. Cover with pastry and bake the pie for 30 minutes in a moderately hot oven, Gas 6, 400°F.

**Miss P. M. Cherry,
Penkridge.**

## THATCHED HOUSE PIE

*3 oz. butter or margarine*
*2 oz. vermicelli*
*12 oz. puff pastry*
*1 dressed wood pigeon*
*Pepper and salt*

1. Take an oven-to-table dish, deep enough to hold a whole pigeon, pastry etc. A 5-inch soufflé dish is ideal, depending on size of pigeon. Rub the inside of the dish with 1 oz. of the butter or margarine.

2. Spread vermicelli on base of the dish.

3. Roll out a piece of pastry and line the base and sides of dish.

4. Fill the pigeon with remaining butter. Season with pepper and salt. Lay the pigeon breast side down in the pastry-lined dish.

5. Cover with a pastry lid sealing the joins.

6. Bake in a moderate oven, Gas 5, 375°F. until the pigeon is cooked, about 1½ hours. When pastry has risen heat may be reduced to Gas 2, 300°F. if pastry is browning too much.
7. Take a hot serving dish and turn out the pie. The vermicelli will appear like thatch—hence the name of the recipe.

**Mrs. Sybil Norcott,
Cheshire.**

## MUSHROOM PIE
**Short Crust Pastry:**
*8 oz. plain flour*
*2 oz. firm margarine*
*2 oz. lard*
*½ teaspoon salt*
*2 full tablespoons water*
Rub fats into flour and salt until like fine breadcrumbs. Mix to a firm dough with the water. Do not be tempted to add more water. Knead lightly until smooth and basin becomes clean.
**Filling:**
*2 rashers bacon*
*8 oz. mushrooms*
*Salt, pepper and a little dried sage*
*2 eggs, beaten*
1. Grease an 8-inch pie dish and line with pastry.
2. Cut bacon small and cover the bottom of pie.
3. Fill up with sliced seasoned mushrooms and sage.
4. Pour over the beaten eggs (reserving a little to brush pie top).
5. Cover with pastry lid and decorate. Brush top with beaten egg.
6. Bake in moderate oven, Gas 6, 400°F. about 1 hour, reducing heat to Gas 3, 325°F. after first half hour if pastry is browning too much before bacon is cooked.

**Mrs. Sybil Norcott,
Cheshire.**

## MINCE MERINGUE TARTS
**Short Crust Pastry Cases:**
*8 oz. soft plain flour*
*½ level teaspoon salt*
*2 oz. firm margarine*
*2 oz. lard*
*2 full tablespoons water*
1. Rub fats into flour and salt.
2. Mix to a firm dough with water. Allow to rest 15 to 20 minutes.
3. Roll out thinly.
4. Line patty tins with pastry and prick base with a fork.
5. Stand a grease-proof paper bun case with a tablespoon of baking beans* in each.
6. Bake at Gas 7, 425°F. for 15 minutes until set and just golden. Remove from patty tins on to rack to cool.
The cases freeze very well and can be made a few weeks in advance. They will keep for 1 week in an air-tight tin.
**Filling:**
*Mincemeat*
*1 egg white*
*2 oz. castor sugar*
(This is sufficient for 8 tarts).
1. Place 1 to 2 teaspoons mincemeat in cases.
2. Whisk egg white very stiffly, fold in castor sugar.
3. Using large star nozzle, pipe this meringue round edge of tarts.
4. Place on a baking sheet in cool oven, Gas 2, 300°F. for about 12 to 15 minutes until meringue is set.
**\*Baking beans** (or peas) for baking pastry cases blind. Haricot beans or dried peas may be used. Keep in a jar for use again—they cannot be eaten after baking.

## RICHMOND MAIDS OF HONOUR
Makes 18
*1 pt. milk*
*1 teaspoon rennet*
*2 oz. butter*
*2 oz. castor sugar*
*1 egg*
*1 oz. very finely chopped almonds*
*2 teaspoons brandy, optional*
*1 level teaspoon grated lemon rind*
*¼ level teaspoon cinnamon*
*Pinch of salt*
*1 small (7½ oz.) packet puff pastry*

1. Warm milk to blood heat, add rennet.
2. Pour into a dish and leave in a warm place to set.
3. When set, roughly cut up junket and place in a nylon sieve over a bowl. Cover and leave in refrigerator overnight.
4. Discard whey and place curds in a bowl.
5. Cream butter and sugar together until light.
6. Beat in curds, egg, almonds, brandy (if using), lemon rind, cinnamon and salt.
7. Roll out pastry thinly and line 18 tartlet tins.
8. Divide curd mixture between tins and bake in a hot oven Gas 7, 425°F. for 15 to 20 minutes until pale golden brown.
9. Carefully lift on to a wire rack and leave to cool.

**Ruth Morgan,
Surrey.**

## RABBIT PIE

*1 rabbit or 1½ lb. rabbit portions*
*12 oz. belly pork*
*2 onions*
*Salt and pepper*
*1 oz. flour*
*A little sage*
*1 teaspoon chopped parsley*
*¼ pt. stock from the rabbit bones.*
*12 oz. made-up rough puff or flaky pastry (see page 29).*

**First prepare the rabbit:**
1. Skin, draw and wash the rabbit well.
2. Bone it and cut into portions.
3. Soak the portions in water for 1 hour.
4. Meanwhile, put into a pan the bones and any bony trimmings from the pork, one of the onions roughly-chopped, salt and pepper. Add water just to cover, bring to boil and simmer for at least one hour.
5. Drain water from the rabbit portions and wipe them on a cloth.

**The Pie:**
1. Put the rabbit into a pie dish, sprinkle with salt and pepper and dredge with flour and sage.
2. Cut the pork into pieces and place them over the rabbit.
3. Sprinkle with parsley and the remaining onion, chopped fine.
4. Add enough stock from the bones to come three quarters up the dish.
5. Cover with pastry. Decorate in the usual manner and make a small hole in the centre.
6. Cook in a fairly quick oven, Gas 5, 375°F. for half an hour until pastry is a good brown then reduce to Gas 3, 325°F. for a further hour.
7. Remove from oven. If liquor has evaporated, add a little more heated bone stock taking care that it does not touch the pie crust. This pie is excellent and usually eaten cold, the bone stock making a good jelly.

**Mrs. M. Pettitt,
Ousden, Suffolk.**

## SAVOURY LAMB PIE

*1 lb. lean lamb, cut into ½-inch cubes (shoulder will do)*
*1 dessertspoon plain flour*
*1 teaspoon Salt and Pepper Mix\**
*8 oz. sliced onions*
*1 large cooking apple, peeled, cored and thickly-sliced*
*¼ pint water, or stock made from bones removed from lamb*

1. Toss meat in flour mixed with Salt and Pepper Mix. Place in shallow 1½ to 2 pint casserole, sprinkle on remaining flour.
2. Layer onion on top, then apple, add water or stock.
3. Cover tightly (a piece of lightly-greased foil will do).
4. Cook at Gas 4, 350°F., 1½ to 2 hours until lamb is tender. The time depends on quality of lamb.
5. Increase heat to Gas 7, 425°F. ready for scone top.

**Scone Top:**
*6 oz. self-raising flour*
*¼ teaspoon salt*
*1 teaspoon mixed herbs*
*1 oz. margarine*
*1 oz. lard*

*\*See page 9.*

*3 to 4 fluid oz. milk*
1. Place flour in a bowl, add salt and herbs.
2. Rub in fats, mix to a smooth dough with the milk.
3. Roll out a quarter inch thick, cut into 2 to 2½ inch rounds.
**To finish the pie:**
Arrange scone rounds on top of casserole, return to oven and bake for 25 to 30 minutes until scone top is crusty and golden.


## LEEK PUDDING
*6 oz. self-raising flour*
*3 oz. grated suet*
*Water to mix, about 6 tablespoons*
*Pinch of salt*
**Filling:**
*Chopped leeks and any cold meat left from another meal.*
1. Chop or mince the meat and mix with the leeks. There should be enough to spread thickly on the rolled out pastry.
2. Mix suet into flour and salt adding enough water to make a softish dough which is still firm enough to roll out.
3. Roll out on a floured board to about 12 by 7 inches.
4. Spread on the filling to within half an inch of edges, sprinkling liberally with salt and pepper. Damp edges with water.
5. Roll up loosely to make a roll 7 inches wide. Nip the ends firmly to seal.
6. Wrap the roll loosely in a large piece of greased foil enclosing it completely and sealing ends well.
7. Scald a strong close-woven cotton cloth at least 12 inches square.
8. Roll pudding in cloth, tie ends securely with string making a strong handle across top also. This helps when removing pudding from water.
9. Have a saucepan two-thirds full of boiling water. Put pudding in, lid on pan and bring back quickly to boil.
10. Boil for 2 hours, keeping water boiling and replenishing if necessary with more boiling water. Serve with a good gravy.

**Mrs. M. White,**
**Northumberland.**

## KIPPER SAVOURY
*2 large kippers*
*2 oz. butter*
*1 tablespoon chopped chives*
*½ clove of garlic crushed with a few grains of salt*
**For the pastry:**
*8 oz. plain flour*
*3 oz. lard*
*3 oz. peeled and grated raw potato*
*About 1 tablespoon cold water*
**To finish:**
*A little melted butter*
1. Steam kippers between 2 plates over a pan of simmering water for about 20 minutes. Remove flesh, discard bones and skin.
2. Soften butter in a basin, but do not let it melt to oil.
3. Add flaked kipper-flesh, chives and garlic. Mix well.
4. Rub lard into flour, add potato and mix to a firm dough with water.
5. Roll out half the dough and line a pie plate 7 to 8 inches in diameter.
6. Spread on filling to within a half inch of edge, dampen edge with cold water.
7. Roll out remaining dough to cover, press edges to seal, trim and flute.
8. With a sharp knife, using tip only, make a criss-cross pattern on top of pie cutting through lid to filling.
9. Brush with melted butter.
10. Bake at Gas 6, 400°F. for about 35 minutes.
Good served with parsley sauce. Can also be served in slices for a buffet.

**Mrs. Joan Ireland,**
**West Suffolk.**

## CHESHIRE ONION PIE
**Shortcrust Pastry:**
*6 oz. plain flour*

¼ teaspoon salt
1½ oz. lard
1½ oz. margarine
3 dessertspoons water
**Filling:**
2 oz. butter
1 to 1¼ lbs. peeled and sliced
onions
1 oz. plain flour (very bare weight)
1 level teaspoon salt
A good quantity of black pepper
Grated nutmeg
¼ pint top of the milk or cream
1 large egg
1. Place flour and salt in mixing
bowl, rub in fats, mix to a firm
dough with the water.
2. Roll out on floured board.
3. Line an 8-inch flan ring on a
baking tray. Leave to rest while
preparing filling.
4. Melt butter in saucepan, add
onions, cook gently until soft,
about 15 minutes. Do not brown.
5. Add flour, let it sizzle then
add salt and pepper and a little
nutmeg.
6. Stir in milk, bring to boil and
cook 2 minutes. Remove from
heat.
7. Beat egg lightly, spoon into it a
little mixture from pan and stir in,
then return to pan and mix in.
Taste for seasoning.
8. Spoon into flan case, level and
grate a little more nutmeg on top.
7. Bake at Gas 6, 400°F. for 45 to
50 minutes. After about 30 minutes
when pastry is set, remove flan
ring to allow crust to brown. Cool
on wire tray.

**Mrs. Sybil Norcott,**
**Irlam.**

## STAFFORDSHIRE
## YEOMANRY PUDDING
**Sweet Shortcrust Pastry:**
1 egg yolk
1 oz. castor sugar
3 teaspoons water
8 oz. soft plain flour
½ level teaspoon salt
5 oz. firm margarine
**Filling:**
4 oz. butter
4 oz. castor sugar

¼ teaspoon almond essence
1 oz. ground almonds
2 eggs (using 2 yolks and 1 white)
2 tablespoons raspberry jam
1. For the pastry, mix together
egg-yolk, sugar and water.
2. Place flour and salt in a bowl,
rub in margarine.
3. Mix to a firm dough with egg,
sugar and water mixture. Leave
in a cool place for 15 minutes.
4. Meanwhile, make filling. Cream
butter and sugar, mix in essence
and ground almonds.
5. Beat egg yolks and egg white
together, beat into rest of mixture.
6. Roll out two thirds of pastry
just under a quarter inch thick
and line a shallow pie dish. Trim
off surplus pastry and damp edge
with water.
7. Spread on jam, then filling.
8. Roll out remaining pastry and
trimmings, fit on top. Trim, seal
and flute edges. Make 4 or 6 small
cuts in top with point of knife.
9. Bake at Gas 4, 350°F. for 40
minutes covering with foil for last
10 minutes as this pastry browns
quickly.
Nice eaten while just warm but
not too hot. Also very good cold.

**Miss P. M. Cherry,**
**Penkridge.**

## LINCOLNSHIRE POTATO
## CHEESECAKE
First put the potatoes on and
while they are cooking make the
pastry.
**Short Crust Pastry:**
6 oz. soft, plain flour
1½ oz. margarine
1½ oz. lard
Salt
3 brimming dessertspoons water
1. Rub fats into flour and salt
until like fine breadcrumbs.
2. Mix to a firm dough with the
water. Do not be tempted to add
more water.
3. Knead lightly until smooth and
basin becomes clean.
4. Roll out on floured board.
5. Line an 8 inch flan ring on a

baking tray. Prick base of flan. Leave to rest while mixing the filling.

**Filling:**
*8 oz. hot, cooked potatoes (steamed or pressure-cooked are best)*
*Salt*
*Pinch of nutmeg, optional*
*4 oz. softened butter*
*4 oz. castor sugar*
*2 eggs, well-beaten*
*Grated rind and juice of 1 medium-sized lemon*

1. Sieve hot potatoes with salt and nutmeg if used.
2. Add butter, sugar, eggs, grated rind and lemon juice. Beat thoroughly together.
3. Fill flan case almost to top.
4. Bake at Gas 6, 400°F. on middle shelf for 15 minutes. Remove flan ring and bake 10 more minutes until filling is set and browning on top.

Served at Harvest Home suppers.
**Mrs. Hilda Newland,
Louth.**

## GODS KITCHEL CAKE

*1 lb. made-up flaky pastry (see page 29).*
*4 oz. margarine*
*8 oz. currants*
*1 oz. sultanas*
*2 oz. candied peel*
*3 oz. sugar*
*2 oz. ground almonds*
*2 teaspoons powdered cinnamon*
*1 teaspoon grated nutmeg*

1. Melt margarine. Add fruit, peel, sugar, ground almonds and spices. Mix well.
2. Halve the pastry and roll one piece into a square about 12 inches across. Place it on a baking sheet. Quantity and size of pastry depend on your baking sheet but rolled out pastry should be quite thin. Moisten edges with milk or water.
3. Spread filling on this square stopping half an inch short of edges.
4. Cover with second piece of pastry rolled out to fit. Seal the edges, pressing lightly together.
5. Carefully mark the top in 2½ inch squares without cutting through.
6. Bake near top of oven Gas 7, 425°F. for about half an hour until it is a nice golden brown.
7. Leave it on baking sheet when it comes out of oven and sprinkle with castor sugar. Let it cool a little then divide into sections and cool on wire rack.
**Mrs. Margaret Pettitt,
Ousden, Suffolk.**

# CHAPTER 4

# POULTRY AND GAME

## TO BONE POULTRY.

A sharp knife is essential.

1. Cut down the centre of the back of the bird from neck to tail.
2. Taking first one side of the bird, cut and work the flesh off the bones. Take care not to puncture the skin.
3. Work down the leg. To facilitate pulling the drumstick bone through cut off at the joint any remaining lower limb.
4. Work down the shoulder in the same way as the leg.
5. Continue working flesh off until the centre breast bone is reached.
6. Now repeat the process on the other side of the bird from back bone round to breast bone.
7. When all the flesh is loose and ready to be lifted right off the carcass take care not to cut through the skin at the edge of the breast bone where it is thin.

Use the carcass to make stock.

## TRUSSING POULTRY OR GAME BIRDS

1. To remove the sinews, make a circular incision about 1 inch below the hock joint, taking care not to cut into the sinews. Break the legs and pull off the feet, (a loop of strong twine may help here).
2. Trim the extreme portions of the wings.
3. Place the bird on the table breast down, and head away from you. With the finger and thumb grasp the skin between the shoulders, cut a strip of skin about ½ inch wide from that point to half-way up the neck. Sever the neck at the shoulder and the skin half-way up the neck.
4. Remove the crop and wind-pipe.
5. Insert the first finger of the right hand in the opening; by circular movement loosen the lungs and other organs.
6. Place the bird neck down, grasp the tail with the left hand. Make an incision midway between the tail and the vent, cut around the vent. Place the bird back down and tail towards you, remove the fat around the abdomen, then grasp the gizzard with the right hand and draw gently when the whole of the internal organs will come out.
7. Save the neck, gizzard, liver and heart. These should be wrapped in greaseproof paper. The gizzard should be split and the inner tough skin peeled off. Take care not to break the gall bladder in removing the liver.
8. To tie up, fold the flap of skin over the neck and fold the wings back over this, Take a trussing needle, threaded with strong white string about 18 inches long. With back downwards pull the legs back towards the head and press down firmly. Pass the needle through the body where the legs join the body. Then turn the bird over and pass the needle through the joint of one wing, across the back of the bird and through the other wing. Now tie the two strings and cut off. With the back downwards again, and keeping the tail towards you, pass the needle and thread through loose skin underneath and near the tip of the breast bone. Leave the string above the legs. Turn the bird on its breast. The two ends of string are then brought round the legs, crossed and tied tightly round the tail. The trussing complete, strings should not be cut to stuff the bird All stuffings required can be put in at the neck end.

## TO JOINT A CHICKEN

Utensils if you don't have secateurs: A sharp knife.
A 1 lb. weight or similar hard object to help knock the knife through
1. Cut the chicken in half length-

wise through breast bone and then the backbone.

2. To obtain four joints, cut each half diagonally, between the leg and the wing, (upwards from the leg).

3. If six joints required divide drumstick from thigh.

4. With a large chicken the wing joint can be removed with a little breast meat.

## CHICKEN, BONED, STUFFED AND ROASTED

*A 3 lb chicken*

### The Stuffing

*1 lb. pork sausage meat*
*1 tablespoon finely chopped parsley*
*2 chopped shallots (or 1 small onion, finely chopped)*
*2 tablespoons stock, or wine*
Mix all together.

### Garnish

4 hard-boiled eggs
Trim a little off the ends so that they will lie close.

### To Stuff the Boned Bird.

1. Spread the bird out on a board, skin side down.

2. Stuff the legs and shoulders with a little of the stuffing mixture.

3. Spread half the stuffing down the centre of the bird. Place the eggs down the centre end to end. Cover with remaining stuffing.

4. Shape the bird again and stitch with fine string.

5. Wrap in tin foil with a little stock and cook at Gas 5, 375º - 400ºF, allowing 20 minutes to lb. per stuffed weight, plus a further 20 minutes.

May be eaten hot, in which case open foil 30 minutes before end of cooking time to allow to brown.

### For Eating Cold

**Coating Sauce:**
*2 oz. butter*
*2 oz. flour*
*¾ pt. milk*
*salt and pepper*
*2 tablespoons top of the milk, or cream*
*¼ pt. water*
*1 oz. gelatine*

(i) Melt the butter, add flour and allow to sizzle without browning 1 to 2 minutes to cook the flour.

(ii) Pour on milk. Stir until boiling. Simmer 1 to 2 minutes stirring continuously.

(iii) Dissolve gelatine in the water, add to the sauce with cream and seasoning.

(iv) Put through a fine sieve or even a clean, damp tea cloth to be sure sauce is smooth. Stir frequently whilst cooling to keep the sauce smooth and velvety. When the consistency of thick cream, it is ready for coating.

**Decoration:**

Any colourful vegetables, peels, etc. (Carrot, cucumber skin, lemon/orange peel, gherkin, olives.)

1. When the bird is cold, remove strings and skin.

2. Place on a wire tray over a dish. Pour over the coating sauce. Allow to set. Give another coating if necessary, (sauce may need rewarming for this.)

3. Decorate with small cuttings of colourful vegetables, peels, etc., first dipping the pieces in a little dissolved gelatine which will stop them slipping off.

## DOROTHY SLEIGHTHOLME'S CHICKEN WITH APPLE

For this you need a large sauté or frying pan with a good lid.

An electric frying pan is ideal.

*2 level tablespoons plain flour*
*1 level teaspoon salt*
*⅓ level teaspoon pepper*
*1 jointed chicken*

2 oz. bacon fat
1 large sliced onion
1 large carrot, cut in rings
2 sharp eating apples, peeled cored
and cut into quarters
½ lb. peas
½ pt. cider (or sharp apple wine)
¼ pt. chicken stock (from giblets)

1. Mix flour, salt and pepper on a plate and coat joints well in it.
2. Heat fat in large sauté or frying pan until quite hot and brown joints all over, turning once or twice, (about four minutes).
3. Add onion and carrot coated in rest of flour, turn over in pan for one minute. Push aside.
4. Place apple quarters, and peas if fresh, in the pan. Pour over the cider or apple wine. This will sizzle. Add stock, allow to boil, reduce heat until simmering.
5. Cook 30 minutes with lid on. Frozen or tinned peas (well drained) can be added now. Cook another 10 minutes.

Arrange on a hot dish, sprinkle chicken with chopped parsley and arrange triangles of toast round edge. Or serve with new potatoes tossed in butter.

The dish can be cooked in a covered casserole in the oven, transfering contents of frying pan after each stage. The cooking time for this method is 35-40 minutes, Gas 5, 375°F.

## BERKSWELL LEMON CHICKEN

2 oz. butter or margarine
Juice of 1 large or 2 small lemons
Salt and pepper
1 young 2½ to 3½ lb. chicken, jointed*
½ pt. chicken stock
1 tablespoon chopped parsley, chives and mint mixed
1 tablespoon flour

1. Melt butter in a flameproof casserole with lemon juice, salt and pepper and make very hot.
2. Put in chicken joints and ¼ pt. of the stock, slowly turn chicken in the mixture so that every part is covered and the liquid boils.
3. Cover at once and put in a slow oven, Gas 3, 325°F. for 1 hour.
4. Put chicken on hot dish.
5. Add flour to liquid in casserole and stir until smooth.
6. Add other ¼ pt. stock and herbs and bring to boil.
7. Pour over chicken and serve.
*See page 44.

**Mrs. Redgrave,
Warwickshire.**

## CHICKEN AND BACON CROQUETTES

4 oz. cold, cooked chicken
4 oz. cold, cooked bacon
4 oz. cold, mashed potato
Chopped parsley
Salt and pepper
2 small eggs, beaten
Dried breadcrumbs

1. Mince the chicken and bacon.
2. Mix together the minced meat, potato, parsley and seasoning with sufficient beaten egg to bind.
3. Shape into croquettes and leave an hour or two, if possible in the refrigerator, when they will be firmer and easier to handle.
4. Dip in beaten egg then coat with dried breadcrumbs.
5. Fry in deep hot fat until golden. Drain on absorbent kitchen paper.

## COUNTRY CHICKEN CASSEROLE

2 oz. bacon dripping, margarine or butter
4 rashers streaky bacon
1 medium-sized, sliced onion
1 level tablespoon flour
1 level teaspoon Salt and Pepper Mix*
4 chicken joints
4 oz. pork sausage meat
An 8 oz. tin of tomatoes
½ teaspoon oregano, marjoram or mixed herbs
¼ pint stock if necessary

*Chopped parsley*

1. Melt 1 oz. of the fat, fry chopped bacon and onion for a few minutes. Drain into a casserole leaving fat in pan.
2. Mix flour and Salt and Pepper Mix, dust chicken joints well. Put them into the frying pan skin side down, using extra dripping only if necessary. Fry joints turning them over in pan until they are golden. Put them into casserole.
3. Divide sausage meat into 8 small balls, roll in the seasoned flour and fry briskly to seal and brown. Place in between joints in casserole.
4. Measure fat in frying pan. Remove some or add a little so that there is just 1 tablespoon. Add remaining flour.
5. Stir to cook flour 1 minute, add tin of tomatoes, herbs and as much stock as necessary to make a thick sauce. Stir until boiling.
6. Pour over chicken, cover and cook at Gas 4, 350°F. for about 1 hour until chicken is cooked.
Sprinkle with parsley and serve from casserole with plain boiled or new potatoes.

## TO ROAST A TURKEY

**Note:** It is wise to time the cooking so that turkey is removed from oven on to warm dish 10 to 15 minutes before serving the meal. This will allow time to make the gravy and also to "rest" the bird.

**Cooking time:** A slow method is recommended unless instructions given with the bird differ.

| Stuffed weight in lbs. | Total cooking time in hours |
|---|---|
| 6 to 8 | 3 to 3½ |
| 8 to 10 | 3½ to 3¾ |
| 10 to 12 | 3¾ to 4 |
| 12 to 14 | 4 to 4¼ |
| 14 to 16 | 4¼ to 4½ |
| 16 to 18 | 4½ to 4¾ |

1. Choose and prepare 2 suitable stuffings for neck end and body cavity. (See suggestions this page).
**Note:** Body cavity takes more than neck end. Any stuffing left can be

put in a pie dish, covered securely and placed in bottom of oven. It will take no harm there for 1½ to 2 hours.
2. Remove giblets from turkey, wash them and place in pan with sufficient water to cover. Add 6 to 8 peppercorns and a small bay leaf. Bring to boil and simmer for at least 2 hours. Strain and keep stock for gravy. The giblets can now be discarded. (Preparation and cooking of giblets can be done the day before.)
3. Wipe inside of turkey and stuff to a plump, even shape.
4. Truss with skewers and fine clean string folding wings under body and tying legs tightly together.
5. Place on rack in a large roasting tin. Cover well with good dripping or pieces of fat pork or bacon. Press foil round legs as they are inclined to dry before being cooked.
6. Place in oven at Gas 6, 400°F. for 20 minutes. Then lower heat to Gas 4, 350°F. for remainder of cooking time. Baste frequently turning bird on its side once or twice during cooking time. If breast browns too quickly cover with foil.
7. Remove turkey on to warm dish and make gravy with giblet stock and sediment from roasting tin. Serve with bread sauce, (see next page), cranberry sauce, small sausages, bacon rolls etc.

## TWO STUFFINGS FOR TURKEY AND CHICKEN

Adjust quantities for size of bird and cavity to be filled.

**Corn and Bacon Stuffing**
*2 oz. butter*
*1 large finely chopped onion*
*8 oz. bacon pieces*
*1 can sweetcorn, approx. 11 oz.*
*4 tablespoons fresh parsley*
*2 teaspoons Salt and Pepper Mix\**
*1 teaspoon mixed herbs*
*1 small loaf of bread, unsliced but crusts removed*

*See page 9.

*2 small beaten eggs*
1. Melt butter in pan. Fry onion and chopped bacon to soften.
2. Place in bowl, add sweetcorn, parsley, salt, pepper and herbs.
3. Cut bread into small cubes.
4. Stir in, mixing eggs in lightly. Do not pack stuffing into bird too tightly.

### Sausage Meat Stuffing
*1 to 1½ lb. pork sausage meat (according to size of bird)*
*1 teaspoon mixed herbs*
*1 grated onion*
*1 grated apple*
*A little freshly milled black pepper*
*Fresh breadcrumbs*
1. Mix together all ingredients adding 1 to 2 tablespoons breadcrumbs if mixture is too soft.
2. Stuff into bird. Do not pack too tightly.

## BREAD SAUCE
*1 medium onion*
*2 cloves*
*¾ pt. milk*
*½ level teaspoon salt*
*6 peppercorns*
*A small piece of bay leaf*
*6 to 8 oz. fresh white breadcrumbs*
*½ oz. butter*
1. Peel onion, stick into it the cloves.
2. Put in saucepan with milk, salt, peppercorns and bay leaf. Cover, place over very low heat and bring to just below boiling point.
3. Remove from heat and set aside for 30 minutes or longer.
4. Strain milk, bring it to boil, pour over the crumbs, add butter and stir.
5. Place in heat-proof pie dish. Cover and place in oven on low shelf under meat for 20 minutes.

## MRS. HART'S TURKEY IN A CHEESE AND SHERRY SAUCE
*12 oz. cooked turkey or chicken, in bite-sized pieces*
*1½ oz. butter*
*2 oz. flour*
*½ pt. milk, warmed*

*4 tablespoons stock from the bird*
*2 tablespoons sherry*
*Nutmeg*
*Salt*
*Black pepper, quite a lot*
*3 tablespoons grated Parmesan and/or Gruyere cheese*
*2 tablespoons cream*
*Dried breadcrumbs*
1. Remove skin and bone from meat.
2. Melt butter in a pan.
3. Add flour and sizzle 1 minute.
4. Add warmed milk, bring to boil, stirring. Add stock, return to boil. Cook 2 minutes.
5. Add sherry and seasonings, bring just to boil.
6. Stir in 2 tablespoons of the cheese and allow to melt. Stir in cream. Reheat, but do not boil.
7. Put layer of meat in shallow oven dish. Pour over a layer of sauce. Fill dish with layers of meat and sauce.
8. Sprinkle with breadcrumbs and remaining cheese.
9. Put in oven Gas 4, 350°F. for 20 to 25 minutes until turkey is properly heated.
10. Finally put under grill to brown before serving.

## TURKEY OR CHICKEN IN SHERRY SAUCE
*12 oz. cooked turkey or chicken in bite-sized pieces*
*3 ozs. butter*
*1 small chopped onion*
*2 lean rashers of bacon, chopped*
*2 oz. button mushrooms*
*2 level tablespoons flour*
*Salt and pepper*
*½ pt. chicken (or turkey) stock*
*3 tablespoons dry sherry*
*Chopped parsley*
*Triangles of toast*
1. Fry turkey or chicken in hot butter until golden. Drain meat, place it on a hot serving dish and keep warm.
2. Fry onion and bacon in same pan about 2 minutes, add mushrooms, cook 2 minutes.
3. Stir in flour and a shake of salt

and pepper. Cook 1 minute.
4. Add stock, simmer 2 minutes.
5. Add sherry, bring just to boil.
Pour over chicken.
6. Sprinkle on chopped parsley
and serve with toast triangles.

## TURKEY RISOTTO
*2 oz. butter*
*1 medium-sized onion, chopped*
*4 oz. mushrooms*
*8 oz. long-grained rice*
*1 to 1¼ pt. of light turkey or*
*chicken stock*
*1 to 2 oz. sultanas*
*3 tomatoes, skinned and chopped*
*4 oz. cooked peas*
*12 oz. cooked turkey, in bite-*
*sized pieces*
1. Wipe or wash the mushrooms,
but do not peel. If large, cut in
half.
2. Melt butter in large saucepan,
add onion, soften but do not
brown.
3. Add the mushrooms.
4. Add the rice and cook gently
until rice absorbs butter and goes
transparent.
5. Add ¾ pt. stock, bring to boil.
6. Simmer, stirring occasionally,
keeping lid on pan when not
stirring. (If mixture is becoming
too dry before rice is cooked,
gradually add a little more stock.)
7. After 12 minutes add sultanas
and turkey. Allow to cook 2 to 3
minutes more then add tomatoes
and peas. Check for seasoning and
continue cooking till rice is done.
The risotto will take about 20
minutes to cook, depending on
type of rice. It should be soft and
creamy, but not mushy.
2 to 3 oz. ham cut in cubes can
also be added at same time as
turkey pieces. Good also if made
with chicken instead of turkey.

## TURKEY AND HAM LOAF
**To eat hot or cold**
*12 oz. cold, cooked turkey pieces*
*8 oz. ham pieces*
*1 small chopped onion*
*1 teaspoon mixed herbs*

*2 teaspoons Salt and Pepper Mix\**
*1 large beaten egg*
*1 teacup fresh breadcrumbs*
*Stock, if necessary*
*Browned, dried breadcrumbs for*
*coating*
1. Mince turkey, ham and onion.
2. Add seasonings, beaten egg and
fresh breadcrumbs. Use stock if
mixture is very dry.
3. Pack into a greased 1½ lb. loaf
tin. Cover with foil.
4. Cook at Gas 4, 350°F. for 1
hour.
5. Turn out and coat while hot in
browned crumbs.

## COLD TURKEY WITH
## ORANGE AND TOMATO
## SALAD
*Slices of cold, cooked turkey*
*4 tablespoons mayonnaise*
*2 tablespoons thick cream*
*2 teaspoons lemon juice*
*Paprika*
*Chopped parsley*
**For the salad:**
*2 oranges, peeled and separated*
*into segments*
*2 to 3 tomatoes, sliced*
*Cress, and/or lettuce*
1. Arrange turkey down centre of
flat, serving dish.
2. Mix mayonnaise, cream and
lemon juice, spoon over turkey.
3. Garnish with slanting lines of
paprika and chopped parsley.
4. Arrange the salad around the
turkey or serve separately.

## TURKEY, RICE AND CORN
## SALAD
*12 to 16 oz. turkey, cut into*
*bite-sized pieces*
*3 tablespoons French dressing*
*(see page 10)*
*¼ pt. mayonnaise mixed with*
*1 tablespoon lemon juice* **Or** *¼ pt.*
*salad cream*
*A little grated black pepper*
*¼ teaspoon salt*
*6 oz. cooked long-grain rice*
*An 11 oz. tin sweetcorn kernels*
*1 green pepper†, de-seeded and*
*finely diced*

2 tomatoes, skinned, de-seeded
and roughly chopped
Lettuce
1. Mix turkey into French dressing.
2. In another bowl combine mayonnaise and lemon juice (or salad cream) with seasonings. Fold in turkey, rice, drained corn, green pepper and tomatoes.
3. Line a salad bowl with crisp lettuce leaves and pile mixture in centre.
†**Green pepper** may be blanched, as the slightly bitter taste does not appeal to everyone. To blanch: prepare pepper, bring to boil in pan of water, boil 1 minute, drain, plunge into cold water to cool.

### TURKEY OR CHICKEN PÂTÉ
*1 large chopped onion*
*2 oz. butter*
*12 oz. cooked turkey or chicken in pieces*
*1 teaspoon Salt and Pepper Mix**
*4 tablespoons cream*
*1 to 2 tablespoons dry sherry*
*Parsley to garnish*
1. Fry onion in butter until soft.
2. Mix in turkey or chicken, mince all finely (or put in blender).
3. Add cream and just enough sherry to moisten. Taste and season. Beat till smooth.
4. Place in dish, fork top. Garnish with a sprig of parsley.

### COOKING THE GOOSE
**With Sage and Onion Stuffing**
**Note:** Time the cooking so that goose is removed from oven on to heated dish 10 to 15 minutes before serving the meal. This will allow time to make the gravy and also to "rest" the bird.
**Cooking time:** 15 minutes to each lb. weight after stuffing plus 15 to 25 minutes extra depending on age of bird.
1. First make the stuffing, see next recipe.
2. Remove giblets from goose, wash them and place in pan with sufficient water to cover. Add 6 to 8 peppercorns and a small bay leaf. Bring to boil and simmer for at least 2 hours. Strain and keep stock for gravy. The giblets can now be discarded. (Preparation and cooking of giblets can be done the day before.)
3. Wipe inside of goose and fill with sage and onion stuffing, not too tightly packed.
4. Truss goose neatly with skewers and fine clean string. This is simply to keep the stuffing in.
5. Place goose on a roasting rack in oven tin. Rub with salt and sprinkle on a little flour. (The breast can be pricked with a fork to help fat escape, but this is not necessary.)
6. Place in centre of oven pre-heated to Gas 6, 400°F. for 20 minutes to crisp skin. Then lower heat to Gas 4, 350°F. for remainder of cooking time and cover goose with greased, grease-proof paper to prevent excess browning. Remove paper for last 20 minutes if goose is not brown enough.
7. Remove goose on to warm dish and make the gravy, using giblet stock, and onion liquor reserved from preparation of stuffing.

### SAGE AND ONION STUFFING
**For Goose and Duck**
Sufficient for an 8 to 10 lb. goose. Use half quantity for a duck.
*2 lb. onions*
*Water*
*1 oz. butter*
*4 to 6 oz. fresh white breadcrumbs*
*2 teaspoons Salt and Pepper Mix**
*2 to 3 teaspoons dried sage*
1. Skin and chop onions, cook in a little water until just softening, about 15 to 20 minutes. Drain well, reserve liquid for gravy.
2. Add butter, crumbs, Salt and Pepper Mix and sage to taste, using sufficient crumbs to make mixture hold together.
Do not pack stuffing in bird too tightly.

50    *See page 9.

## ROAST DUCK

Traditionally served with Sage and Onion Stuffing, in which case, follow instructions given for Cooking the Goose.

Try also:
## APRICOT STUFFING

**Excellent with duck but good with other poultry**

*4 oz. finely chopped onion*
*2 oz. butter*
*6 oz. fresh white breadcrumbs*
*4 oz. finely chopped dried apricots*
*2 oz. finely chopped salted peanuts*
*1 tablespoon chopped parsley*
*Grated rind and juice of 1 orange*
*1 level teaspoon Salt and Pepper Mix**
*1 small beaten egg*

1. Fry onion in butter to soften.
2. In bowl combine crumbs, apricots, peanuts, parsley and finely grated orange rind. Add onion and any butter in pan, orange juice and Salt and Pepper Mix. Mix with sufficient egg to bind.

## CRISPY DUCKLING —a tip.

Prick the duckling all over with a pin or very sharp fork and then roast in a hot oven, 400°F, Gas 6, 15 minutes per lb.

## A GOOD GRAVY
### For Goose and Duck

Using giblet stock and onion liquor reserved from preparation of Sage and Onion Stuffing. (See page 50).

1. Boil together liquor from giblets and onions.
2. Pour off all fat and sediment from roasting tin into cold basin and fat will rise to top at once.
3. Place 2 tablespoons fat in a pan, remove rest with spoon to dripping jar.
4. Place pan on heat, add 2 level tablespoons flour, sizzle for 1 to 2 minutes.
5. Gradually add hot, not boiling, stock and stir well. Add sediment from basin, taste for seasoning, boil up for 2 minutes.

This is the original method of making gravy and can be applied for all meats, using good vegetable and meat stock, with meat juices and/or sediment from roasting tin.

## CASSEROLED WOOD PIGEON
### Serves 4

*1 oz. lard; 2 oz. belly of pork, finely diced; 4 pigeons, or if plump ones, 2 each split in half; 1 oz. flour; ½ pt. stout (not milk or sweet variety) ½ pt water; 1 chicken stock cube; ½ lb. onions, cut in wedges; 1 clove garlic, crushed; 2 sprigs thyme; 4 oz. mushrooms, sliced; about 1 teaspoon salt; black pepper; gravy browning.*

1. Melt lard and fry pork until pale golden and the fat has run out, lift pieces out into large casserole.
2. Brown pigeons, skin side down, in the fat then add to pork in casserole.
3. Blend in flour to pan, stir in stout and water.
4. Add remaining ingredients (not gravy browning yet), bring to the boil stirring.
5. Pour over pigeons in casserole.
6. Cover and cook at 325°F, Gas 3 for about 3 hours, or until tender.
7. Remove thyme and check seasoning, add a little gravy browning if need be.

This can be cooked just as well, and more economically, on top of the stove, using throughout a good-sized, heavy saucepan. Cover and simmer very slowly for about one hour, or until tender (cooking time can vary from half an hour to 3 hours).

## JUGGED HARE
### Serves 6

This popular classic British dish is surprisingly cheap and not difficult

*See page 9.

to make. It is really only a glorified stew enriched with port, and thickened with a liaison — butter kneaded with flour — and the blood of the hare to give a really smooth sauce. Take care not to over cook the hare. Simmer it slowly. A young hare, leveret, will take about 2 hours and serve 6, whereas an older hare will take over 3 hours and be enough for 8 to 10 people.

*1 hare cut into neat pieces;*
*2 oz. bacon fat; 2 large onions*
*(each stuck with 2 cloves;)*
*1 stick celery, cut in 1 inch*
*pieces; 6 peppercorns; rind of*
*½ lemon; pinch cayenne pepper;*
*1 blade mace; bouquet garni*
*(sprig thyme, bay leaf, 2 sprigs*
*parsley tied together); salt and*
*pepper; 2 pts. water.*
**For the liaison:**
*2 oz. butter; 2 oz. flour;*
*¼ pt. port wine; 1 tablespoon*
*redcurrant jelly; the blood of*
*the hare.*
**For the garnish:**
*Salad oil (for frying); 4 slices*
*bread; chopped parsley.*

1. Divide the hare into neat joints, saving as much of the blood as possible. Your butcher will do this for you and more often than not, will put the blood in a tin for you to carry it home.
2. Melt the bacon fat in a large frying pan and fry the joints briskly until they are a good brown colour; then remove them from the pan.
3. Pack the joints into a heavy ovenproof casserole with the onions, celery, peppercorns, lemon rind, cayenne pepper, mace, bouquet garni, salt and pepper.
4. Pour the water over contents of casserole and cover with a tightly fitting lid. Bake at Gas 3 or 335°F. for 2 hours or until the hare is tender.

5. Pour the gravy through a sieve into a pan, remove spices, lemon rind and herbs from the casserole and keep meat and vegetables warm.
6. To make the liaison, work the butter on a plate with a palette knife until it is soft. Then knead in the flour a little at a time to form a smooth paste.
7. Reheat the gravy, but do not allow it to boil and add the kneaded butter in small pieces, whisking it until it has thickened, stirring all the time.
8. Add the port and redcurrant jelly to the gravy and simmer gently until the jelly has dissolved.
9. Blend two or three tablespoons of the gravy with the blood and then add the blood to the rest of the gravy. The gravy must not be allowed to boil after this stage. Adjust the seasoning with more salt and pepper.
10. Strain the gravy over the hare. Cover bottom of a frying pan with oil, heat, add the slices of bread and fry until golden. Cut the fried bread into kite shapes and decorate with parsley and arrange on top of the hare. Serve with redcurrant jelly and savoury forcemeat balls.

# CHAPTER 5

# FISH

## SOUSED HERRINGS

*6 herrings; salt and pepper;*
*½ pt. mixed distilled malt vinegar*
*and water; 1 tablespoon mixed*
*pickling spice; 4 bay leaves;*
*2 small onions (cut into rings).*

1. Scale, clean and bone herrings.
2. Season well with salt and pepper.
3. Roll up fillets, skin inwards, from tail end.
4. Place neatly and fairly close together in an ovenproof dish.
5. Cover with mixed vinegar and water.
6. Sprinkle with pickling spice.
7. Garnish with bay leaves and onion rings.
8. Cover with baking foil or lid and bake slowly, 300°F, Gas 2 for about 1½ hours.

## JUGGED KIPPERS — a tip.

Place kippers head down in a heated deep jug and cover with boiling water. Cover with lid and stand in warm place for about 8 minutes. Drain well and serve with pat of butter

## CULLEN SKINK

A delicious fish soup from the Moray Firth.

*1 smoked haddock (Finnan is best)*
*Water*
*1 chopped onion*
*1 pint milk*
*Hot mashed potato, quantity*
*depends on desired consistency of*
*soup*
*1 to 2 oz. butter*
*Salt and pepper*

1. Skin haddock and place in pan with just enough water to cover.
2. Bring to boil and add chopped onion. Cook till ready, about 5 to 10 minutes.
3. Lift fish from pan and remove the bones.
4. Return bones to pan and boil for three quarters to one hour.
5. Meanwhile prepare the potatoes, mash them well while hot adding a little butter.
6. Flake the fish and lay aside.
7. Strain the bone stock, add the slightly warmed milk, the fish and enough hot mashed potato to give a creamy consistency. Stir in the butter and season to taste.
Serve very hot.

**Mrs. Muriel Hume,**
**Carmyllie, Scotland.**

## HEREFORDSHIRE COD

Serves 4 people.

*1 lb. cod fillets*
*8 medium-sized mushrooms*
*2 large tomatoes, halved*
*½ pint strong cider*
*Salt and pepper*
*1 oz. butter*
*1 oz. flour*
*Creamed potato, optional*
*2 to 3 oz. grated cheese*

1. Cut the cod into four serving pieces and arrange in a greased ovenproof dish with the mushrooms and tomatoes.
2. Pour the cider slowly over the ingredients in the dish, and then season them with salt and pepper.
3. Bake for 15 minutes in a fairly hot oven, Gas 5, 375°F.
4. Meanwhile, melt the butter, add the flour and cook for a few minutes.
5. Add the liquid from the fish, bring to the boil and cook gently for a few minutes.
6. Pour this sauce over the fish, and, if liked, pipe creamed potatoes round the edge of the dish.
7. Sprinkle with the grated cheese and brown under a hot grill.

**Mrs. A. Searle,**
**Holme Lacy.**

## PILCHARD CRUMBLE

To serve 2.

*A 5½ oz. tin of pilchards in tomato*
*sauce*
*1 beaten egg*
*3 tablespoons milk*
*½ level teaspoon Salt and Pepper*
*Mix**

**Top:**
*3 oz. plain flour*

*See page 9.

*Shake of salt and pepper*
*1½ oz. margarine*
*1 oz. grated cheese*
1. Remove bones and then place the pilchards in a pie dish and break them up lightly.
2. Mix egg, milk and Salt and Pepper Mix and pour over.
3. Shake salt and pepper into flour and lightly rub in margarine. Mix in cheese. Sprinkle over fish.
4. Bake at Gas 4, 350°F. for 20 minutes.

## SAVOURY SARDINES
*4 tablespoons oil*
*1 finely-chopped onion*
*A 15 oz. can tomatoes*
*1 level teaspoon mixed herbs*
*Salt and pepper*
*6 oz. self-raising flour*
*¼ teapsoon baking powder*
*Pinch of salt*
*1½ oz. margarine*
*About 5 tablespoons milk*
*1 tin sardines in oil*
*2 oz. grated cheese*
1. Heat the tomatoes gently in a pan. Drain through a sieve (save the juices to drink or for soup). Rinse the pan.
2. Place 1 tablespoon oil into the rinsed pan, add onion, cook until fairly soft but not brown, about 5 minutes. Add the tomatoes, herbs, salt and pepper. Keep warm.
3. Sieve flour, baking powder and salt, rub in margarine, mix with milk to make a soft but not sticky dough.
4. Pat or roll into a circle to fit a large frying pan.
5. Heat remaining oil in frying pan, place in circle of dough, cook over medium heat to brown underside, about 5 minutes. Turn and cook a further 5 minutes.
6. Meanwhile prepare grill to medium heat.
7. Spread tomato mixture over cooked dough, arrange sardines like spokes of a wheel on top, sprinkling cheese between.
8. Place under grill to heat sardines and melt cheese.
9. Slide on to a warmed plate if you can or serve straight from pan. Serve with green salad.
See also Kipper Savoury, page 40.

## BAKED COD STEAKS
**For 2 persons**
*2 cod steaks, approx. 5 oz. to 6 oz. each*
*Salt and pepper*
*½ oz. margarine*
*1 small, finely-chopped onion*
*1 oz. fresh breadcrumbs*
*1 level teaspoon finely-chopped parsley*
*2 teaspoons lemon juice*
**To accompany**
*2 tomatoes*
*A little melted fat*
1. Prepare 2 pieces of foil, each large enough to enclose a fish steak and to wrap securely. Grease them lightly.
2. Place one piece of cod on each square of foil, dust with salt and pepper.
3. Melt margarine, fry onion until softening—it can be lightly golden. Stir in crumbs, parsley and lemon juice. Divide into 2, place a portion in cavity of cod steak.
4. Wrap foil loosely round fish and secure edges. Place on oven-proof plate.
5. Bake Gas 4, 350°F. for about 20 minutes.
6. Meanwhile prepare tomatoes. Make an incision around each tomato just below the middle. Brush with a little melted fat. Stand them upside down on the plate beside the fish and return to oven for 10 more minutes.
Serve with new or boiled potatoes.

## KIPPER PASTE OR PÂTÉ
Makes a good pâté to start a meal, or a paste for sandwiches.
*8 oz. boneless kippers*
*Boiling water*
*4 oz. butter or margarine, softened*
*1 tablespoon lemon juice*
*1 tablespoon grated onion*
*A good grating of black pepper*

1. Place kippers in a large basin, cover with boiling water, leave 5 to 8 minutes.
2. Drain kippers, discard liquid. Remove skin and fin bones if any, and flake the fish.
3. Add remaining ingredients, beat to a smooth consistency, tasting for seasoning. No salt is required, but use lots of pepper.
4. Place in small dish, fork over the top.

**As a pâté,** serve with toast or brown bread or small savoury biscuits and garnish with small pieces of tomato, lettuce or watercress.

### HERRINGS IN OATMEAL
*4 herrings*
*2 oz. medium oatmeal*
*½ teaspoon of salt*
*1 to 2 oz. butter*
*Juice of ½ lemon*
*Parsley*
1. Clean and bone herrings. Dry.
2. Dip in oatmeal and salt.
3. Melt 1 oz. of the butter in pan, fry herrings about 3 minutes each side, adding the extra butter as necessary. Place on hot dish.
4. Add a little more butter to pan, heat frothy, add the lemon juice, pour over fish and sprinkle with chopped parsley.

### CREAMED HADDOCK WITH MUSHROOMS
**To serve 4 to 5**
*2 lb. filleted fresh haddock*
*¾ lb. mushrooms*
*1 oz. onion, chopped & parboiled*
*Parsley*
*2½ oz. butter or margarine*
*4 tablespoons dry white wine or dry cider*
*½ oz. flour*
*¼ pint hot milk*
*Salt and pepper*
*Juice of ½ lemon*
*Red pepper*
*Paprika*
*2 oz. grated cheese*
**To Serve:** *Boiled potatoes*
1. Skin the fish and divide into 4

or 5 portions. Put into a shallow ovenware dish and pour on the wine or cider.
2. Wash the mushrooms, but do not peel them. Slice one good-sized mushroom and sprinkle it on fish.
3. Cover with a lid, or greased paper, and cook in a hot oven, Gas 8, 450°F., for 15 minutes.
4. Fine-chop the rest of mushrooms and mix with the chopped onion and a dessertspoon of chopped parsley.
5. Melt 2 oz. of the butter or margarine in a saucepan, add the mushroom mixture and cook gently for 2 to 3 minutes.
6. When fish is cooked keep it hot but strain off the juices for the sauce.
7. Now make the sauce. Melt ½ oz. butter, add the flour and pour on gradually ¼ pint of the fish juices and the hot milk. Simmer for 5 minutes, season to taste, stir in the lemon juice, a pinch of red pepper and a teaspoon of paprika.
8. Add the grated cheese. Reheat but do not boil.
9. Stir about a ¼ pint of this sauce into the mushroom mixture and cover the bottom of a shallow serving dish with it. Arrange the fish on top and coat with the remaining sauce. Sprinkle with grated cheese.

Surround with plain boiled potatoes, sprinkled alternately with chopped parsley and paprika. Garnish with sprigs of parsley.

### KEDGEREE
*12 oz. smoked haddock*
*½ pint milk and water mixed*
*4 oz. long grained rice*
*2 oz. butter or margarine*
*A good shake of pepper*
*2 tablespoons cream or top of milk*
*2 hard boiled eggs*
*Chopped parsley*
1. Poach the haddock in milk and water until just beginning to flake. Drain.

2. Remove skin, and flake roughly.

3. Cook rice in plenty of boiling, salted water until a grain will crush between the fingers. Do not overcook—12 minutes is usually enough.

4. Drain well in sieve, pour over boiling water to separate grains.

5. Mix into fish, with butter, pepper, cream, and 1 chopped egg. Heat through carefully, stirring. If a little firm add more cream or top of milk.

6. Pile into hot serving dish. Garnish with sliced egg and chopped parsley.

Freezes well.

## FISH PUFFS & A PIQUANT SAUCE

*8 oz. fresh or smoked cod*
*or haddock*
*Milk and water*
**For the Fritter Batter**
*4 oz. plain flour*
*Pinch salt*
*1 tablespoon cooking oil*
*¼ pint of tepid water*
*1 tablespoon lemon juice*
*1 egg white*

1. Poach the fish in even quantities of milk and water sufficient almost to cover. Flake it.

2. Make the batter.
Beat together flour, salt, oil, water and lemon juice. Leave 15 minutes, beat again, then fold in firmly whisked egg white.

3. Stir in the fish.

4. Deep fry in hot fat, dropping mixture in a dessertspoon at a time. Fry about 3 minutes until golden. Drain on kitchen paper.

**Piquant Sauce**
*1 oz. margarine*
*1 oz. plain flour*
*¼ teaspoon Salt and Pepper Mix**
*½ pint milk*
*2 teaspoons lemon juice*
*1 egg yolk*
*Chopped parsley or capers*
*(optional)*

1. Melt margarine, add flour and seasonings, sizzle one minute.

2. Stir in milk, boil one minute.

3. Add lemon juice.

4. Mix 2 tablespoons sauce into egg yolk, return this to pan, hold over heat—do not boil.

5. Add chopped parsley or capers if desired.

Serve the sauce separately.

## CIDERED HADDOCK CASSEROLE
**Good with cod also**

*1 to 1½ lb. haddock or cod fillet, skinned*
*8 oz. tomatoes, skinned and sliced*
*2 oz. mushrooms, sliced*
*1 tablespoon chopped parsley*
*Salt and pepper*
*¼ pint cider*
*2 tablespoons fresh white breadcrumbs*
*2 tablespoons grated cheese*

1. Wipe the fish, cut into cubes and lay these in an ovenproof dish.

2. Cover with the sliced tomatoes and mushrooms, the parsley and seasonings and pour the cider over.

3. Cover with foil and cook in the centre of the oven at 350°F. Gas 4 for 20 to 25 minutes.

4. Remove from the oven and sprinkle with breadcrumbs and cheese, and brown in a hot oven, 425°F. Gas 7 or under a hot grill.

**Mrs. Elspeth Foxton,**
**Kirby Misperton,**
**Yorkshire.**

## FISH PIE

*1 lb. filleted haddock or cod, skinned and cut into serving pieces*
*1 tablespoon lemon juice or dry white wine*
*1½ oz. margarine or butter*
*Salt and pepper*
*1 lb. potatoes, weighed after peeling*
**For the sauce**
*1 oz. margarine*
*1 oz. flour*
*½ teaspoon Salt and Pepper Mix**
*½ pint liquid, the fish liquor made up with milk*
*3 oz. grated cheese*

*\*See page 9.*

### To garnish

*2 or 3 tomatoes, skinned, sliced*
*A little melted margarine, about*
$\frac{1}{2}$ *oz.*

1. Lay fish in a greased, shallow dish just to fit in a single layer. Sprinkle on juice or wine, salt and pepper and dot with $\frac{1}{2}$ oz. of the margarine or butter.
2. Cover, foil will do, and cook at Gas 5, 375°F. for 15 minutes, or until cooked.
3. Meanwhile. boil the potatoes and mash them with $\frac{1}{2}$ teaspoon salt and 1 oz. margarine.
4. When fish is cooked spoon off liquor into a measure and add milk to make up quantity to $\frac{1}{2}$ pint.
5. **Now make the sauce.** Melt margarine, add flour and cook for 1 minute.
6. Add salt and pepper. Stir in liquid. Bring to boil, stirring, and simmer for 2 minutes.
7. Beat in cheese. Do not let sauce boil again. Pour it over the fish.
8. Pipe potato round edge of fish.
9. Arrange tomato down centre. Brush potato and tomato with melted margarine.
10. Place dish under grill to tinge potato golden.

### A TURBAN OF COD

**Or Baked Cod and Egg Sauce but this dish looks so good it needs a better name!**

*1 large cod fillet, about 1$\frac{1}{2}$ lb.*
*Salt and pepper*
*Juice of 1 lemon*
*2 oz. butter*
*2 oz. flour*
*$\frac{3}{4}$ pt. milk*
*2 hard-boiled eggs*

### Garnish

*Lemon slices*
*Parsley*

1. Wash and dry the fillet of cod, sprinkle with salt and pepper.
2. Coil the fish round into a turban shape with the skin inside and place in a shallow ovenproof dish just large enough to hold it, securing the "turban" in place with a wooden cocktail stick or skewer if necessary.
3. Brush the outside of the fish with a little of the lemon juice.
4. Put into the oven Gas 4, 350°F. and cook for 20 to 25 minutes or until fish is tender.
5. Meanwhile make the sauce. Melt the butter, stir in flour and allow it to sizzle a little. Add the milk, season to taste with salt and pepper and continue stirring until the mixture forms a thick smooth sauce, cook for 2 minutes. Add strained lemon juice.
6. Remove the cooked fish from the oven, pour off most of the liquor which will have formed in cooking.
7. Strain the liquor into the sauce. Stir until smooth then add the roughly-chopped, hard-boiled eggs.
8. Pour a little of the egg sauce into the centre of the "turban". Serve the rest in a sauce boat.
9. Make a slit in each lemon slice, form into a cone and place on top of the turban. Sprinkle with chopped parsley and decorate with parsley sprigs.

### CRISP FISH BALLS

*8 oz. cooked and flaked fish*
*6 oz. mashed potato*
*1 oz. melted margarine*
*1 teaspoon lemon juice*
*$\frac{1}{2}$ teaspoon Salt and Pepper Mix\**
*2 beaten eggs*
*1 tablespoon chopped parsley*

1. Combine all ingredients.
2. Drop spoonfuls into deep hot fat. Cook until golden.

Serve with a piquant parsley sauce, see below.

### A PIQUANT PARSLEY SAUCE

*1 oz. butter*
*1 oz. flour*
*$\frac{1}{2}$ teaspoon Salt and Pepper Mix\**
*$\frac{1}{2}$ pint milk*
*1 teaspoon lemon juice*
*A nut of butter*

*\*See page 9.*

*2 tablespoons freshly-chopped parsley*

1. Melt butter in saucepan, stir in flour and cook 1 minute.
2. Add salt and pepper and milk. Stir until boiling and cook 1 to 2 minutes.
3. Remove from heat, beat in lemon juice and a nut of butter. Stir in lots of parsley.

# CHAPTER 6

# MEAT

## ABERDEEN ROLL

May be eaten hot or cold
*8 oz. streaky bacon*
*8 oz. minced beef*
*1 large onion*
*1 clove of garlic, optional*
*but try it*
*3 oz. rolled oats*
*1 tablespoon Worcestershire sauce*
*1 teaspoon made mustard*
*1 teaspoon Salt and Pepper Mix\**
*1 beaten egg*
*¼ pint stock*

### For eating cold:
*Stock*
*Dried breadcrumbs*

1. De-rind bacon and cut into strips. Skin and chop onion, crush garlic to a cream with a little salt. Mix well with minced beef and mince all using fine cutters.
2. Add oats, sauce, mustard and Salt and Pepper Mix. Mix in beaten egg and a little stock if mixture is dry.
3. Grease a 1 lb. loaf tin and press mixture in firmly.
4. Cover with foil. Stand in a small roasting tin containing enough hot water to come well up sides.
5. Cook at Gas 4, 350°F. for 2 hours.

### To eat hot:
Remove from tin, smother with fried onion rings and serve with tomato or brown sauce and jacket potatoes.

### To eat cold:
1. Do not remove from tin but pour in at once as much boiling stock as it will asborb, pressing mixture gently with back of a spoon.
2. Cover with foil and place a weight on top. Leave overnight in a cool place.
3. Turn out of mould, roll in dried breadcrumbs and serve sliced with potato salad (see page 12).

## BEEF CASSEROLE WITH DUMPLINGS

To serve 4
*12 oz. lean stewing beef*
*8 oz. onions*
*8 oz. carrots*
*4 to 6 oz. swede or turnip*
*1 level tablespoon plain flour*
*1 teaspoon Salt and Pepper Mix\**
*1 oz. beef dripping*
*1 pint hot stock*
*2 teaspoons vinegar*
*Brown colouring if desired*

1. Cut stewing beef into 1 inch cubes.
2. Slice onions thickly and cut the carrots and swede or turnip into 1 to 2 inch chunks.
3. Mix flour and salt and pepper and coat beef well.
4. Melt dripping in large saucepan, stir in beef, turning to seal and brown slightly.
5. Add onion and any remaining flour, stir for 1 minute.
6. Add remaining vegetables, stock and vinegar, stir until boiling. Stir in a few drops of colouring.
7. Cover and simmer gently for 1½ hours or until meat is tender. Or, transfer to a large casserole with lid, and cook at Gas 4, 350°F. for 1½ hours or until meat is tender. *At this stage the casserole can be frozen. Cool very quickly, place in suitable freezer container, label and place in fridge to become quite cold, then transfer to freezer. When re-heating, the casserole must boil again before dumplings are added.*
8. If casserole method is used now turn oven to Gas 6, 400°F. while mixing dumplings.

### Dumplings:
*4 oz. self-raising flour*
*¼ teaspoon salt*
*2 oz. suet*
*1 tablespoon freshly chopped parsley or ½ teaspoon dried mixed herbs*
*3 to 4 tablespoons water*

1. Mix flour, salt, suet and parsley.

*\*See page 9.*

Mix to a softish dough with water.
2. Turn on to well-floured board, cut into 8 pieces. Roll into balls using a little flour.
3. Drop dumplings into pan or casserole. Replace lid.
4. Simmer in pan for 20 minutes or in casserole for 25 minutes.

## HEREFORD HAM
Serves 2 to 3
*An 8 oz. tin lean sweetcure ham*
*½ oz. margarine or butter*
*1 medium-sized onion, chopped coarsely*
*1 small cooking apple*
*1 level teaspoon plain flour*
*2 tablespoons apple juice or cider*
*A 6 oz. tin double cream*
*Salt and pepper*
*Chopped parsley*
1. Prepare a cool oven, Gas 2, 300°F. Place a medium-sized serving dish on centre shelf to heat through.
2. Cut the ham into 6 to 8 slices and arrange down the centre of the heated serving dish.
3. Cover, foil will do, and place in the oven until the sauce is ready.
4. Melt the margarine or butter in a frying pan, add the onion, and cook without browning for 5 minutes.
5. Peel, quarter and core the apple. Cut into fairly thin slices.
6. Add the apple to the onion and cook for 5 minutes until the onion is soft but the apple still a little crisp.
7. Sprinkle the flour over the onion and apple mixture.
8. Stir in the apple juice or cider, the cream, salt and pepper. Cook gently, stirring, for 1 minute.
9. Spoon over the ham, sprinkle with the chopped parsley.
**Mrs. A. Searle,**
**Holme Lacy.**

## LIVER PUFFS
Makes about 12.
*4 oz. pig's liver*

*3 oz. macaroni*
*½ oz. butter*
*1 tablespoon flour*
*¼ pint milk*
*1 tablespoon chopped parsley*
*2 eggs*
*Oil or fat for frying*
**Note:** If flavour of liver is too strong, soak it in some milk and water for 1 hour before cooking. Discard the liquid.
1. Parboil liver.
2. Boil macaroni in salted water till cooked. Drain well.
3. Mince liver and macaroni finely.
4. Melt butter in a pan, stir in flour and cook till golden brown.
5. Add the quarter pint of milk, stir and cook till thick.
6. Add liver, macaroni and parsley and heat through.
7. Add well-beaten eggs.
8. Drop large tablespoonfuls into hot fat deep enough to cover. They puff up lightly when cooked.
**Kate Easlea,**
**Hampshire.**

## LOVE IN DISGUISE
*3 sheep's hearts*
*1 oz. vermicelli*
*3 bacon rashers*
*1 small egg yolk*
*Dried breadcrumbs*
**Stuffing:**
*2 oz. fresh breadcrumbs*
*2 tablespoons shredded suet*
*Pinch of mustard*
*2 oz. minced ham or bacon*
*2 tablespoons chopped parsley*
*1 teaspoon marjoram*
*A grating of lemon rind*
*Salt and pepper*
*Water*
1. Remove pipes from hearts and discard. Wash hearts well and steep in cold water.
2. Break vermicelli and cook in boiling salted water. Leave to cool.
3. Combine the stuffing ingredients with a little water.
4. Dry the hearts and fill with stuffing. Wrap rashers of bacon around them and fasten with small skewers.

5. Stand in a small baking tin so that they prop each other up. Cover with foil and bake in a moderate oven, Gas 5, 375°F., for 1½ hours.

6. Remove the foil, carefully lift each heart out of tin, brush with beaten egg-yolk and roll in mixed breadcrumbs and vermicelli.

7. Replace in baking tin without foil. Return to the oven and bake till lightly brown, about 10 minutes.

Serve with freshly-made tomato sauce, (see page 24).

**Mrs. A. Searle,
Holme Lacy,
Herefordshire.**

## PORK WITH PUREE OF TOMATOES

*1 lb. fresh tomatoes or 14 oz. tin of tomatoes*
*2 bay leaves*
*10 peppercorns or a good shake of black pepper*
*Nut of butter*
*Salt*
*2 or 3 slices belly of pork or spare rib chops*
*1 teaspoon sugar*

**For thickening:**
*About 1 tablespoon rolled oats or 1 to 2 tablespoons soft white breadcrumbs*

1. Put tomatoes (skinned and chopped if fresh are used), bay leaves, peppercorns and butter into a casserole.

2. Add salt and place pork on top.

3. Cover closely (foil will do) and cook in the oven very gently, Gas 2, 300°F. for 1½ to 2 hours, turn and baste meat occasionally.

4. When meat is tender remove it from casserole for a moment. Remove bay leaves.

5. Add sugar to the tomato mixture and stir in oats or breadcrumbs.

6. Replace meat on top of tomato mixture, do not cover. Return casserole to oven for 10 to 15 minutes.

**Mrs. W. A. Sharman,
Norton Lindsay,
Warwickshire.**

## RABBIT PASTE

*1 jointed rabbit*
*2 oz. margarine*
*2 teaspoons sugar*
*12 allspice*
*6 peppercorns*
*3 blades mace*
*1 onion stuck with 12 cloves*
*2 tablespoons water*
*8 oz. butter or margarine*
*1 dessertspoon Worcestershire sauce*
*Pinch of cayenne pepper*
*Melted butter*

1. Cut rabbit into small pieces and put in a casserole with the 2 oz. margarine, 1 teaspoon of the sugar, allspice, peppercorns, mace, onion and water.

2. Cover closely and cook slowly at Gas 3, 325°F. until meat will leave bones, about 1 hour.

3. Mince meat finely twice.

4. Put it in a bowl and beat with the 8 oz. butter or margarine, Worcestershire sauce, cayenne and remaining teaspoon sugar.

5. Put into small dishes. Either cover and freeze or pour melted butter over and store until required in refrigerator where it will keep 3 or 4 days.

Spread on hot toast to serve.

**Kate Easlea,
Hampshire.**

## STUFFED BELLY PORK
**A good cheap roast**

*2½ lbs. Belly Pork, boned and with rind finely scored.*
**Stuffing:**
*3 oz. fresh breadcrumbs; 1 grated apple; 1 grated onion;*
*1 oz. shredded suet; 2 teaspoons powdered sage; 1 egg yolk;*
*1 teaspoon Salt and Pepper Mix\**

*\*See page 9.*

1. Mix stuffing ingredients together to a firm consistency.
2. Spread stuffing on pork.
3. Tie up or sew loosely with fine string. This will allow for expansion during cooking so that stuffing does not squeeze out at ends.
4. Brush rind with softened pork dripping (or lard) and sprinkle with salt.
5. To keep meat out of fat, place on rack in roasting tin. Cook at Gas 5, 375°F, allowing 50 minutes to the lb. (stuffed weight) — approx. 2 hours.

## PEASE PUDDING

*½ lb. yellow split peas; 1 chopped onion; 1 oz. butter; 1 beaten egg; flavoured stock (bacon stock is excellent)*

1. Soak peas overnight, then drain.
2. Put peas and onion in pan with enough stock to cover.
3. Simmer together with lid on until peas are quite soft, replenishing stock if necessary.
4. Sieve or liquidize.
5. Beat in butter and egg. Test for seasoning.
6. Pour into a greased pie dish, cover and cook ½ hour, Gas 3, 325°F.

Serve hot with roast pork, ham or bacon.

When cold, fry in bacon dripping, serve with breakfast bacon.

The mixture will freeze well but put in freezer before butter and egg is added.

## BREAST OF LAMB
### A good cheap roast

*A Breast of Lamb, boned.*
**Stuffing:**
*3 oz. fresh breadcrumbs; 1 teaspoon each of chopped parsley and mint; 1 teaspoon of rosemary (if available); 1 chopped onion; 1 oz. grated suet;*

*1 oz. dripping; 1 teaspoon of Salt and Pepper Mixture*; beaten egg to bind.*

1. Melt dripping and fry onion until softening. Mix in dry ingredients and sufficient egg to form a firm consistency.
2. Spread stuffing on lamb and roll up like a Swiss Roll and tie or sew as for the Pork, (page 64).
3. Place on rack in roasting tin. Cook at Gas 4, 350°F allowing 35 minutes to the lb. (stuffed weight).

## THIN RIB OR FLANK OF BEEF
### A good cheap roast

*3–4 lbs. thin rib or flank on the bone.*

1. Score the top and sprinkle with salt.
2. Place on rack in roasting tin, with ¼ pt. of water.
3. Cook at Gas 3, 325°F allowing 50 minutes to the lb. The meat can be covered loosely with foil, allowing an extra 30 minutes cooking time.
4. Remove bones from meat whilst hot.

Equally good eaten cold.

## YORKSHIRE PUDDINGS

*4 oz. strong, plain flour; ¼ teaspoon salt; 1 large egg; ½ pt. skimmed milk (i.e. skim off the creamy top).*

1. Beat all well together until bubbles appear. Can be left to stand until required, but this is not necessary.
2. Heat a little dripping in 12 deep patty tins, half fill with batter. Cook, Gas 7, 425°F, about 30 minutes.

## GOLDEN POTATO BAKE

*¾ pt. Onion Sauce; 2 lbs. potatoes, peeled and thinly sliced; 3 oz. grated cheese.*

*See page 9.

### Onion Sauce

*1 oz. margarine; 1 oz. plain flour;*
*½ teaspoon salt; shake of pepper;*
*1 medium sliced onion;*
*¾ pint milk.*

(i) Melt margarine in saucepan, add onion and soften but do not brown.
(ii) Stir in flour and sizzle for 1–2 minutes. Gradually add milk, salt and pepper and allow to boil and thicken.

1. Layer potatoes in a 2½ pint (approx.) pie dish. Pour sauce over.
2. Cover and cook for 1½ hours at Gas 3, 325°F.
3. Uncover, sprinkle on cheese, place in oven until cheese melts and begins to bubble.

Serve with any roast joint.

### POT ROAST BRISKET

Boned and rolled brisket may be used or a piece on the bone.

1. Add to the meat in the pan a stock cube and three quarters of an inch of water.
2. Season well with salt and pepper.
3. Cover with lid or tin foil.
4. Put in oven at 425°F, Gas 7.

In about half an hour, when you begin to smell it, reduce heat to 325°F, Gas 3, and leave it for 2 hours.

5. When you raise the heat and put your Yorkshire pudding in the oven take the lid or covering off the meat to let it brown. The juices make a good gravy which may be thickened if preferred.

### SHIN OF BEEF CASSEROLE

*2 lb. shin of beef in 1 inch cubes;*
*1½ oz. flour seasoned; 1½ oz.*
*beef dripping; 1 clove garlic,*
*crushed; 2 sticks celery, sliced;*
*1 pt. beef stock; ½ pt. light beer;*
*14 oz. can tomatoes; salt; pepper;*
*gravy browning; small green pepper;*
*seeded and diced; 2 oz. mushrooms,*
*sliced.*

1. Toss meat in seasoned flour in plastic or paper bag.
2. Heat dripping, fry meat until golden.
3. Add any remaining flour, cook for 1 minute.
4. Stir in all ingredients except browning, peppers and mushrooms.
5. Add a little gravy browning.
6. Cover and cook for 3½ hours, simmering very slowly.
7. Add peppers and mushrooms, cook for further ½ hour.
8. Check seasoning and serve.

### BRAISED STEAK

*1 - 2 lb. braising steak, cut at*
*least 1 inch thick and as lean as*
*possible.*

#### Marinade

*Oil and vinegar in equal*
*quantities; 6–8 black pepper-*
*corns; 1 crushed clove of garlic*
*or 1 finely chopped onion.*

Place meat with the marinade in a strong polythene bag and seal securely. Leave at least 2 hours, turning from time to time.

Other ingredients:
*A little flour; 1–2 lbs. mixed*
*vegetables – onions, carrots,*
*leeks, turnip, celery, as preferred;*
*Pepper and salt; 1 oz. beef*
*dripping; ¼ pt. cheap red wine;*
*¼ pt. beef stock.*

1. Remove meat from marinade. Pat dry and dust lightly with flour.
2. Clean vegetables and cut coarsely and put these first into the casserole. Season with a good shake of pepper and a teaspoon of salt.
3. Heat dripping in heavy frying pan, seal meat quickly on both sides
4. Place meat on top of vegetables.
5. Pour wine into frying pan, sizzle, and add to casserole.
6. Add just enough stock so that liquid comes halfway up vegetables.

It is advisable to use a casserole just large enough to contain the contents.

7. Cover tightly. Cook at Gas 3, 325°F. for 1–1½ hours, depending on size and thickness of meat.

Serve on meat dish, placing vegetables around. Suggest jacket potatoes as extra vegetable.

## OXTAIL CASSEROLE WITH PARSLEY DUMPLINGS

*1 oxtail (jointed); 1 oz. dripping; ½ lb. each of onion, carrot and turnip; 1 pt. boiling water; 1 level teaspoon salt; \*bouquet garni; 2 sticks celery; ¼ lb. butterbeans (soaked overnight); 2 level tablespoons cornflour; 3 tablespoons water; 1 dessert- spoon vinegar.*

\*The bouquet garni may be made by taking a small piece of muslin and tying up in it a piece of bay leaf, a few peppercorns, some parsley stalks and a sprig of thyme.

1. Wash and dry oxtail, cut away excess fat.
2. Prepare carrot and turnip, cutting coarsely. Peel and slice onion.
3. Melt dripping in large pan or flameproof casserole. Add onion, fry golden. Add oxtail, fry 1 to 2 minutes, turning over in fat.
4. Add carrot, turnip and boiling water, salt and bouquet garni. Cover and bring to boil. Simmer for 1½ hours.
5. Remove bouquet garni. Add drained beans, also celery cut in pieces. Simmer until oxtail is tender, check seasoning. Remove from oven.
6. Leave overnight if possible. Next day remove fat from top and bring to boil. Mix cornflour, water and vinegar, add to casserole, stirring lightly and bring to boil. (If you wish, the casserole may be left overnight before Stage 5).

### Parsley Dumplings

*4 oz. self raising flour; 2 oz. suet; Pinch of salt; 1 tablespoon chopped parsley.*

Mix ingredients with sufficient water to make a firm dough. Form into small balls, place on top of casserole. Cover and simmer for 15 minutes.

## STUFFED HEARTS

*2 lamb's or sheep's hearts; 2 oz. fresh breadcrumbs; 2 oz. suet; 1 teaspoon dried sage; 1 onion; salt and pepper; 1 beaten egg; stock.*

**To serve:**

*Redcurrant jelly, creamed potato and peas.*

1. Wash hearts, cut away all gristle and membrane and make a single cavity in centre. Soak in salted water for ½ hour.
2. Mix crumbs, suet, sage 1 table- spoon of the onion, grated, salt and pepper with sufficient egg to bind. Stuff the hearts, skewering tops, tying or sewing up with fine string if hearts will not stand up in your casserole.
3. Place in small casserole, add any onion left over, cover with stock.
4. Cover lightly with a lid or foil and cook at 350°F, Gas 4. Contents should simmer gently until hearts are tender – 1½ to 2 hours.
5. Place hearts on hot serving dish, remove string. Strain stock into small pan and thicken. Check season- ing.
6. Pipe potato round dish, garnish with peas. Spoon a little sauce over hearts – these can be cut into 2 portions each. Serve the rest of sauce and redcurrant jelly separately.

## KIDNEYS IN RED WINE SAUCE

*6 to 8 lamb's kidneys; 1½oz. seasoned flour (Herb Seasoning may be used for this); 2 oz. butter; 2 oz. mushrooms; ¼ pt. light stock; ¼ pt. red wine (Home-made light red wine that has not cleared properly is ideal!)*
**To serve:**
*Rice and a little chopped parsley.*
1. Skin kidneys, remove core, and cut into pieces.
2. Toss in seasoned flour, saute in melted butter until the colour changes, add mushrooms and any left over flour. Cook for 1 minute.
3. Add stock and wine. Simmer for 10 minutes. Check seasoning.
4. Serve in a border of boiled rice. Sprinkle with parsley.

## PIG'S KIDNEY STUFFING

This may be used in roast leg of pork if you get the butcher to remove the bone from the fleshy end. It may also be used to stuff other boned pork joints.
1. Skin, core and chop the pig's kidney.
2. Add chopped fresh herbs; mostly parsley but also thyme and a few chives, even a little garlic.
3. Add salt and pepper and mix well.
4. Stuff into the joint. Use tin foil round the fleshy end to keep the stuffing in place.

## MARY BERRY'S FARMHOUSE PÂTÉ

*Sprig of parsley; 6 rashers streaky bacon (de-rinded); 1 egg; 4 thin slices yesterday's white bread broken into pieces (without crusts); 4 tablespoons port or madeira or, if unavailable, sherry; ½ lb. chicken livers; 1 clove garlic (peeled); ½ lb. pig's liver; ⅛ level teaspoon freshly ground black pepper; ½ level teaspoon ground nutmeg; ¼ level teaspoon dried mixed herbs; ½ level teaspoon dried marjoram; 4 oz. bacon trimmings (or streaky bacon cut in small pieces); 4 oz. lard or bacon fat, melted; 2 level teaspoons salt.*
1. Well grease a 2 pt. ovenproof dish and put a sprig of parsley in the centre.
2. Stretch the 6 rashers of streaky bacon with the back of a knife on a board, then use them to line the base and sides of dish.
3. Put all the other ingredients into the blender and reduce to pulp.
4. Pour pâté into prepared dish, cover tightly with a lid or foil, place dish in a meat tin containing ½ inch warm water and bake for about 2½ hours at 325°F, Gas 3.
5. Remove from oven and turn out of dish when cold.

## BACON MOULD

*2 green bacon shanks or hocks (soaked at least 6 hours); 1 carrot; 1 onion; 1 small bay leaf; 12 black peppercorns.*
1. Place shanks in pan with fresh water to cover. Add chopped carrot and onion, bay leaf and peppercorns.
2. Cover and simmer gently until meat will leave the bones quite easily but clings a little. (Time taken depends on size and quality of bacon and could be 3 to 4 hours).
3. Remove shanks from pan and boil stock rapidly to reduce by about a quarter.
4. Meanwhile separate meat and skin from bones and break it up into neat (not too small) pieces.
5. Strain stock and pour over sufficient to cover the meat. Check seasoning, adding salt or pepper if necessary.
6. Spoon into 1 large mould or

3 to 4 small ones and leave overnight in a cool place to set.
7. Turn out and serve with chutney
or salad.

## PRESSED BRISKET
*3–3½ lb. brisket. 1 pig's trotter.*
Buy the brisket on the bone. Ask
the butcher to loosen the bone but
not entirely remove it and to place
it in brine for 3–4 days.
*1 carrot, chopped; 1 onion,*
*chopped; bouquet garni*
*(8–10 black peppercorns, piece*
*of bay leaf, a small sprig of*
*parsley and one of thyme – tied*
*firmly in a piece of scalded*
*muslin).*
1. To remove excess salt, soak
brisket overnight in cold water, together with trotter if also brined.
2. Next day, place brisket and
trotter in large pan, cover with
cold water, add carrot, onion and
bouquet garni.
3. Cover pan, bring quickly to boil,
lower heat and simmer very gently
until the meat is tender, (about
2–2½ hours).
4. Transfer the beef to a dish – the
trotter is not used and may have
cooked away. Remove bones, gristle
and any excess fat from meat.
5. Pack into a mould to fill it and
pour over about ¼ pt. of the
strained liquid. Place a board on
top and weight down (not too
heavily). Leave overnight to set.

## STOCK
The liquid from the brisket should
be strained into a bowl and left overnight in a cool place. Lift off the fat
and use the stock for soups etc. It
will freeze well in an airtight container.

## TO KEEP AND USE LEFT-OVER FAT
The fat can be removed from stock
after boiling beef, bacon or ham, or
from the dripping tin after roasting
but do not mix the fats from different meats.
**To clarify:**
1. Place fat in a saucepan with a
little water. Bring slowly to boil.
2. Strain into a basin and allow to
set. All sediment will sink into the
water.
3. The fat can be removed from
the top. Scrape clean, melt and
pour into labelled pots.
It is advisable to use beef dripping
when cooking beef dishes, pork or
bacon dripping for pork, etc. In
this way the flavour of the meat is
not impaired.
Pork and bacon dripping makes
good pastry for using with a savoury
filling.
Beef dripping is delicious on toast.
Mutton fat will seal chutneys in
the same way as wax.
When fat is clarified it will keep if
covered for several weeks. If not
covered is inclined to develop an
"off flavour". Should not be frozen.

## CASSEROLE OF PORK
At one time this dish used the pork
trimmings after the ribs had been
lifted prior to salting the meat for
bacon. As this may be hard to
get it is suggested that meat from
the shoulder is used.
*1 to 1½ lb. of lean pork slices*
*about ½ inch thick, from the*
*shoulder*
*1 heaped tablespoon flour*
*seasoned with salt and pepper*
*Dripping for frying*
*1 lb. onions, sliced*
*3 or 4 cooking apples*
*½ to ¾ pt. stock or water*
*2 tablespoons brown sugar*
1. Dip the pork slices in seasoned
flour and fry them gently until
browned on both sides. Put into a
casserole.
2. Fry the sliced onions until

softened but not brown and add as a layer on top of the pork.

3. Core the unpeeled apple and slice into thick rings. Fry for a few minutes on each side and put into casserole on top of the onions.

4. Make a gravy with the residue from frying pan and left-over seasoned flour and stock. Strain into casserole—it should just cover the **meat** only.

5. Sprinkle the apples with the brown sugar.

6. Cover the casserole tightly and cook in a slow oven Gas 3, 325°F. for about 45 to 60 minutes depending on maturity of meat, testing to see if pork is tender.

Serve with vegetables.

Pork chops are very good this way, but tend to be greasy.

**Miss G. S. Davies,**
**Flintshire.**

## HEREFORD SAUSAGES

*1 lb. pork sausages*
*1 oz. cooking fat or oil*
*2 medium onions, finely chopped*
*2 rashers back bacon, cut in strips*
*1 heaped teaspoon plain flour*
*3 tablespoons cider, made up to*
*½ pt. with stock*
*1 bay leaf*
*Salt and pepper*
*4 oz. mushrooms*
**To serve:**
*1½ lb. creamed potatoes*
*Finely chopped parsley*

1. Fry sausages in fat or oil for about 20 minutes, until golden brown. Remove from pan and pour away some of the fat.

2. Add the onion and bacon and cook gently for 5 minutes.

3. Sprinkle on flour and cook 2 to 3 minutes, stirring well.

4. Pour on stock and cider. Bring to boil.

5. Add bay leaf, sausages and seasoning. Cover and simmer for 20 minutes, adding mushrooms for the last 10 minutes.

6. Pipe a border of creamed potatoes round a hot serving dish.

Fill centre of dish with sausage mixture, removing bay leaf. Sprinkle with chopped parsley. Serves 4.

**Mrs. A. Searle,**
**Holme Lacy.**

## LANCASHIRE HOT POT

**Serves 3**
*2 oz. mushrooms*
*1 small onion*
*12 oz. potatoes*
*1 sheep's kidney*
*1 oz. lean bacon*
*3 lamb neck chops*
*Seasoning*
*Knob of butter or fat from chops*
*Parsley, to garnish*

1. Wash and halve the mushrooms. Slice the onions and potatoes.

2. Skin, core and quarter the kidney. Dice the bacon.

3. Lay the cleaned chops on the base of a deep ovenproof dish.

4. Place a layer each of onions, kidneys, mushrooms, bacon and potatoes over the chops.

5. Season well. Repeat to use all ingredients, topping off the Hot Pot with overlapping potato slices and dot with butter or fat.

6. Add water to ⅔ fill the casserole dish.

7. Cover and bake at Gas 5, 375°F. for 2 hours, removing the lid for the last ½ hour to brown the top.

8. Serve garnished with parsley.

**Mrs. M. J. Harkins,**
**Garstang.**

## LINCOLNSHIRE HASLETT

*6 oz. pig's liver*
*6 oz. lean and fat bits of pork*
*3 oz. pig's heart*
*1 small, or half a large, onion*
*About 1½ oz. fresh breadcrumbs*
*2 or 3 leaves of sage, chopped*
*1 teaspoon salt*
*Pepper*
*A piece of pig's veil, optional*

1. Mince liver, pork, heart and onion.

2. Add breadcrumbs and sage. Season with salt and pepper.

3. Mix all together then wrap in

veil or foil and place on small baking tray.

4. Cook in a moderate oven, Gas 4, 350°F. for about 1½ hours.

**Mrs. Bailey,
Ruskington.**

## CASSEROLE OF PORK AND BEANS

*4 to 8 oz. haricot beans, exact quantity depends on personal taste*
*1 lb. minced shoulder pork*
*8 oz. diced carrots*
*1 large chopped onion*
*¼ teaspoon chilli powder* } Or ¼ *teaspoon*
*¼ teaspoon tabasco sauce* } *cayenne pepper*
*1 teaspoon curry powder*
*Salt and pepper*
*¼ pint stock*

1. Soak beans overnight in plenty of water.
2. Next day, drain beans and put them into a large pan with fresh water. Boil for 15 minutes then drain.
3. Put pork, carrots, onion and beans into a casserole with all the seasonings. Pour over the stock.
4. Cover the casserole and cook at Gas 3, 325°F. for 1½ to 1¾ hours.

## STEAK AND KIDNEY PIE
### with Potato Pastry Crust

*1 oz. beef dripping*
*4 oz. chopped onion*
*1 lb. lean, pie beef, cut into 1-inch cubes*
*4 oz. kidney, trimmed and cut slightly smaller than the beef*
*1 level tablespoon flour seasoned with 1 teaspoon Salt and Pepper Mix\**
*¾ pint water*
*2 teaspoons Worcestershire sauce*
*4 oz. mushrooms*

**Note.** Use a pressure cooker (trivet removed) for this if you have one. It saves 1½ hours' cooking time.

1. Melt dripping in pan, add onion, cook 1 minute.
2. Mix beef and kidney into seasoned flour coating well. Add

to pan and stir over heat to seal— it will change colour.

3. Add water and Worcestershire sauce, stir until boiling.
4. Cover and simmer for about 2½ hours until meat is tender. Stir occasionally.

If using a pressure cooker, pressure cook for 40 minutes. Allow to cool at room temperature before removing lid.

5. Place meat in a 1¼-pint pie dish with about 4 tablespoons of the gravy and set aside to cool. Keep remaining gravy to serve with pie.
6. When meat is cold cover with sliced mushrooms.

**Potato Pastry**
*6 oz. self-raising flour*
*½ teaspoon salt*
*4 oz. lard*
*6 oz. cold, dry, mashed potato*

1. Mix flour and salt, rub in lard.
2. Work in potato using a strong fork or hands. Do not add any water.
3. Knead lightly, roll out on floured board to fit pie dish.

**To finish the pie**
*A little milk*

1. Brush edges of pie dish with water, lift pastry on top and press firmly in place. Flute edges, brush top with milk.
2. Bake at Gas 7, 425°F. for about 20 minutes until turning golden. Reduce heat to Gas 5, 375°F. for a further 15 minutes.
3. Heat reserved gravy and serve with pie.

## SAUSAGES IN SWEET AND SOUR SAUCE

*1 lb. sausages*
*½ oz. margarine*
**For the sauce**
*1 oz. margarine*
*1 medium-sized onion, finely-chopped*
*1 large stick of celery, finely-sliced*
*1 medium-sized carrot cut into matchstick pieces*
*1 large, finely-diced apple*

*See page 9.

½ pint light stock
1 heaped teaspoon cornflour
½ teaspoon dry mustard
1 teaspoon Salt and Pepper Mix*
1 heaped teaspoon Demerara
sugar
2 teaspoons Worcestershire sauce

**To serve**
*Rice or mashed potato*
1. Start with the sauce. Melt margarine in saucepan, fry onion, celery, carrot and apple gently to soften.
2. Add stock.
3. Mix cornflour, mustard, Salt and Pepper Mix, sugar and Worcestershire sauce with just enough water to blend.
4. Stir this mixture into pan of vegetables and bring to boil. Simmer for 5 minutes.
5. Meanwhile, fry sausages in ½ oz. margarine until nicely brown. Drain away fat.
6. Pour sauce over the sausages. Cover and simmer for 15 minutes. A little water can be added if mixture becomes too thick. Re-season if necessary.
7. Serve in a bed of rice or piped potato.

## BEEF OLIVES
1¼ to 1½ lb. top-side beef cut into 8
thin slices measuring not less than
3 × 4 inches
8 small slices streaky bacon
1 oz. beef dripping
1 level tablespoon flour
½ pint stock
1 teaspoon Worcester sauce
**Stuffing**
2 oz. fresh white breadcrumbs
1 oz. shredded suet
1 small grated onion
1 teaspoon chopped parsley
1 teaspoon mixed herbs
A good grating of pepper
1 egg yolk
1. Combine the stuffing ingredients and divide into 8 rolls.
2. Beat slices of beef until thin. A rolling pin is ideal for this.
3. Place a piece of bacon on top and a roll of stuffing. Roll up and tie with a length of fine string.
4. Melt dripping in large frying pan. When hot put in beef rolls and turn over in fat to seal.
5. Pack neatly into a shallow casserole, if possible just large enough to contain them.
6. Stir flour into fat in pan, cook 1 minute. Add stock gradually stirring to prevent lumps forming. Add Worcester sauce. When boiling, pour over the meat rolls. Cover.
7. Cook at Gas 4, 350°F. until tender, 1¼ to 1½ hours.
8. Remove strings and place rolls on hot serving dish. A few drops of gravy browning can be added to the sauce if a little more colour is required. Trickle 1 to 2 tablespoons over Beef Olives. Strain the rest into a sauceboat.
Serve with a border of piped, creamed potatoes or try Jamie Jackson's Bien Pommes de Terre on page 82.

## DURHAM LAMB CUTLETS
8 oz. cold cooked lamb
1 medium-sized onion
1 cooking apple
8 oz. mashed potato
1 teaspoon Salt and Pepper Mix*
1 tablespoon chopped parsley
2 teaspoons tomato ketchup or
1 teaspoon tomato purée
Flour
1 beaten egg
Dried breadcrumbs
Fat for deep frying
1. Mince together lamb, onion and apple.
2. Add potato, Salt and Pepper Mix, parsley and ketchup or tomato purée. Mix well.
3. Shape into "cutlets", dust with flour, brush with beaten egg, roll in dried crumbs.
4. Deep fry for 3 to 4 minutes. Drain on paper.

## HIGHLAND LAMB STEW
1 oz. pearl barley
3 sticks of celery
8 oz. carrots

*See page 9.

1 large onion
1 oz. margarine
1¼ to 1½ lb. of lean lamb cut into
1-inch cubes
¼ pint cider
¼ pint light stock
1 teaspoon Salt and Pepper Mix*
1 sprig fresh thyme or
½ teaspoon dried thyme

**Sauce**
1 oz. margarine
1 oz. flour
1 heaped teaspoon parsley

1. Rinse barley in a sieve under running water. Place in small pan, just cover with water and simmer 10 minutes or so.
2. Meanwhile, prepare vegetables, cutting them into chunks.
3. Melt margarine in large pan, soften vegetables without browning for 7 to 8 minutes.
4. Add lamb and turn it over in fat to seal.
5. Pour in cider and stock, add Salt and Pepper Mix and thyme, then drained barley. Cover and cook until meat is tender, about 1 to 1¼ hours.
6. Place meat and vegetables on a serving dish and keep warm. Remove sprig of thyme if used.
7. Now make the sauce. Melt margarine in pan, add flour, cook 1 minute.
8. Strain liquid in pan, pushing any loose vegetables through sieve. Mix into the roux—that is, the cooked flour and margarine in the pan—bring to boil and simmer 2 minutes. Stir in parsley. Taste for seasoning.
9. Spoon a little sauce over meat, serve remainder in a sauce-boat.

## RABBIT CASSEROLE
1½ lb. rabbit joints
6 oz. streaky bacon
1 to 2 oz. bacon dripping or firm margarine
12 oz. chopped onion
12 oz. carrot
2 good sticks celery
⅓ pint light ale
4 oz. button mushrooms

1 level tablespoon cornflour
1 teaspoon Salt and Pepper Mix*
Chopped parsley

**Forcemeat Balls**
4 oz. fresh white breadcrumbs
1½ oz. shredded suet
1 tablespoon grated onion
2 teaspoons chopped fresh thyme, or ½ teaspoon dried thyme
½ teaspoon Salt and Pepper Mix*
1 beaten egg
A little flour

1. Soak rabbit in lightly-salted water for half an hour, drain and dry.
2. Cut bacon into 1-inch pieces, fry gently to extract fat.
3. Add 1 oz. dripping or margarine to pan, fry rabbit joints until golden.
4. Lift out joints and transfer to casserole.
5. Fry onion in fat and transfer to casserole.
6. Add to casserole the carrot cut into chunks and celery in 1-inch pieces. Pour over the light ale.
7. Cover and cook at Gas 4, 350°F. for 1 hour.
8. Wash mushrooms and add to casserole. Mix cornflour and Salt and Pepper Mix with a little water, mix in.
9. Cover casserole and return it to oven for half an hour.
10. Meanwhile, make the forcemeat balls. Mix breadcrumbs, suet, onion, thyme and seasoning and bind together with the egg. Make into 12 balls, roll in flour.
11. Fry lightly in fat to seal.
12. Place in casserole. Cover and cook for half an hour.
Sprinkle on chopped parsley just before serving.

## A tip with fresh suet
Buy fresh suet from the butcher. Put it in an oven-proof basin, cover and when the oven is on put it at the bottom. As the suet gradually melts pour it off into another basin. When it has set put it in a polythene bag, store in the

refrigerator and grate off as needed. Keeps a long time.

**Mrs. M. Wright,
Cleethorpes,
Lincolnshire.**

## SMOTHERED LIVER HOT-POT

3 rashers streaky bacon
1 lb. liver
1 level tablespoon plain flour
mixed with 1 level teaspoon Salt
and Pepper Mix*
2 sliced onions
1 sliced apple
1 teaspoon sugar
¼ pint light stock
¼ pint cider
1 oz. bacon fat if necessary
4 oz. fresh white breadcrumbs

1. De-rind bacon, cut it into one-inch pieces and fry lightly to extract a little fat.
2. Wash and slice liver, coat well in seasoned flour and place in a shallow casserole.
3. Drain bacon, scatter on top of liver. Add onions and apple and sprinkle on sugar.
4. Pour over the stock and cider.
5. Add a little fat to pan to make up to a good tablespoonful, tip in crumbs and stir to combine.
6. Spread crumbs over casserole. Cover, foil will do.
7. Cook at Gas 5, 375°F. for 45 minutes. Test with a skewer to ensure liver is cooked—pig and beef liver take longer than lamb's.
8. Uncover, cook 10 to 12 minutes to crisp top.

## CURRY SAUCE

½ pint light stock
1 heaped tablespoon coconut
1 oz. butter or good dripping
1 finely-chopped onion
1 thinly-sliced apple
1 level tablespoon curry powder
1 level tablespoon plain flour
1 tablespoon sultanas
1 tablespoon chutney
1 dessertspoon brown sugar
1 dessertspoon lemon juice
1 Boil stock and pour it over the coconut. Leave to infuse for 10 to 15 minutes. Strain stock, discard coconut.
2. Melt fat in pan, add onion and apple, soften a little, stir in curry powder and flour, allow to sizzle and cook, stirring, for 2 minutes.
3. Stir in the stock, bring to boil, simmer 15 minutes.
4. Add remaining ingredients, simmer a further 15 minutes. If becoming too thick, add a little more stock, but the sauce should not be thin.
Serve over hot hard-boiled eggs. Or add cooked meat and vegetables towards end of cooking time, making sure these are thoroughly heated through before serving.

## TO RE-HEAT RICE

1. Grease a suitable oven dish lightly with butter, tip in cooked rice, put a few shavings of butter on top, cover tightly.
2. Put in the oven, Gas 4, 350°F. for about 30 minutes. Stir lightly with fork before serving.

## BACON JOINT WITH CIDER SAUCE AND SUET CRUSTIES

This will provide a meal on 2 days for 4 people. On second day: soup for first course and cold bacon (with pickles) to follow.

3 lb. collar bacon
1 bay leaf
12 peppercorns
2 to 3 parsley stalks
1 lb. medium-sized onions
1 lb. carrots
1 lb. parsnips
1 lb. swede
**Sauce:**
1 level tablespoon cornflour
1 teaspoon dry mustard
½ pt. cider
¼ pt. bacon stock
**Suet Crusties:**
8 oz. self-raising flour
½ teaspoon salt
4 oz. shredded suet
Water
1. Soak bacon at least 4 hours or

*See page 9.

overnight.

2. Place in large pan, cover with fresh water, add herbs tied in muslin.

3. Bring to boil, skim if necessary, simmer 40 minutes.

4. Meanwhile, prepare vegetables, leaving onions whole, cutting rest to similar size.

5. When bacon has simmered 40 minutes add vegetables to pan, bring back to boil, simmer 20 minutes. The vegetables should be slightly undercooked so test at 15 minutes.

6. Take vegetables from pan, drain, then place in a baking dish.

7. Take out bacon, skin, score top into diamonds and place with vegetables. (Save the stock for an excellent soup—see next recipe.)

8. Heat oven to Gas 6, 400°F.

9. Meanwhile mix sauce ingredients in small pan, bring to boil and pour over vegetables.

10. Place in oven, middle shelf, for 35 to 40 minutes.

11. **Now make the Suet Crusties:**
(a) Lightly mix, with a knife, flour, salt and suet with 7 to 8 tablespoons of water. The dough should be soft, but not too sticky.
(b) Turn on to a floured board and roll out half an inch thick either round or square. Mark into 8 pieces.
(c) Place on greased tray. Bake on top shelf of oven 25 to 30 minutes until outside is crisp.

12. Set bacon and vegetables on a warm dish. Arrange Crusties around edge. Serve the sauce separately.

## BACON AND VEGETABLE SOUP FOR THE NEXT DAY

1. Strain bacon stock into bowl. Leave overnight and then remove any fat from top.

2. Sieve or liquidize any vegetables left-over (or prepare and cook more in the stock if necessary).

3. Mix 1 to 1½ pts. bacon stock into vegetable puree, check for seasoning, add any cider sauce left over.

4. Bring to boil. If consistency is a little too thick, add more stock or a little cider according to taste. Or even add a 14 oz. tin of tomatoes, sieving them first to remove pips.
Freezes well.

## MEAT BALLS IN TOMATO SAUCE

*1 lb. finely minced beef*
*2 oz. fresh white breadcrumbs*
*1 large grated onion*
*1 beaten egg*
*1 level tablespoon plain flour*
*1 teaspoon salt*
*½ teaspoon pepper*
*1 oz. beef dripping*
*14 oz. tin of tomatoes*
*½ pt. beef or bacon stock*

1. Mix together beef, crumbs, half the onion and the beaten egg.

2. Form into 16 even-sized balls. Roll in flour mixed with salt and pepper.

3. Heat dripping in pan, add meat balls, turn over in hot fat to seal for 1 to 2 minutes, allow to brown a little. Drain on to a plate.

4. Add remaining onion to pan, stir in any seasoned flour left and cook, stirring for 2 minutes.

5. Pour in can of tomatoes, mix well, add stock, and bring to boil.

6. Sieve into a casserole, add meat balls, cover tightly. Cook at Gas 4, 350°F., for 45 minutes.

Serve in ring of potatoes or rice, with green vegetables. Pour a little sauce over the meat balls, serve the rest separately.

This dish can also be cooked on top of stove. At paragraph 6 above, use saucepan instead of casserole, cover with lid. Simmer gently for 35 minutes, checking from time to time in case it sticks. This dish freezes well. Thaw slowly—it is better done in refrigerator overnight—then heat through in a pan, stirring from time to time. If sauce has thickened too much, add a little more stock. Remove meat balls on to dish and whisk sauce a little if it shows signs of curdling.

## STUFFED MARROW RINGS

*Vegetable marrow*
*Cooked meat—any left over*
*meat, even small quantities*
*can be used*
*Onion*
*Soft white breadcrumbs*
*Shredded suet (only if meat is lean)*
*Made mustard*
*Salt and Pepper Mix\**
*Mixed dried herbs*
*Beaten egg*
*Gravy*

1. Cut required number of marrow rings about 1½ inches wide, peel and remove seeds. Place in greased oven tin.
2. **Make a filling:**
(a) Put meat through mincer.
(b) To ½ lb. of meat add 1 grated onion, 2 oz. soft white crumbs, 1 oz. shredded suet (only if meat is lean), 1 teaspoon of made mustard, 1 teaspoon Salt and Pepper Mix, 1 teaspoon mixed dried herbs, 1 beaten egg. Mix well together.
3. Fill rings with mixture. Bake at Gas 5, 375°F. 30 to 40 minutes until marrow is soft.
Serve with a good thick gravy.
A good idea for slimmers.

## LIVER RAGOUT

*1 lb. lamb or calf liver*
*½ oz. seasoned flour*
*1 oz. dripping*
*1 finely chopped onion*
*Juice of ½ a lemon*
*5 tablespoons dry red or*
*white wine*
*4 oz. mushrooms*
**To Serve:** *1½ lb. creamed potatoes*
　　　　**Or:** *8 oz. Patna rice*
*Chopped parsley*

1. Wash liver, remove skin and any tubes. Cut into 1 inch cubes.
2. Coat in flour seasoned with a shake of salt and pepper.

3. Melt dripping in pan, add liver and onion turning it over to seal the liver.
4. Cook gently for 8 to 10 minutes with lid on pan but stirring occasionally to prevent catching.
5. Add lemon juice, wine and washed and sliced mushrooms. Cook with lid on about 8 minutes more until liver is tender.
Meanwhile, cook potatoes and beat until creamy. Form into a ring on warm dish, pour ragout in centre. Sprinkle with chopped parsley.
If using rice—cook about 12 minutes, using bacon stock instead of water if this is available. Form into ring, pour ragout in centre. Sprinkle with chopped parsley.

　　*\*See page 9.*

# CHAPTER 7

# VEGETABLES

## BEETROOT AS A HOT VEGETABLE

1. Choose small even-sized beetroot.
2. Remove tops and roots, but do not break skin. Wash well.
3. Simmer gently for about $1\frac{1}{2}$ hours until tender.
4. Peel and keep hot.

**To Serve with White Sauce:**
*1 oz. margarine*
*1 oz. plain flour*
*$\frac{1}{2}$ teaspoon Salt and Pepper Mix\**
*$\frac{1}{2}$ pint milk*

1. In pan, melt margarine, add flour and Salt and Pepper Mix, sizzle for one minute.
2. Gradually stir in milk and simmer for 1 minute.
3. Pour over the peeled beetroot.

**To Serve Glazed:**
*1 oz. butter*
*1 teaspoon sugar*
*Grated rind of 1 lemon*
*Juice of $\frac{1}{2}$ lemon*
*2 teaspoons chopped parsley*

1. Melt butter in pan, add beetroots, sugar, lemon rind, parsley and lemon juice.
2. Toss over medium heat until hot.


## CAULIFLOWER WITH CHEESE AND BACON SAUCE

*A cauliflower*
**For the Sauce:**
*4 oz. streaky bacon*
*1 oz. margarine*
*1 oz. plain flour*
*$\frac{1}{2}$ teaspoon Salt & Pepper Mix\**
*$\frac{1}{4}$ pint milk*
*$\frac{1}{4}$ pint of the cauliflower water*
*3 oz. grated cheese*

**To Serve 'Au Gratin':**
*1 to 2 oz. grated cheese*
*Crisp breadcrumbs (optional)*

1. Remove stalk end and all but the delicate young leaves. Wash well in salted water. Do not leave to soak.
2. Cut a cross at the stalk end to allow both stalk and flower to be evenly cooked.
3. Place in deep pan just big enough to hold the cauliflower with enough boiling, salted water to reach about one inch up the sides. Cover and cook for about 10 to 15 minutes until tender but still firm.
4. Cut the bacon into small pieces and fry till crisp.
5. Melt the margerine in a pan, add flour and Salt and Pepper Mix and sizzle for one minute.
6. Gradually stir in milk and cauliflower water and simmer for one minute.
7. Add cheese, reheat but do not boil. Stir in crisp bacon.
8. Have the well-drained cauliflower in a warm dish and pour over the cheese and bacon sauce.

**To Serve 'Au Gratin':**
Place cooked cauliflower in a heat-resistant casserole. Pour over cheese sauce, sprinkle on cheese and breadcrumbs, place under a medium grill to melt cheese and brown a little.


## MARROW AND ONION SAVOURY

*$1\frac{1}{2}$ lb. marrow, peeled,*
*de-seeded, and cut into*
*1 inch cubes*
*1 lb. onions thinly sliced*
*Salt*
*Pepper*
*Mixed herbs*
*Butter*

1. Layer marrow and onion in a greased pie-dish, sprinkling seasoning between layers, and ending with marrow. Dot with butter.
2. Cover (foil will do) and cook at Gas 4 or 350°F. until tender, usually about $1\frac{1}{2}$ hours.
This will cook in lower part of oven, under meat.
Serve with lamb or roast pork.


## SCALLOPED TOMATOES

*1 onion*
*$\frac{1}{2}$ oz. margarine (or*
*good dripping)*
*1 lb. tomatoes*

80      *\*See page 9.*

2 oz. grated cheese
2 oz. breadcrumbs
1 teaspoon sugar
1 teaspoon Salt and Pepper Mix*
A little butter
1. Chop the onion and cook gently in fat for about 5 minutes.
2. Meanwhile, skin the tomatoes by placing in a basin and pouring over boiling water. Leave 10 seconds. Pour away water and refresh with cold water. Skins should now come away easily.
3. Thickly slice the tomatoes.
4. Remove onions from heat. Add cheese and crumbs.
5. Place tomatoes in 1½ pint greased pie-dish, sprinkling with sugar, salt and pepper between layers.
6. Spread onion mixture on top, dot with butter.
7. Cook at Gas 4 or 350°F. 25 to 30 minutes.

## STUFFED PEPPERS
Allow 1 pepper per person.
**To Prepare Peppers:**
1. Cut a piece from stalk end, cut out all membrane and seeds.
2. Blanch pepper by dropping into a pan of boiling water, cook 3 minutes. Drain and dry.
3. Brush outside with a little melted oil or fat, and arrange in lightly greased, shallow casserole.
**Filling for 4 Large Peppers**
1 oz. butter or good dripping
1 large grated onion
2 oz. finely sliced mushrooms
8 oz. chopped ham, chicken, turkey or minced cooked beef
2 oz. white breadcrumbs or cooked long-grain rice
2 teaspoons Worcester Sauce
1 teaspoon Salt & Pepper Mix*
A little stock to moisten
1. Melt fat in pan, cook onion and mushrooms for 2 to 3 minutes.
2. Add rest of ingredients but use stock only if mixture is a little dry.
3. Stuff the mixture into the peppers. Add 2 tablespoons of water to casserole. Cook at Gas 5 or 350°F. about 40 minutes.

A sprinkling of grated cheese can be added before cooking for extra flavour.

## POTATOES
**Choosing:**
Should be reasonably clear of soil, firm and sound, but washed potatoes do not keep. They are better bought from a sack as exposure to daylight causes green patches.
**Storing:**
Keep in brown paper bag in a cool place. Heat causes them to go soft and sprout.
**Preparation:**
**New Potatoes**
Should scrub or scrape easily. Do not prepare too long in advance.
**Old Potatoes**
Most nutritious if scrubbed and baked in jackets. If peeling, use a peeler that takes away the minimum of peel. Cut to size, place in cold salted water, replacing this for cooking.
**Cooking:**
**New Potatoes**
Place in boiling, salted water with a sprig of mint. Cook 15 to 20 minutes, according to size. Drain, place in hot dish with a good nut of butter. Turn over to coat, sprinkle on chopped parsley.
**Old Potatoes**
Place in cold, salted water, bring to boil. Cook 20 to 30 minutes, according to size. Drain. While keeping warm, place a clean, folded tea-towel on pan to absorb moisture.

## MASHED OR CREAMED POTATOES
Add 1 oz. butter to each 1 lb. potatoes and salt and pepper to taste. Mash until creamy. A little top of the milk may also be added to give a softer consistency.
## CREAMED POTATO FOR PIPING
**Duchesse and Potato Baskets**

For each 1 lb. potatoes allow 1 oz. butter and 1 egg yolk with salt and pepper to taste and a grate of nutmeg, one beaten egg white.

1. Mash the potatoes entirely free from lumps—a potato ricer is good for this method—and then mix in the butter, egg yolk, salt, pepper and nutmeg.
2. Use a large forcing bag and a large serrated nozzle. Pipe rosettes of potato or basket shapes on to a greased baking tray.
3. Brush with beaten egg white and bake in hot oven Gas 7, 425°F. for 10-15 minutes.

Filled with peas the potato baskets make a good garnish for a joint of meat.

A large potato basket can be filled with cheese sauce and vegetables.

## POTATO CROQUETTES

For each 1 lb. potatoes:
*1 oz. butter*
*1 egg, separated*
*Salt and pepper*
*1 to 2 teaspoons chopped parsley*
*A grate of nutmeg*
*A little flour*
*Dried breadcrumbs*

1. Mash the potatoes free from lumps and mix in the butter, egg yolk, salt, pepper, parsley and nutmeg. The mixture should be firm, but not dry.
2. Form into cork-shaped pieces about 3 inches long and 1 inch in diameter.
3. Flour, dip in lightly beaten egg white and roll in dried breadcrumbs.
4. Deep fry for 3 to 4 minutes.

These freeze well, but this must be done before they are fried.

## ROAST POTATOES

Peel, cut into even-sized pieces and boil for 10 minutes. Drain well and dry. Place round meat, rolling over in fat in tin and allow 30 to 40 minutes cooking time at Gas 6, 400°F.

These can also be placed in a separate tin, allowing fat to become hot first, and roasted at Gas 6, 400°F on top shelf of oven. If potatoes are not crisp enough when cooked through, place under medium grill for 5 minutes, turning to ensure even browning.

## STUFFED JACKET POTATOES
### A Meal on Its Own

1. Choose even-sized potatoes. Scrub well.
2. Prick with fine skewer and rub with beef or bacon dripping.
3. Bake at Gas 6, 400°F. for 1 to $1\frac{1}{4}$ hours (according to size).
4. Cut in half, lengthways. Remove most of inside.
5. Mash with a good piece of butter, adding salt and pepper and 2 oz. grated cheese per potato.
6. Spoon into shells, place in oven 5 to 10 minutes to heat through.

Nice topped with a bacon roll. De-rind rashers of streaky bacon, roll up and place on large skewer on a baking tray. Cook in oven with potatoes. Will take 15 to 20 minutes.

Try also with an egg. After spooning mashed potato and cheese back into potato case, make a hollow with back of spoon, crack in an egg, put on a nut of butter to stop egg going hard on top and return to oven to reheat potato and set the egg.

## BIEN POMMES DE TERRE
### Or good spuds French-style!

*$1\frac{1}{2}$ lb. old potatoes*
*1 onion*
*Salt and Pepper Mix**
*3 to 4 tablespoons milk*
*1 oz. butter*

1. Slice potato thickly.
2. Slice onion into thin rings.
3. Use some of the butter to grease a fairly deep ovenproof dish—a $2\frac{1}{2}$ pint pie or soufflé dish is suitable.
4. Place the potato and onion in the dish in layers, seasoning to taste.

*See page 9.

5. Pour over the milk.
6. Dot with small bits of butter.
7. Cover and put in the oven at Gas 4, 350°F. for 1 hour. Remove cover to let it brown a little for a further 8 to 10 minutes.
**Jamie Jackson,
London.**

## TATWS LLAETH
### New Potatoes in Buttermilk
*New potatoes*
*Buttermilk*
Traditionally, the first new potatoes to be lifted were used for this delicate and nourishing dish. Nowadays, obtaining buttermilk may be difficult for some people but it is produced for sale by several dairies and sold in many parts of the country.
1. Cook the scraped potatoes in boiling salted water with a sprig of mint.
2. When cooked, drain thoroughly and then put enough for one serving in a basin and just cover with buttermilk. Eat at once.
**Miss G. S. Davies,
Flintshire.**

## POTATO AND CELERY SOUP
*2 oz. butter*
*1 lb. potatoes, peeled and*
*cut into pieces*
*2 onions, peeled and quartered*
*5 stalks celery, washed and*
*cut into pieces*
*1½ pints chicken or bacon stock*
*Salt and pepper*
*¼ pint milk*
*Nutmeg*
1. Melt butter and fry vegetables gently for 4 minutes.
2. Add stock, salt and pepper, bring to boil, cover and simmer for 40 minutes.
3. Sieve or liquidize.
4. Add milk, reheat, adjust seasoning and grate in a little nutmeg.
Garnish with a few chopped celery leaves.

## CHEESE ONION AND POTATO PIE
*8 oz. potatoes*
*2 to 3 oz. cheese*
*Half an onion*
*1 oz. margarine*
*Salt and pepper*
*⅛ pint or 2½ fluid oz. milk*
*Chopped parsley*
1. Put the potatoes on to boil until they soften.
2. Meanwhile grate cheese and chop onion finely.
3. Fry onion till golden in half of the margarine.
4. Drain the potatoes and add salt, pepper, milk and remaining margarine. Mash well.
5. Add onion, all but 2 tablespoons of the cheese and a little parsley. Mash well, put into a warmed, oven-proof dish and smooth top.
6. Sprinkle on remaining cheese and put under grill to brown a little before serving. Add final touch of parsley.
**Miss Jackie Brindley,
Biddulph,
Stoke-on-Trent**

**A delicious variation** to Miss Brindley's recipe.
1. Before sprinkling the cheese on top (paragraph 6), make 4 hollows in the mixture with the back of a spoon.
2. Drop an egg into each hollow and put a dot of butter on each.
3. Sprinkle the grated cheese between the eggs.
4. Put in the oven Gas 5, 375°F. until eggs set, about 15 minutes.

## BUTTERED CABBAGE
*Cabbage*
*Salt and pepper*
*Butter*
*A little boiling water*
1. Cut the cabbage in half. Place it cut side down on a board and slice carefully into thin segments. Do not remove the core because this holds the segments together and stops them falling to pieces

during cooking.

2. Stand the segments together on edge in a saucepan small enough to hold them upright.

3. Sprinkle on a little salt and plenty of pepper. Dot with tiny pieces of butter.

4. Pour into the pan half an inch only of boiling water. Cover pan tightly. Bring to the boil, reduce heat at once and allow to simmer for 5 to 8 minutes.

5. Drain well and using a suitable utensil serve unbroken slices on to the plates.

## BRAISED RED CABBAGE

*1 small red cabbage, 1½ to 2 lbs.*
*2 oz. of butter or good bacon dripping.*
*1 medium-sized onion, sliced*
*1 large cooking apple*
*¼ pint cheap red wine, or stock*
*2 teaspoons salt*
*1 tablespoon vinegar*
*½ level teaspoon powdered cloves*
*½ teaspoon grated nutmeg*
*Plenty of black pepper, to taste*
*1 level tablespoon soft brown sugar*

1. Cut the cabbage into quarters removing outer leaves, white root and any large pieces of white pith. Shred the cabbage finely.

2. Place in a large bowl, pour over sufficient boiling water to cover. Leave 1 minute, drain.

3. Melt butter in a large heavy pan, add onion, cook gently to soften but not brown, about 5 minutes.

4. Add apple, peeled, cored and thickly sliced, the wine or stock, salt, vinegar, cloves, nutmeg and a good grating of black pepper. Add cabbage and turn over to mix into liquid. Cover tightly.

5. Cook gently until tender, turning over from time to time, about 1 hour.

6. Stir in sugar and serve.

Serve with a hot joint, especially pork or bacon.

This heats very well the following day, losing none of its flavour.

## VEGETABLE HOT POT

**Ratatouille**
*3 large onions*
*1 small green pepper*
*1 good-sized aubergine*
*4 tablespoons cooking oil*
*1 lb. ripe tomatoes or a 14 oz. tin of tomatoes*
*1 clove of garlic*
*1 teaspoon sugar*
*Salt*
*1 bay leaf and/or ½ teaspoon basil*
*Black pepper*

1. Cut the onions into chunks. Cut the green pepper into very small pieces and the aubergine into ½ to 1 inch cubes. Skin and roughly chop the tomatoes. Crush the garlic.

2. Heat oil in a large heavy-based pan. Turn the onions over in the oil for a couple of minutes.

3. Add the pepper and the aubergine and mix well.

4. Add tomatoes, garlic, sugar, salt, bay leaf, basil and a good grating of black pepper. Mix all together.

5. Cover tightly and simmer very gently for at least half an hour. An hour is not too long to cook this dish.

Serve with rice or pasta or even large chunks of crusty bread. Particularly good with an omelette or a cheese soufflé. Reheats well.

## LENTIL ROAST

*8 oz. lentils*
*2 tablespoons oil*
*2 onions*
*2 large tomatoes*
*1 large cooking apple*
*2 oz. breadcrumbs*
*1 egg*
*1 teaspoon sage or mixed herbs*
*Salt and pepper*

1. Soak lentils overnight in enough water just to cover.

2. Next day, cook lentils in same water until soft, beat smooth.

3. Heat oil in pan and fry finely-chopped onions gently until soft.

4. Peel, core and finely slice apple. Skin and chop tomatoes. Add both to onion and fry till soft.
5. Add to lentils with breadcrumbs, beaten egg, herbs and seasonings.
6. Press into greased loaf tin and cover.
7. Bake at Gas 5, 375°F. about 50 minutes.
Serve as a main course with green vegetables, gravy or tomato sauce.

## SAVOURY PUDDING

*1 lb. white bread, without crusts*
*½ pint hot, light stock*
*1 lb. finely chopped onions*
*3 oz. shredded suet*
*1 teaspoon mixed herbs*
*2 beaten eggs*
*Salt*
*Black pepper*
*1 tablespoon chopped parsley*
1. Cut the bread into 1 inch cubes and soak for 1 hour in hot stock.
2. Add rest of ingredients and beat well. Place in a small, greased roasting tin or pie dish.
3. Cook at Gas 4 to 5, 350° to 375°F. for 30 to 40 minutes.
Serve on its own with thick gravy or serve it with pork or poultry.

## CUMBERLAND HERB PUDDING

*1 heaped tablespoon pearl barley*
*1 lb. spring cabbage*
*4 oz. nettles, optional but worth trying*
*2 medium-sized onions*
*2 medium-sized leeks*
*1 oz. butter*
*1 egg*
*Salt and pepper to taste*
1. Soak barley overnight in 1 pint water.
2. Next day, boil until tender in the same water.
3. Place washed and shredded vegetables in a large heavy saucepan, add cooked barley and the liquid in which it cooked. Add a little more water if necessary.
4. Boil quickly until tender with lid on pan stirring occasionally to prevent barley sticking to base of pan. This can take from 20 to 30 minutes depending on age and quality of vegetables.
5. Drain through a colander discarding liquid and tip vegetables back into the pan.
6. Add butter and beaten egg, mix in and season to taste with salt and pepper.
7. Turn into a 2-pint heat-proof basin or pie dish.
8. Cover and re-heat in moderate oven, Gas 4, 350°F., about 10 to 15 minutes.
Serve hot, turned out of basin on to a warmed plate.
**Miss H. Holmes,**
**Crosby on Eden.**

## GLAZED PARSNIPS
**Quite a sweet dish. Nice with pork or poultry**
*1½ lb. parsnips*
*1½ oz. butter*
*1 tablespoon brown sugar*
*¼ teaspoon salt*
*2 teaspoons lemon juice*
*Juice of 1 orange (or 4 tablespoons cider)*
1. Wash the parsnips and boil them until just tender. Then peel, slice and leave them to drain well.
2. Choose a shallow baking dish, butter it well and arrange half the parsnip slices in a single layer in the dish.
3. Melt 1 oz. of the butter, remove from heat and mix with it the sugar, salt, lemon and orange juice (or cider).
4. Pour half the mixture over the sliced parsnips. Cover with remaining parsnip slices and pour over them the rest of the sugar mixture.
5. Dot with the rest of the butter.
6. Bake in the oven at Gas 5, 375°F. for 20 minutes or until the top is nicely glazed.
**Mrs. Sybil Norcott,**
**Irlam, Nr. Manchester**

## LEEKS IN RED WINE

*Leeks as required, not too large,*
*preferably all the same size*
*1 tablespoon oil*
*1 oz. butter*
*1 glass (about ¼ pint) cheap red*
*wine*
*¼ to ½ pint well-flavoured stock*
*Salt and pepper*

1. Trim leeks and wash very well in cold, running water to remove any grit.
2. Heat oil and butter in a wide shallow pan, lay leeks in side by side. Gently turn them over until golden all over.
3. Pour on the wine, allow to bubble.
4. Boil stock and pour on just enough to cover leeks. Check seasoning.
5. Cover pan and cook until leeks are tender.
6. Remove leeks to a hot dish, boil liquid rapidly to reduce to about ¼ pint. Pour over leeks.

## CUCUMBER AND YOGURT

*1 cucumber*
*1 tablespoon salt*
*Garlic, optional*
*1 teaspoon vinegar (wine vinegar is*
*best)*
*1 dessertspoon dried mint*
*1 teaspoon salad oil (olive oil is*
*best)*
*10 to 12 oz. best quality, natural*
*yogurt*
*A little black pepper*

1. Peel the cucumber and chop it finely.
2. Put it in a bowl or colander, sprinkle on the salt and leave it 1 to 2 hours.
3. Take a shallow serving dish and rub around it the raw edge of half a clove of garlic. (Or, crush a quarter of a clove of garlic and put in dish).
4. Put less than a teaspoon of vinegar into the dish and shake it around.
5. Drain as much liquid as possible from the cucumber.
6. Put the cucumber in the dish,

crumble over it the dried mint, shake over the salad oil.
7. Now spoon over the yogurt and stir very well adding lastly a little black pepper.
8. Chill for about 1 hour but do not serve it too cold.
Keeps in refrigerator for a day or two. If any separation occurs stir before serving.
Particularly good to eat on its own following a rich main course, but also nice with cold meats.

# CHAPTER 8

# HOME BAKING

## WHITE BREAD DOUGH
**And a number of different ways to shape, bake and vary it.**

*2 lb. strong plain flour*
*3 teaspoons salt*
*3 oz. margarine*
*3 level teaspoons dried yeast, or 1½ oz. fresh yeast*
*1 teaspoon sugar*
*½ pint tepid water*
*½ pint tepid milk*

This quantity makes approximately 3¼ lbs. of risen dough.

**Note:** Different brands of flour require differing quantities of water to produce a good elastic dough. The quantity of water listed gives a general indication but may be modified slightly as required.

1. Mix together the flour and salt and rub in the margarine.
2. Mix the dried yeast and the sugar into the water. Leave it in a warm place until quite dissolved and beginning to froth.
If using fresh yeast mix it and the sugar into the water stirring to dissolve the yeast. It is now ready for use. Unlike dried yeast it is not necessary to wait until the mixture froths up.
3. Add the yeast mixture with milk to the flour mixture.
4. Mix to a pliable dough and turn on to a floured board.
5. Knead well until the dough is no longer sticky, and is smooth and shiny. If the dough is a little soft, extra flour may be added, whilst kneading (up to 2 oz.), but it is difficult to add water if too firm.
6. Lightly grease the bowl and place dough in it. Cover, or place inside a large polythene bag, keep away from draughts, and leave to rise (or "prove") until doubled in size.
7. Turn on to a floured board and knead lightly to let out air and to make dough pliable again.
The dough at this stage is referred to as "risen dough". Cut off quantity required for any of the following:

### Standard 1 lb. Loaf
Approximately 1 lb. risen dough. Grease a 1 lb. loaf tin with a little lard. Lightly shape dough to fit into the tin, cover with muslin or light cloth, or place in polythene bag and leave to rise to the top of the tin. Bake at Gas 7, 425°F., 40 minutes. Reduce heat to Gas 6, 400°F. if it browns too quickly.

### Cottage Loaf
12 oz. risen dough.
Divide into 2 portions of about 8 oz. and 4 oz. each. Pat each piece out until 1 inch thick, placing smaller piece on top. Make a hole down centre with finger. Put loaf on to a greased baking tray. Cover with muslin or light cloth, or place in polythene bag, and allow to rise until puffy. Bake at Gas 7, 425°F. 35 minutes.

### Muffins
Roll out 12 oz. of risen dough into a square, half an inch thick. Cut into 3-inch rounds (will make 4). Place on greased and floured baking tray. Cover. Allow to rise until quite puffy. Heat a thick frying pan or girdle until moderately hot, grease with a piece of suet. Transfer muffins with a spatula, and cook 6 minutes each side until golden brown both sides.

### Bread Sticks
8 oz. risen dough will make at least 12. Break off small pieces, roll out with floured hands until finger thickness. Put them on a greased baking tray. Cover and leave to rise until puffy. Bake at Gas 7, 425°F. until crisp, 12 to 14 minutes.

### Bread Buns, Swiss Buns, Devonshire Splits
12 oz. risen dough will make 8 of any of these. Shape, place on greased baking tray, cover and leave to rise until puffy. Bake at

Gas 7, 425°F. for 10 to 12 minutes.
**Bread Buns** for dinner rolls, should be glazed with beaten egg before rising.
**Swiss Buns.** When cold, ice tops with pink icing.
**Devonshire Splits.** When cold, fill with whipped cream and strawberry jam, dust with icing sugar.

### Sultana Loaf
Take 12 oz. of risen dough. Work in 2 oz. sultanas and 1 oz. of vanilla sugar*. Place in greased 1 lb. loaf tin, cover, allow to rise until doubled in size. Bake at Gas 6, 400°F. for about 40 minutes.

### Apricot and Walnut Twist
Take 12 oz. of risen dough. Add 2 oz. dried apricots, cut up finely, and scalded (by placing in sieve and pouring over boiling water), 1 oz. chopped walnuts, and 1 oz. of vanilla sugar*. Work together and make into a twist or finish as for Sultana Loaf. Cover and rise until double the size. Bake at Gas 6, 400°F. for about 40 minutes. Ice when cold.

### Tea Cakes
Take 12 oz. risen dough, work in 2 oz. currants, 1 oz. vanilla sugar*. Divide into 4 portions. Roll out with rolling pin, until half an inch thick. Cover and leave to rise until puffy. Bake at Gas 7, 425°F. for 12 to 15 minutes.

### Lardy Cake
*12 oz. risen, white, bread dough*
*2 oz. lard*
*2 oz. castor sugar*
*2 oz. currants*
*A little honey*
1. Roll out dough to an oblong about 5 inches by 12 inches.
2. Spread on lard and sprinkle on sugar and currants.
3. Roll up like a Swiss Roll.
4. Roll this out into a square and place in a greased, shallow, 7-inch baking tin. Make light diagonal

cuts in top to give a diamond pattern.
5. Cover and leave to rise to the top of the tin.
6. Brush lightly with honey and bake at Gas 5, 375°F. for about 35 minutes.
7. Serve hot with butter.

### Oatcakes
*8 oz. risen dough*
*8 oz. rolled oats (packet porridge oats will do)*
*3 oz. melted lard*
*1 oz. castor sugar*
*1 level teaspoon of salt*
Work all ingredients together, roll out quite thinly on floured board, cut into squares or triangles with sharp knife. Place on greased baking tray. Do not leave to rise. Bake at Gas 6, 400°F. for about 10 minutes until just golden.

### Mary Berry's Savoury Tart
*12 oz. risen, white, bread dough*
*1 large onion, sliced*
*A little butter*
*14 oz. tin of tomatoes*
*12 oz. Cheddar cheese, sliced or grated*
*Salt and pepper*
*A little chopped fresh thyme*
*8 slices short back bacon*
1. Roll out dough on a large, floured baking sheet into a 12-inch circle. If you do not have a large baking sheet make two small tarts.
2. Fry the onion in the butter until soft.
3. Spread onion over dough. Cover with the tomatoes including most of the juice. Cover tomatoes with the cheese. Sprinkle with salt, pepper and thyme. Arrange the bacon over the top.
4. Cover and put in a warm place to rise for 15 minutes.
5. Cook at Gas 7, 425°F. for 15 to 20 minutes until the edges are golden. Serve at once.

**\*Vanilla Sugar.** Break up 1 vanilla pod and put it in a screw-top jar with 1 lb. castor sugar. Replenish sugar and vanilla pod as necessary but vanilla will retain its aroma for some time.

If you cannot make your own vanilla sugar, most recipes can be made using castor sugar and a few drops of vanilla essence.

## JANET'S QUICK WHOLEMEAL BREAD

*1½ lb. wholemeal flour*
*1 dessertspoon salt*
*1 tablespoon dried yeast or 1 oz.*
*fresh yeast*
*1 teaspoon soft brown or white*
*sugar*
*¾ pint milk*
*¼ pint tepid water*

The quantity of dough made with these ingredients is enough for a 2 lb. and a 1 lb. loaf-tin, or, three 1 lb. loaf-tins, or, of course, other shapes may be made, such as bloomers, bread rolls etc. using a baking sheet.

**Note:** Different brands of flour require differing quantities of water to produce a good elastic dough. The quantity of water listed gives a general indication but may be modified slightly as required.

1. Put the flour and salt into a bowl and stand it in a warm place.
2. Warm the milk to blood heat and put half of it into a small bowl. Mix in the dried yeast and sugar. Leave it in a warm place until yeast is quite dissolved and beginning to froth.

If using fresh yeast, warm the milk to blood heat and put half of it into a small bowl. Add the yeast and sugar to the small bowl of milk stirring to dissolve the yeast. It may now be used. Unlike dried yeast it is not necessary to wait until the mixture froths up.
3. Grease 2 lb. or 1 lb. loaf-tins and/or a baking sheet.
4. Make a well in the centre of the flour. Pour in yeast mixture and mix it into the flour gradually

adding the remaining milk and most of the water, enough to make a soft pliable dough.
5. Turn dough out on to a floured board. Knead only lightly making sure your hands are warm. It will only take a few minutes as this dough does not require heavy kneading like white bread dough.
6. Divide dough into 2, 3 or more pieces. Shape them lightly but do not overhandle. Put into tins or on to baking sheet, cover with a clean cloth or a piece of polythene, stand in a warm, draught-free place and leave to rise. Do not put it near direct heat.

Depending on the warmth of your kitchen it could take about an hour to 1½ hours for dough to rise until doubled in size. Slow rising makes better bread.

If you leave it too long and dough begins to drop down again do not attempt to bake it. Knock it back, re-shape and put to rise again.
7. Bake above centre of oven— try to get all one shelf—at Gas 7, 400°F. to 425°F:

2 lb. loaf-tins about 45 minutes. Look in the oven after 30 minutes and reduce heat a little if getting too brown.

1 lb. loaf-tins, about 30 to 35 minutes.

Loaves or rolls cooked on baking sheet vary according to size. Small bloomer, about 15 to 20 minutes. Bread rolls, about 12 to 15 minutes.

To test: If it is done it will feel firm and sound hollow when tapped on the bottom.
8. Turn out of tins etc. at once on to a cooling rack and leave in a warm place until cooled.

Provided it is not overbaked this bread keeps moist and good to eat for 4 or 5 days.

## BASIC SCONE MIXTURE

*8 oz. self-raising flour*
*¼ teaspoon salt*
*2 oz. margarine*
*5 to 6 tablespoons milk*

1. Sift flour and salt into a bowl, rub in margarine.
2. Mix to a soft but not sticky dough with milk.
3. Turn out on to a floured board, knead very lightly, roll out half an inch thick.
4. Cut into 2-inch rounds, re-rolling and cutting the trimmings, and place on a lightly greased baking tray.
5. Bake at Gas 7, 425°F. 12 to 14 minutes until lightly golden and firm to the touch.

**Try also the following based on the Basic Scone Mixture recipe:**

**Herb Scones**
1. After rubbing in the margarine, add a shake of pepper and 1 level teaspoon of mixed dried herbs, then mix to a soft but not sticky dough with the milk.
2. Turn out on to a floured board, knead very lightly, roll out half an inch thick.
3. Cut into about 10 fingers, place them on a lightly-greased baking tray and brush with milk.
4. Bake at Gas 7, 425°F. for 12 to 14 minutes as for basic scone recipe.
**Serve with a savoury filling such as:—**
2 oz. softened margarine, 2 oz. finely-grated cheese, ½ level teaspoon mixed mustard beaten together.
**Or,** beat together 2 oz. softened margarine and 1 good teaspoon chopped, fresh parsley with salt and pepper to taste.

**Sweet Scones**
After rubbing margarine into flour and salt, add 1 oz. castor sugar and 2 oz. sultanas. Finish according to basic recipe.

**Cheese Scones**
After rubbing margarine into flour and salt, add ½ teaspoon dry mustard, a pinch of cayenne pepper, 3 oz. finely grated cheese. Finish according to basic recipe.

## OATEN BISCUITS
Makes about 32 biscuits
*4 oz. self-raising flour*
*4 oz. medium oatmeal or porridge oats*
*¼ teaspoon salt*
*3 oz. firm margarine*
*2 teaspoons sugar*
*1 beaten egg*
1. Mix together flour, oatmeal and salt.
2. Rub in margarine, add sugar and bind to a firm dough with the beaten egg.
3. Divide mixture into 2 portions for easier rolling and roll out quite thinly on a floured board.
4. Cut into rounds with a plain cutter about 2½-inch diameter. Re-roll and cut the trimmings.
5. Place on a lightly-greased baking sheet.
6. Bake at Gas 4, 350°F. for 10 to 12 minutes until firm but not coloured. Do not overbake.

## RICH BREAD DOUGH
*¼ oz. (2 level teaspoons) of dried yeast OR ½ oz. fresh yeast*
*8 liquid oz. warm milk*
*1 teaspoon sugar*
*1 oz. butter*
*1 lb. strong plain flour*
*1 teaspoon salt*
*1 egg*

NOTE
Different brands of flour require differing quantities of liquid to produce a good elastic dough. The quantity of milk listed gives a general indication but may be modified slighly as required.
1. If using **dried yeast**, prepare first:
(a) Add half the warmed milk to the yeast and sugar in a small basin.
(b) Put remaining milk in another small basin and add butter.
(c) Place basins in a container of warm water so that contents will be at blood heat when ready to use. Leave like this until yeast is frothy, stirring occasionally to soften yeast

granules. This can take from 12 to 15 minutes.

1. If using **fresh yeast**:
(a) Mix in a small bowl the sugar and half the warm milk.
(b) Put the butter with warm milk remaining in the pan.
(c) You can proceed with the recipe as soon as yeast is liquified. It is not necessary to wait for it to froth.
2. Mix flour and salt in a large warm bowl.
3. Add liquids and beaten egg and knead firmly until dough is smooth and elastic.
4. Place·to rise in a large, greased, warm bowl inside a large polythene bag. Leave until double in size when you can push a finger into the dough and the impression will remain.
5. Turn on to floured board, knead lightly and shape. This quantity, if divided into 3 even-sized portions. will make 8 dinner buns and 2 small loaves.
6. This mixture is not suitable for baking in loaf tins. Place on greased tray, cover and allow to rise until doubled in size. It should be puffy when lightly touched.
7. Bake at Gas 6, 400°F. Dinner buns require approximately 12 minutes. Loaves: 25 to 30 minutes depending on size. The base should sound hollow when tapped with knuckles.

### QUICK WHOLEMEAL BREAD
Sufficient for a 2 lb. loaf or a 1 lb. loaf, twist, bread rolls.
*1 lb. wholemeal flour; 4 oz. strong plain flour; 2 teaspoons salt; ½ pt. plus 4 tablespoons tepid water; 1 oz. fresh baker's yeast; ½ oz. lard; 1 dessertspoon dark treacle.*
NOTE
Some wholemeal flours absorb more liquid than others. An extra table-spoon of water may be required to produce a good elastic dough.

1. Mix together in a large bowl the flours and salt.
2. Using a small bowl whisk yeast into half of the water.
3. Using another small bowl dissolve lard and treacle in the remainder of the water.
4. Pour the two liquid mixtures on to the dry ingredients and make into a softish dough.
5. Turn on to a floured board and knead well until smooth and elastic.
6. The dough can now be shaped as required for baking.
7. After shaping put into greased tins or on greased baking sheets. Keep covered and away from draughts and allow to rise until doubled in size.
8. Bake the loaves at 425°F. Gas 7, reducing to 370°F. Gas 5 after 15 minutes. A 2 lb. loaf will take one hour. 1 lb. loaves: 40 minutes. A twist (depending on size): 25 minutes. Tap the loaves which will sound hollow when ready. Small bread rolls take 12 to 15 minutes at 425°F. Gas 7.

### SAVARIN AND RHUM BABA
Baking moulds for these dishes are available in 2 sizes. Quantities of ingredients are given for both.
**Small Mould**
*¼oz. fresh yeast or 1 level teaspoon dried yeast; ½ teaspoon sugar; ⅛ pint (3 tablespoons) tepid milk; 2 oz. butter; 4 oz. plain flour; ¼ teaspoon salt; 1 large beaten egg. For Rhum Baba – 1 oz. currants.*
**Large Mould**
*Bare ½ oz. fresh yeast or 2 level teaspoons dried yeast; 1 level teaspoon sugar; ⅛ pint tepid milk; 3 oz. butter; 6 oz. plain flour; ¼ teaspoon salt; 2 small eggs.*
1. Grease and flour mould.
2. Mix yeast and sugar in the milk. If using dried yeast leave

mixture in a warm place until it begins to froth up.

3. Rub butter into flour and salt.

4. Mix in yeast mixture and beaten eggs, adding 1 oz. currants if making Rhum Baba. Beat well until bubbles appear in batter.

5. Pour into tin. Cover and rise until tin is ¾ full.

6. Bake, centre oven, Gas 6. 400°F., 20–25 mins, until springy, golden brown, and will leave tin. If browning too quickly, reduce heat after 15 mins. to Gas 4, 350°F.

**To finish**

**Rhum Baba.** Place on wire over a deep plate, prick all over with skewer, and soak with warm syrup. Syrup: dissolve 2 oz. sugar in ¼ pint hot water. Simmer a few minutes until glossy. Add rum to taste.

Pleasant if served slightly warm.

**Savarin.** As above, soaking in warm syrup flavoured with sherry if liked. Allow to cool and decorate with fruit and whipped cream. If using tinned fruits the syrup from the tin may be used.

## SPONGE CAKE (OR SANDWICH)

*2 large eggs; 3 oz. vanilla sugar\*; (If no vanilla sugar, use castor sugar, but in this case do not add vanilla essence).; 3 oz. soft plain flour.*

1. Grease two 6½ inch sandwich tins and line the bases with rounds of greaseproof paper which should also be greased.

2. Whisk eggs and sugar until pale in colour and holding the impression of the whisk. The eggs should be at room temperature, not straight from the fridge. The whisking can be done in an electric mixer, first warming the bowl. If using a rotary whisk, place the bowl over, but not touching, some hot water in a saucepan.

3. Carefully fold in sifted flour.

Divide mixture between tins, level the tops.

4. Bake at Gas 5, 375°F. centre oven, about 22–23 minutes. It is cooked when shrinking from side of tins and feels firm.

This mixture will make a variety of cakes, baked in different tins, e.g. a Swiss Roll baked at Gas 7, 425°F. 7 to 8 minutes; or, again baking in a Swiss Roll tin, cut cake into even-sized pieces, sandwich with butter icing and decorate to make a gateau.

## SOMERSET APPLE CAKE

*3 oz. butter*
*6 oz. castor sugar*
*1 orange rind, grated*
*8 oz. self raising flour*
*1 lb. Bramley apples, peeled cored and cubed*
*2 eggs, beaten*
*2 tablespoons milk*
*1 oz. candied peel, chopped*
*About 1 tablespoon granulated sugar*

1. Grease and flour a 9 inch cake tin.

2. Cream butter, sugar and orange rind, and beat until light and creamy.

3. Mix 1 tablespoonful of the flour with apples in a dish.

4. Put eggs, milk in bowl with creamed butter.

5. Add remaining flour, peel and apples to the creamed mixture and blend well with a metal spoon.

6. Turn into prepared tin, sprinkle with granulated sugar.

7. Cook at 350°F, Gas 4, for 40 to 50 minutes until golden brown.

8. Serve cold as a cake or hot as a pudding with cream.

## DATE AND WALNUT LOAF

*8 oz. chopped dates; 4 oz. castor sugar (\*vanilla sugar preferable); a pinch of salt; 1 level teaspoon bicarbonate of soda; 2 oz. margarine; 6 liquid oz. water (or*

8 brimming tablespoons);
1 beaten egg; 2 oz. chopped
walnuts; 8 oz. self raising flour;
1 teaspoon vanilla essence (if
vanilla sugar not used.)

1. Place dates, sugar, salt, soda and margarine (cut into small pieces) in a mixing bowl.
2. Boil water, pour over, and mix well to melt margarine. Cool a little.
3. Add beaten egg, walnuts and flour, and vanilla essence if used, and mix to a smooth, batter-type consistency.
4. Grease and line base of 2 lb. loaf tin, pour mixture in.
5. Bake, centre oven, Gas 3, 325°F. for approximately 1¼ hours until firm. Cool in tin 10–15 minutes.

Eat cold sliced and buttered. Ideal for picnics or packed lunches as well as teatime. Keeps well.

### MARY BERRY'S HONEY AND ALMOND LOAF

6 oz. butter; 3 oz. castor sugar;
3 tablespoons clear honey;
3 eggs, beaten; 8 oz. self-raising flour, sifted; 5 oz. glacé cherries, quartered; 3 tablespoons milk.

**Topping:**
1 oz. blanched split almonds, toasted; 1 oz. glacé cherries, quartered; 2 level tablespoons clear honey.

1. Well grease and line 2 lb. loaf tin, about 8 inches by 4½ inches by 3 inches deep.
2. Cream together butter, sugar and honey until it is light and creamy.
3. Beat in the egg a little at a time, beating well after each addition. Add a tablespoon of the flour with the last amount of egg.
4. Blend cherries with flour and fold in with milk.
5. Turn mixture into the prepared loaf tin and bake at 350°F, Gas 4 for 55 to 60 minutes. Turn loaf out to cool on a wire rack.
6. Heat honey for topping in a pan

until warm. Add almonds and cherries, then spoon over loaf.

N.B. The topping is delicious but if you prefer leave it plain and serve sliced with butter instead.

### YORKSHIRE PARKIN

9 oz. plain flour
7 oz. plain white sugar
3½ oz. porridge oats
2 heaped teaspoons powdered ginger
3 oz. soft margarine
2 oz. lard
7 oz. golden syrup *
3 oz. black treacle *
1 slightly rounded teaspoon bicarbonate of soda
A few drops (about 1 dessertspoon) vinegar
¼ pint milk

1. Mix the flour, sugar, oats and ginger together in a bowl and make a well in centre.
2. Melt the fats in a pan. Before they get too hot, add the syrup and treacle and let it melt a little. Do not overheat, certainly do not boil.
3. Pour this mixture into dry ingredients in bowl. Drop bicarbonate of soda into centre, sprinkle the vinegar on the soda and watch it fizz.
4. Put the milk into the syrup pan, warm it a little to clean syrup from pan and then add to bowl.
5. Now stir it all up well. When mixed it should pour like a batter mixture. Pour it into large greased and floured roasting tin.
6. Bake between Gas 3 and Gas 4, 335°F., slightly above the middle of the oven for 1 hour. Look at it in 15–20 minutes to see if middle has lifted. If so, shake it to let it sink again, turn tin round and allow to continue cooking.
7. Allow to cool in tin. Cut into quarters. Store 3 days for

preference before eating. Keeps well.

* If you have no treacle use 10 ozs. golden syrup. Add gravy browning when you stir the mixture at Paragraph 5, to get the true dark Parkin colour.

## WHOLEWHEAT GINGERBREAD

4 oz. plain flour
¼ teaspoon salt
½ level teaspoon ground cinnamon
3 level teaspoons ground ginger
1 level teaspoon
bicarbonate of soda
4 oz. wholewheat flour
1½ oz. demerara sugar
1½ oz. sultanas
1½ oz. candied peel
4 oz. butter
4 oz. golden syrup
4 oz. dark treacle
1 large egg
¼ pint milk
½ oz. flaked almonds

1. Sieve into a bowl, the plain flour salt, cinnamon, ginger and bicarbonate of soda.
2. Add the wholewheat flour, demerara sugar, sultanas, candied peel.
3. Warm in pan - butter, golden syrup and dark treacle.
4. Beat the egg and to it add ¼ pint milk.
5. Mix liquids into dry ingredients.
6. Pour into tin, lined with greased, greaseproof paper and sprinkle on the flaked almonds.
7. Bake centre oven, 300°F, Gas 2, for about 1 hour until just firm and slightly springy to touch. This is best baked in a tin 7 inches square and about 2½ inches deep or a small dripping tin 9 inches by 5½ inches.
8. Store for a few days. Cut into squares to serve.

## SUGAR BISCUITS

4 oz. butter or firm margarine
4 oz. castor sugar
1 teaspoon lemon rind
1 egg (separated)
¼ teaspoon salt
6 oz. plain flour
1 oz. semolina
Extra castor sugar for dredging

1. Lightly cream together butter, sugar and lemon rind.
2. Work in egg yolk and salt until blended.
3. Add flour and semolina and combine to make a firm paste. If a little soft, wrap in greaseproof paper and leave in a cool place for a short while.
4. Roll out thinly on a floured board and cut into shapes. Place on a lightly greased baking tray.
5. Whisk egg white lightly to liquify. Brush tops of biscuits and dredge with castor sugar.
6. Bake near top of oven, at Gas 4, 350°F. for 12 to 15 minutes until pale golden. They may require checking half way through baking as sugar browns easily.
7. Leave on tray 1 - 2 minutes to crisp. Remove carefully on to a cooling wire. When quite cold, store in airtight tin.
**Variations:**
Use orange rind instead of lemon.
Use vanilla sugar* in place of plain castor sugar and omit lemon rind.

## PLAIN BISCUITS

7 oz. plain flour
¼ teaspoon salt
1 oz. semolina
4 oz. margarine
4 oz. castor sugar
1 beaten egg

1. Mix flour, salt and semolina.
2. Rub in margarine.
3. Add sugar
4. Bind with beaten egg to make a firm paste. If a little soft, wrap in greaseproof paper and leave in a

*See page 89.

cool place for a short while.

5. Roll out thinly on a floured board and cut into shapes. Place on a lightly greased baking tray.

6. Bake near top of oven at Gas 5, 375°F. for 12 minutes approximately until pale golden.

7. Leave on tray 1 - 2 minutes to crisp. Remove carefully on to a cooling wire. When quite cold, store in airtight tin.

These can be glacé iced and decorated

**Variations:**
Use vanilla sugar* in place of castor sugar.

Add 1 teaspoon lemon or orange rind with the castor sugar.

Add 1 oz. currants with the castor sugar, (an unfluted cutter is easier to use with this mixture). ½ level teaspoon mixed spice or powdered cinnamon can be sieved with the flour if desired.

**A tip**
Biscuits should never be stored in a tin containing cakes or pastry. They will lose their crispness.

## SHORTBREAD

*8 oz. butter; 4 oz. vanilla sugar*; (If no vanilla sugar, use castor sugar, but in this case do not add vanilla essence).; 12 oz. plain flour*

1. Work the butter until soft in mixing bowl.

2. Mix in sugar until creaming but do not beat in any more air than necessary.

3. Mix in flour using hands if necessary. The mixture should be firm — the consistency of short crust pastry. Knead lightly until smooth and free from cracks, leave to rest, if possible until a little firmer and easy to roll.

4. Using half quantity, roll out ½ to ¾ inch thick in a neat round, flute edges, mark with knife into 8 sections. Prick with skewer to

prevent bubbling during baking. Place on lightly greased baking tray.

5. Use second half to make shortbread fingers. Roll out ½ inch thick, cut into oblongs 1 inch by 2 inches. Prick.

6. Bake at Gas 4, 350°F. centre oven, until straw-coloured and firm, about 30 minutes.

Shortbread is broken into wedges, not cut.

## BRANDY SNAPS

*2½ oz. golden syrup (measure or weigh carefully)*
*2 oz. butter*
*2 oz. castor sugar*
*2 oz. plain flour*
*½ level teaspoon ground ginger*
**Filling**
*¼ pint double cream*
*1 teaspoon brandy*

1. Warm together in a pan syrup, butter and sugar, until all are melted, but not too hot. Sieve flour and ginger and mix in.

2. Well grease a large baking sheet and place mixture in teaspoonfuls well apart to allow for spreading, not more than 4 at a time.

3. Bake at 325°F., Gas 3, for about 8 to 10 minutes until golden.

4. Remove tray on to a damp cloth on table and have ready a large wooden spoon, with the handle greased. Leave for a few seconds for brandy snaps to become firm enough to lift from tray with palette knife. Roll each one quickly round spoon handle and slide off on to wire cooling rack.

5. Follow same procedure until all mixture is used. Will make about 24.

6. Whip the cream, fold in brandy and pipe a rosette of cream at each end of Brandy snap.

## CHEESE SCONES

*8 oz. self raising flour*
*½ teaspoon salt*
*½ teaspoon dry mustard*

¼ teaspoon (very level)
cayenne pepper
2 oz. margarine
3 oz. finely grated Cheddar cheese
4 to 5 tablespoons milk

1. Sieve flour, salt, mustard and pepper into a bowl. Rub in margarine, mix in cheese. Add sufficient milk to make a soft but not sticky dough.
2. Roll out ⅜ inch thick, cut into 2½ inch rounds. Place on greased baking tray.
3. Bake at 400°F, Gas 6, near top of oven for about 12 minutes. Makes 1 dozen scones.

## FRUIT SCONES

*8 oz. plain flour; ½ level teaspoon salt; ½ teaspoon bicarbonate of soda; 1 teaspoon cream of tartar; 1½ oz. margarine; 1 oz castor sugar; 1–1½ oz. sultanas, or currants; Bare ¼ pint milk.*

1. Sieve together flour, salt, soda and cream of tartar into a bowl.
2. Rub in margarine.
3. Add sugar, sultanas (or currants).
4. Mix to a soft but not sticky dough with as much milk as necessary. It could leave a tablespoon of milk. Knead lightly until smooth.
5. Roll out ½ inch thick, cut into 2½ inch rounds.
6. Bake on greased tray at Gas 7, 425°F. above centre of oven, about 12 minutes.

## WHOLEMEAL SCONES

*4 oz. wholemeal flour; 4 oz. plain flour; ½ level teaspoon salt; ½ teaspoon bicarbonate of soda; 1 teaspoon cream of tartar; 1½ oz. lard; 1 oz. castor sugar; Bare ¼ pint milk.*

1. Sieve together plain flour, salt, soda and cream of tartar into a bowl.
2. Add wholemeal flour and sugar.
3. Rub in lard.

4. Mix to a soft but not sticky dough with as much milk as necessary. It could leave a tablespoon of milk. Knead lightly until smooth.
5. Roll out ½ inch thick, cut into 2½ inch rounds.
6. Bake on greased tray at Gas 7, 425°F. above centre of oven, about 12 minutes.

## SCOTCH PANCAKES OR DROP SCONES

*6 oz. plain flour*
*pinch of salt*
*½ level teaspoon bicarbonate of soda*
*1 level teaspoon cream of tartar*
*1 tablespoon castor sugar*
*1 beaten egg*
*1 teaspoon golden syrup*
*¼ pint plus about 3 tablespoons milk*
*A piece of beef suet for greasing*

1. Sieve dry ingredients. Add egg, syrup and enough milk to make a batter which will pour from spoon, but must not be thin.
2. Heat a heavy frying pan or hot plate and grease it with the suet. Pour batter on 1 tablespoon at a time, not too close together. When bubbles appear on top of scone and just start to burst turn over with palette knife, and cook about 1 minute until golden. It is a good idea to test one scone before doing a batch. If the pan is too hot it will brown too quickly before bubbles burst. If too cool bubbles will burst but scone will not be brown.

## GIPSY BREAD

*10 oz. self-raising flour*
*Pinch of salt*
*Pinch of mixed spice*
*½ teaspoon ground ginger*
*4 oz. soft brown sugar*
*6 oz. sultanas*
*1 to 2 oz. chopped peel*
*6 oz. black treacle*
*1 tablespoon milk and a little extra*

*1 egg*
*¼ teaspoon bicarbonate of soda*
1. Grease a 2 lb. loaf tin well.
2. Mix together in a bowl flour, salt, mixed spice, ginger, sugar, sultanas and peel.
3. In a pan, warm treacle with 1 tablespoon milk. Do not boil. Remove from heat, add egg and whisk.
4. Dissolve bicarbonate of soda in a little milk and add with treacle mixture to ingredients in bowl.
5. Mix well and pour into loaf tin.
6. Bake at Gas 4, 350°F. for three quarters of an hour. Then reduce heat to Gas 3, 325°F. for a further half hour.
7. Cool in tin for 10 minutes. Turn out on to wire cooling rack.
Eat sliced and spread with butter.

**Kate Easlea,
Hampshire.**

## MRS. ROBIN'S FRUIT CAKE
*4 oz. margarine*
*6 oz. granulated sugar*
*6 oz. currants*
*6 oz. sultanas*
*2 oz. chopped peel*
*1 cup (8 liquid oz.) water*
*1 level teaspoon bicarbonate of soda*
*1 heaped teaspoon of mixed spice*
*2 beaten eggs*
*4 oz. plain flour*
*4 oz. self-raising flour*
*Pinch of salt*
1. Place margarine, sugar, currants, sultanas, peel, water, bicarbonate of soda and mixed spice in a pan, bring to boil and simmer 1 minute. Pour into large mixing bowl. Allow to cool.
2. Line a 7 inch square (or 8 inch round) tin with greased, grease-proof paper.
3. Add eggs, flours and salt to cooled mixture, mix well, pour into tin.
4. Bake, centre oven at Gas 4, 350°F. for 1¼ hours.

## VICTORIA SPONGE
*4 oz. margarine*

*4 oz. castor sugar*
*2 large eggs*
*4 oz. self-raising flour*
**To finish:**
*2 tablespoons raspberry jam*
*2 teaspoons castor sugar*
1. Grease two 6½ to 7-inch sandwich tins and line their bases with greased grease-proof paper.
2. Beat margarine and sugar until creamy.
3. Add eggs one at a time, beating and adding 2 teaspoons of the flour to prevent curdling.
4. Fold in rest of flour.
5. Bake at Gas 5, 375°F. about 20 to 25 minutes until firm on top and shrinking slightly from edges of tins.
6. Remove to wire to cool.
7. When cold, peel off paper and spread raspberry jam on base of one cake. Place the other cake on top so that both bases are together.
8. Sprinkle castor sugar lightly on top.

## GRANTHAM GINGERBREADS
Makes 24 biscuits.
*4 oz. butter or firm margarine*
*4 oz. castor sugar*
*2 level teaspoons ground ginger*
*4 oz. self-raising flour*
1. Cream the fat and sugar lightly together until softening.
2. Add the ginger and then the flour and make into a stiff dough.
3. Roll into balls about half the size of a golf ball.
4. Put these on ungreased baking trays well apart and bake at Gas 1½, 250°F. for about three quarters of an hour in the lower part of the oven.

**Mrs. J. Wilcox,
Harlaxton, Lincolnshire.**

## WARWICKSHIRE CHOCOLATE BISCUITS
Quick to make.
*3 oz. margarine*
*2 oz. soft brown sugar*
*2 teaspoons cocoa*
*Pinch of salt*
*Vanilla essence*

4 oz. self-raising flour
1 oz. cornflakes, crushed
**To decorate:**
*Melted chocolate*
*Almonds, optional*
1. Cream together margarine and sugar.
2. Stir in cocoa, salt and vanilla essence. Mix well.
3. Beat in gradually and alternately the self-raising flour and crushed cornflakes.
4. Knead well. Shape into balls about the size of a walnut.
5. Place on a lightly greased baking sheet and flatten a little. Allow space for them to spread.
6. Bake in moderate oven, Gas 3, 325°F., for 15 minutes until just firm.
7. When cool ice with melted chocolate. Decorate with almonds if liked.

## SCOTTISH OATCAKES
*1 tablespoon bacon fat*
*4 oz. fine to medium oatmeal*
*A generous pinch of salt*
*A generous pinch of bicarbonate of soda*
*Tepid water to mix*
1. Melt fat and add to dry ingredients.
2. Bind to a softish dough with water.
3. Sprinkle a little oatmeal on to a board. Turn dough on to it and knead to remove cracks. Roll out thinly into a round.
4. Cut into three "farls" or even-sized 3-sided pieces. True Scottish oatcakes are always shaped this way.
5. Bake on a hot, ungreased girdle till edges start to curl.
6. Toast second side under the grill till crisp but not brown.
> **Mrs. Anne Wallace,**
> **Dunlop, Scotland.**

## SCOTTISH CRUMPETS
Makes 10 to 12.
*1 large egg*
*1 tablespoon castor sugar*
*¼ pint milk and 1 extra*
tablespoonful
*4 oz. plain flour*
*1 good level teaspoon cream of tartar*
*1 scant level teaspoon bicarbonate of soda*
*Pinch of salt*
1. Beat egg and sugar to a thick cream.
2. Mix in the quarter-pint of milk then the sieved flour.
3. Dissolve cream of tartar, bicarbonate of soda and salt in 1 tablespoon milk and stir gently into mixture.
4. Pour on to a heated, ungreased girdle in large tablespoonfuls, cook till brown, flick over (I use a paint scraper for this) and brown second side.
5. Cool in a cloth and serve with butter and jam.
> **Mrs. Anne Wallace,**
> **Dunlop, Scotland.**

## TREACLE GIRDLE SCONES
*8 oz. plain flour*
*A pinch of salt*
*1 teaspoon cream of tartar*
*1 level teaspoon bicarbonate of soda*
*¼ teaspoon ground cinnamon*
*¼ teaspoon ginger*
*¼ teaspoon mixed spice*
*1 large tablespoon black treacle*
*Approximately ¼ pint milk*
1. Sieve dry ingredients together and make a well in the centre.
2. Pour in slightly-warmed black treacle.
3. Pour milk on top of treacle and gradually draw in flour to make a fairly soft dough.
4. Turn on to a floured board and knead very lightly till smooth and free from cracks.
5. Roll out to a round barely half an inch thick.
6. Place on a hot, ungreased girdle. When browned turn over and continue baking till cooked – 4 to 5 minutes each side.
7. Cool in a cloth on a wire tray.
> **Mrs. Anne Wallace,**
> **Dunlop, Scotland.**

## DOUGHNUTS

½ oz. fresh yeast*
½ teaspoon sugar
3 to 4 fluid oz. milk, warmed
8 oz. strong plain flour
½ teaspoon salt
1 oz. margarine
1 small beaten egg
3 to 4 oz. castor sugar
Powdered cinnamon

*If using dried yeast, use ¼ oz. and follow manufacturer's instructions.

1. Cream yeast and sugar in a basin, stir in most of the milk and mix well to dissolve yeast.
2. In a large bowl, mix flour and salt, rub in margarine.
3. Make a well in centre, add yeast mixture and beaten egg. Mix to a pliable dough, adding remaining milk if necessary. The mixture should be softish but firm enough to knead.
4. Turn out on to a floured board, knead until smooth and elastic, using a little flour if necessary.
5. Grease the bowl, place mixture in and cover. A good idea is to place bowl in a large polythene bag.
6. Prove (which means leave to rise) until doubled in size, preferably in a warm place away from draughts or direct heat.
7. Turn on to floured board and knead smooth.
8. Roll out half an inch thick, cut into 3-inch rounds with a plain cutter. Cut out centres with 1½-inch cutter and put these with the trimmings to roll out again.
9. Place doughnuts on a greased and floured baking tray spacing them carefully. Cover with muslin and leave to rise until just about doubled in size and quite puffy.
10. Heat a pan of oil or good clarified dripping or lard which should be 2½ to 3 inches deep. It is hot enough when a 1-inch cube of bread will sizzle at once and gradually turn golden.
11. Using a spatula or broad knife carefully lift doughnuts into fat, a few at a time, leaving room to turn them over. Fry for 3 minutes, turning 2 or 3 times.
12. Lift on to kitchen paper and then toss in castor sugar sifted with a little cinnamon.

## BATTENBERG CAKE
### Cake
4 oz. margarine
4 oz. castor sugar
2 beaten eggs
4 oz. self-raising flour
A few drops of pink colouring
1 tablespoon raspberry jam
2 tablespoons apricot jam (or use all raspberry jam throughout)
### Almond Paste
3 oz. ground almonds
1 oz. semolina
3 oz. castor sugar
3 oz. sifted icing sugar
A few drops of almond essence
Beaten egg to bind
### To finish
A little castor sugar

1. Grease two 1 lb. loaf tins and line the base of each with a piece of greased greaseproof paper.
2. Cream margarine and sugar, beat in eggs, fold in flour.
3. Divide mixture exactly into 2 portions and colour one pink.
4. Place a portion of mixture in each tin.
5. Bake centre oven, Gas 4, 350°F. for about 25 minutes until firm and beginning to leave the sides of the tins.
6. Remove from tins and cool.
7. Remove paper, trim sides and level tops.
8. Cut each cake exactly in half lengthways. All the pieces must be the same size.
9. Using raspberry jam sandwich the four portions together, arranging pink and white squares alternately.
10. **For the paste.** Combine ingredients using enough egg to make a firm paste.
11. Use a piece of waxed paper,

sprinkle well with castor sugar and roll out paste to fit round the sides of cake.

12. Spread the paste with sieved apricot or raspberry jam, place cake on at one end. Carefully wrap paste round cake, pressing so that it adheres. Press edges together to seal.

13. Trim ends of cake, flute along the two top edges, make a diamond pattern on top with back of knife. Dredge lightly with castor sugar.

## BRIGHTON SANDWICH

*8 oz. self-raising flour*
*1 oz. semolina, optional*
*4 oz. castor sugar*
*4 oz. butter*
*1 egg, well-beaten*
*2 tablespoons apricot jam*
*1 oz. almonds, blanched and split*

1. Grease an 8-inch cake tin and line with greased greaseproof paper, or use an 8-inch flan ring placed on a baking sheet.
2. Put flour, semolina and sugar in a bowl. Rub in butter.
3. Add beaten egg and bind together. Divide mixture in half.
4. Roll out one half of mixture and fit it into tin or flan ring. Spread jam in centre.
5. Roll out second half of mixture and place on top. Cover with split almonds.
6. Bake centre oven Gas 4, 350°F. for 15 minutes, then reduce heat to Gas 3, 325°F. for a further 20 minutes.

**Miss V. M. Secker,**
**Bury St. Edmunds.**

## CHERRY CAKE

*6 oz. glacé cherries*
*6 oz. margarine or butter*
*6 oz. castor sugar*
*3 eggs*
*2 oz. ground almonds*
*4 oz. self-raising flour*
*3 oz. plain flour*

1. Wash and dry cherries, cut in halves or quarters.

2. Cream margarine and sugar.
3. Add eggs, one at a time, beating after each addition.
4. Stir in ground almonds.
5. Mix cherries into flour and stir into creamed mixture. Do not beat.
6. Grease a 7-inch square or 8-inch round tin and line base with greased greaseproof paper. Spoon in mixture.
7. Bake at Gas 3 to 4, 360°F. for $1\frac{1}{4}$ hours or until firm and beginning to leave sides of tin.

## BUN LOAF

*8 oz. mixed dried fruit*
*6 fluid oz. cold strained tea*
*8 oz. self-raising flour*
*Pinch of salt*
*4 oz. soft brown sugar*
*1 beaten egg*

1. Soak fruit in tea overnight.
2. Place flour, salt and sugar in bowl, mix.
3. Drain the fruit, reserving liquid.
4. Mix fruit and beaten egg into flour using a little liquid to make a firm dropping consistency. Depending on size of egg, about 1 to 2 tablespoons of liquid will be required.
5. Grease a 1 lb. loaf tin and line base with greased, greaseproof paper. Tin ought to be at least $1\frac{1}{2}$ pints capacity.
6. Bake at Gas 4, 350°F. for about 1 hour, until firm.
7. Leave in tin about 5 minutes. Then turn on to wire rack to cool.

**Mrs. V. Nation,**
**Lambeth, London.**

## NUTTY TREACLE BREAD

*2 oz. soft margarine*
*3 oz. sugar*
*6 oz. (6 level tablespoons) dark treacle*
*8 fluid oz. milk*
*3 oz. plain flour*
*3 teaspoons baking powder*
*1 small teaspoon salt*
*8 oz. wholemeal flour*
*3 oz. chopped walnuts*

1. Grease a 2 lb. loaf tin and line base with greased greaseproof paper.
2. Beat together margarine, sugar and treacle, beat in milk.
3. Sift together plain flour, baking powder and salt. Add with whole-meal flour and walnuts to milk mixture. Mix to a dough.
4. Spoon into tin, level top.
5. Bake at Gas 3, 325°F. for about 1¼ hours until firm to the touch and shrinking slightly from sides of tin.

### GRANDMA'S 1234 BUNS
*1 egg*
*2 oz. margarine*
*3 oz. castor sugar*
*4 oz. self-raising flour*
*A little milk*
1. Beat the egg.
2. Cream margarine and sugar until fluffy.
3. Add half the egg, half the flour, mix well and add remaining egg, flour and 1 tablespoon of milk.
4. Place in greased bun tins. This quantity will make 12 of the shallow type or 9 deeper buns.
5. Bake at Gas 6, 400°F. 15 to 16 minutes until firm.
Try serving these hot as a pudding with a fruit sauce, see page 123.
**Miss K. A. Butterworth, Leeds.**

### POTATO SCONES
*4 oz. mashed potato*
*Pinch of salt*
*1 teaspoon cream or ¼ oz. butter*
*1 oz. plain flour*
1. Mix potato, salt and cream or butter adding sufficient flour to make a dough dry enough to roll out.
2. Roll out on a floured board as thinly as possible, to a round about 10 inches across. Trim round a dinner plate if a perfect circle is desired.
3. Prick all over with a fork and divide into four pieces.

4. Bake on a hot girdle 2 minutes each side.
5. Cool in a clean tea towel.
Serve with butter and jam or fry quickly in bacon fat to eat with bacon.
**Mrs. Anne Wallace, Dunlop, Scotland.**

### CHEESE CRACKERS
*8 oz. self-raising flour*
*½ teaspoon salt*
*3 oz. margarine*
*Approx. 5 tablespoons water*
*3 oz. finely-grated cheese*
1. Place flour and salt in a bowl and rub in margarine.
2. Mix to a pliable dough with water. Leave to rest for 5 minutes.
3. Roll out on a floured board to an oblong three times as long as wide.
4. Sprinkle 1 oz. of the cheese on bottom two-thirds of pastry, fold top third down, then fold down again. Turn once to the left.
5. Roll out, sprinkle on an ounce of cheese as before, fold and turn twice more. Pastry may need to rest before final rolling.
6. Divide dough into 2 pieces. Using a floured board, roll out thinly, less than ¼ inch thick is best. Prick well all over with a fork.
7. Cut into squares about 2½ inches across.
8. Place on very lightly-greased baking tray. Bake at Gas 5, 375°F. for about 15 minutes.

### CHOCOLATE BROWNIES
*3 oz. margarine*
*2 oz. plain cooking chocolate*
*2 beaten eggs*
*6 oz. castor sugar*
*1 teaspoon vanilla essence*
*2 oz. walnuts, chopped*
*3 oz. plain flour*
*½ level teaspoon baking powder*
1. Grease a 7-inch square, shallow tin, line base with greased grease-proof paper.

2. Stand a large basin over hot water, put in the margarine and chocolate and allow it to melt. Cool.
3. Stir in eggs, sugar, vanilla essence and walnuts. Mix well. Sift flour and baking powder, and fold into mixture.
4. Pour into tin. Bake at Gas 4, 350°F. for about 40 minutes until firm. Leave in tin to cool. While still just warm sprinkle with castor sugar.
5. Cut into 12 pieces when cold.

## COCONUT MACAROONS
*2 sheets rice paper, optional*
*2 egg-whites*
*2 level teaspoons cornflour*
*4 oz. castor sugar*
*5 oz. dessicated coconut*
*9 almonds, blanched and split into halves*
1. Place rice paper on baking trays, smooth side downwards. Or, lightly grease the trays.
2. Beat egg whites until frothy but not firm.
3. Mix cornflour and sugar, fold into egg-whites, then mix in coconut.
4. Place in teaspoons a little apart on rice paper, smooth tops with a pastry brush dipped in cold water. Makes 18.
5. Place a halved almond on each.
6. Bake at Gas 4, 350°F. for about 20 minutes until firm and golden.
7. Tear away surplus rice paper. Allow to cool. Store in airtight tin.

## GARIBALDI BISCUITS
*4 oz. self-raising flour*
*A pinch of salt*
*1 oz. quick-creaming fat, ordinary lard is not as good*
*2 tablespoons milk*
*2 oz. currants*
*1 oz. castor sugar*
1. Combine flour, salt, fat and milk in a bowl, using a fork. Mix to a smooth dough.
2. Cut into 2 even-sized pieces, roll out one piece on a floured board, about a quarter of an inch thick, no more.
3. Lift this on to a lightly-greased baking sheet. Use a baking sheet without sides.
4. Chop currants and mix in with 1 teaspoon of the sugar and sprinkle them over the pastry leaving a half inch edge. Damp edges with water. Scatter remaining sugar over filling.
5. Roll out second piece of pastry to same size, place on top, seal edges.
6. Roll the rolling pin lightly over top until currants are just showing but not quite breaking through the pastry.
7. Mark into 9 squares, then across diagonally to make 18 triangles, brush with water and sprinkle on a little extra sugar.
8. Bake at Gas 5, 375°F. for about 15 minutes until firm and crisp.

## APPLE FRUIT CAKE
*1 lb. cooking apples*
*Water*
*½ lb. plain flour*
*1 level teaspoon bicarbonate of soda*
*1 level teaspoon powdered cinnamon*
*½ level teaspoon mixed spice*
*½ level teaspoon ground ginger*
*6 oz. sultanas*
*2 oz. peel*
*2 oz. seedless raisins*
*2 oz. chopped walnuts*
*2 oz. chopped glacé ginger*
*5 oz. butter*
*6 oz. soft brown sugar*
*Rind of 1 lemon, finely grated*
*2 eggs*
*Castor sugar*
1. Cook apples until quite soft, using a minimum of water, 1 to 2 tablespoons.
2. Sieve or liquidize.
3. Measure 8 liquid oz. (1 breakfast cup). Cool.
4. Grease and line base of 8 inch round or 7 inch square cake tin.

5. Sieve together flour, bicarbonate of soda, cinnamon, mixed spice and ginger.
6. Add sultanas, peel, seedless raisins, walnuts and glacé ginger. Mix.
7. Cream together in another bowl butter, soft brown sugar and finely grated lemon rind. Beat in eggs.
8. Fold in dry ingredients alternately with apple sauce.
9. Place in tin. Dredge top with castor sugar. Bake in centre oven Gas 3, 325°F., 1¼ hours.

## FRUIT LOAF

*8 oz. self-raising flour*
*Pinch salt*
*4 oz. firm margarine*
*Grated rind of 1 lemon*
*4 oz. castor sugar*
*2 oz. currants*
*2 oz. sultanas*
*2 oz. quartered cherries*
*1 large egg*
*4 to 5 tablespoons milk*

1. Grease a 2 lb. loaf tin or 6 inch cake tin, and line base with greased greaseproof paper.
2. Put flour and salt in a bowl and rub in margarine.
3. Add lemon rind and sugar, mix together.
4. Add fruit. Mix to a firm dropping consistency with beaten egg and 4 tablespoons milk, adding extra milk if mixture will not fall from spoon with a flick of the wrist.
5. Place in tin, smooth top with the back of a spoon.
6. Bake, centre oven, Gas 4, 350°F. 1 to 1½ hours until firm and leaving sides of tin.
7. Cool on wire.
Try also using 4 oz. vanilla sugar* instead of the castor sugar in which case omit the lemon rind.

## LAGER LOAF

*3 oz. butter*
*1 tablespoon golden syrup or treacle*
*3 oz. soft brown sugar*
*2 eggs*
*10 oz. self-raising flour*
*¼ teaspoon bicarbonate of soda*
*½ teaspoon cream of tartar*
*Pinch salt*
*¼ pint (5 fluid oz.) lager*
*2 bananas, peeled and mashed*
*4 oz. dates, chopped*
*2 oz. walnuts, chopped*

1. Well grease a 2 lb. loaf tin or two 1 lb. loaf tins.
2. Gently heat the butter, syrup and sugar in a saucepan until melted. Remove from heat and whisk the eggs into the mixture.
3. Sift flour, bicarbonate of soda, cream of tartar and salt into a bowl.
4. With a wooden spoon briskly mix in the syrup mixture and add the lager. Mix to a smooth batter then quickly add the mashed bananas, chopped dates and walnuts. Pour into the prepared loaf tin.
5. Bake in the centre of a moderate oven, Gas 4, 350°F. for 1½ hours. Turn out on to a cake-rack and cool.
Serve sliced and buttered.
This loaf smells delicious whilst cooking and is even more delicious sliced and buttered for tea. It will keep well as it does not go dry quickly.

## DECORATED CHOCOLATE CAKE

*2 oz. plain cooking chocolate*
*2½ oz. soft margarine*
*2½ oz. vanilla sugar\**
*1 level tablespoon golden syrup*
*½ level teaspoon bicarbonate of soda*
*⅛ pint milk, warmed just to blood heat*
*5 oz. self-raising flour*
*1 large beaten egg*

1. Grease two 6 inch or 6½ inch sandwich cake tins, and line base with a circle of greased greaseproof paper.
2. Place chocolate to melt in a basin over hot water.
3. Thoroughly beat margarine and

sugar until creamy.

4. Beat in syrup and melted chocolate.

5. Dissolve bicarbonate of soda in milk.

6. Fold flour, egg and milk alternately into creamed mixture, mix but do not beat.

7. Divide mixture evenly between the two tins.

8. Bake second shelf down in oven, Gas 4, 350°F. for 20 to 25 minutes. Remove to wire tray to cool.

9. When cold, remove papers. Sandwich with butter icing, and decorate top if desired.

### Butter Icing
*4 oz. soft margarine*
*A few drops vanilla essence*
*8 oz. sifted icing sugar*
Beat together until creamy.
This will make filling and also enough to decorate top. Could sprinkle on grated chocolate. Or, make half this quantity of butter icing, for filling only, and decorate as follows:—
### Glacé Icing
*6 oz. icing sugar*
*5 teaspoons warm water*
*1 level teaspoon cocoa*
1. Mix the icing sugar and water. The mixture should coat the back of a spoon, a ½ teaspoon more water may be needed.

2. Remove 2 heaped teaspoons of the mixed icing to a separate basin. Add to it sieved cocoa and 2 to 3 drops warm water. This is the piping mixture and should be a bit firmer than the white icing.

3. Spread the white icing on the cake, using a wet palette knive to obtain a smooth finish.

4. Take a 10 inch square of greaseproof paper, fold to make a triangle, make into a cone, leaving a tiny hole at the point.

5. Spoon the chocolate icing into cone. Pipe parallel lines approximately 1 inch apart across cake.

6. **For feather icing:** draw the point of a knife or a skewer in alternate directions across the piped lines.

7. To make a spider's web: pipe a spiral from the centre out to the edge leaving approximately 1 inch between lines.

8. Starting in centre, draw a knife across the lines, to the edge of the cake in alternate directions, making 8 sections.

### VICTORIA SANDWICH MIXTURE FOR SMALL ICED CAKES
*4 oz. margarine*
*4 oz. vanilla sugar**
*4 oz. self-raising flour*
*Pinch salt*
*1 teaspoon cornflour*
*2 large beaten eggs*
**To ice and decorate:**
*Butter icing (this page)*
*Coconut .*
*Chocolate vermicelli*
*Nuts, cherries, etc.*
1. Beat margarine until soft.

2. Beat in sugar until fluffy.

3. Sieve flour, salt and cornflour into another bowl.

4. Add egg and flour alternately to creamed mixture.

5. Grease a tin 7 inches square and approximately 1½ inches deep, line base. Put in the mixture.

6. Bake centre oven Gas 4, 350°F., approximately 40 minutes until firm and springy and shrinking from tin.

7. Next day cut into small rounds or squares, spread butter icing around sides, roll in coconut or chocolate vermicelli and pipe butter icing on top. Decorate with nuts, cherries etc.

These cakes will freeze. Pack into shallow foil containers—1 layer only. Place in freezer overnight. Place in polythene bags next day. Remove from bag before thawing.

### ROCK BUNS
*8 oz. self-raising flour*
*½ level teaspoon salt*

4 oz. firm margarine
3 oz. vanilla sugar*
1½ oz. currants
½ oz. candied peel
1 beaten egg
2 tablespoons milk
1. Put flour and salt in a bowl. Rub in margarine. Add sugar and fruit.
2. Mix to a stiff consistency with beaten egg and milk.
3. Grease 2 baking trays. Place mixture on trays using 2 forks dipped in milk. Leave rough. Dredge with castor sugar.
4. Bake at Gas 7, 425°F. about 12 to 15 minutes until firm and slightly golden.
5. Cool on wire rack.
Makes 18 to 20 buns.
These will freeze very well.

### CHOCOLATE BUTTONS
4 oz. margarine
2 oz. vanilla sugar*
Pinch of salt
4 oz. self-raising flour
1 oz. drinking chocolate powder
Approx. 2 oz. plain chocolate
1. Cream margarine and sugar until fluffy.
2. Add salt, work in flour sieved with chocolate powder.
3. With damp hands roll into balls about the size of a walnut.
4. Place on greased baking tray, leaving room for spreading. Mark tops with a fork dipped in cold water, and flatten slightly.
5. Bake at Gas 4, 350°F 8 to 10 minutes. They will rise a little at first, then flatten, and are soon baked when this happens. Do not overbake, it spoils the flavour.
6. Leave on tray for 1 minute to crisp, remove carefully with spatula on to a wire tray. Leave until cold. Sandwich in pairs with melted chocolate.

### BISCUITS
#### Using the Viennese Mixture
6 oz. soft margarine (or butter)
2 oz. vanilla sugar*
6 oz. soft plain flour

**To decorate:**
Plain chocolate
Cherries
Jam or lemon curd
Icing sugar
1. Cream butter and sugar very soft, work in flour.
2. Use a large forcing bag and fluted nozzle:—
**Fingers**
1. Pipe 2½ inches long on to greased baking tray.
2. Bake at Gas 4, 350°F about 10 minutes until firm, but only very slightly coloured.
3. Allow to cool.
4. Dip ends in melted chocolate.
**Stars**
1. Pipe star shapes, place a small piece of cherry in centre.
2. Bake as above.
**Tea Cakes**
1. Pipe mixture into paper baking cases in a spiral, leaving a small dent in centre.
2. Bake as above, for approx. 20 minutes. Cool, leaving in paper cases.
3. Before serving, place a little jam or lemon curd in centre, sift on a little icing sugar.

### GINGER NUTS
4 oz. self-raising flour
2 level teaspoons ground ginger
Pinch salt
1 level dessertspoon castor sugar
½ level teaspoon bicarbonate of soda
2 oz. margarine
2 oz. golden syrup
A little milk
1. Sieve dry ingredients into a bowl.
2. Melt margarine and syrup over very low heat, do not allow to boil. Cool a little, mix into dry ingredients.
3. Grease a baking sheet. Roll mixture into small balls, place well apart on sheet to allow for spreading.
4. Flatten slightly with pastry brush dipped in milk.
5. Bake second shelf of oven at

Gas 4, 350° F. 12 to 14 minutes until firm but not hard.

6. Leave on tray to crisp—1 to 2 minutes. Remove with spatula to cooling wire.

Makes 24-26 biscuits.

## BUN LOAF AND HOT CROSS BUNS

*1 oz. fresh or ½ oz. dried yeast*
*2 oz. castor sugar*
*¼ pt. tepid water*
*1 lb. strong plain flour*
*1 level teaspoon salt*
*½ teaspoon ground cinnamon*
*1 teaspoon mixed spice*
*A grate of nutmeg*
*2 oz. margarine*
*3 oz. mixed currants, sultanas and peel*
*Warm milk and 1 beaten egg to make ¼ pt. bare measure.*

**Glaze:**
*2 tablespoons milk boiled with 1 tablespoon sugar.*

1. Cream the fresh yeast with 1 teaspoon of the sugar and dissolve in water. If using dried yeast follow instructions on packet.
2. Sift into a large bowl flour, salt and spices.
3. Rub in margarine.
4. Mix in the rest of the sugar and the prepared fruit.
5. Mix to a pliable dough with liquids.
6. Knead till smooth and elastic in texture.
7. Place to rise in greased bowl, away from draughts. Cover with polythene or clean tea-towel. It should double in size and take about 1 hour.
8. Turn on to a floured board and knead smooth again.
9. **For Bun Loaf:**
Weigh off 1 lb. dough, shape into a loaf and put into a greased 1 lb. loaf tin, or round tin of similar capacity. Place to rise, covered, and away from draughts.
10. **For Hot Cross Buns:**

Divide remaining dough (approx. 1 lb) into 8 even pieces. Shape into buns, round or oval. Roll lightly, make a cross on top with knife.
11. Place on greased baking tray, cover, and rise until puffy.

**For rising:**
A slightly warm atmosphere (like above the stove, or even the airing cupboard) is an advantage as this type of dough rises more slowly than plain bread.
12. Bake buns for approx. 15 minutes at Gas 6, 400°F. until nicely browned. Remove from oven and turn out on to cooling rack. Brush with glaze while hot.
13. Bake loaf at Gas 6, 400°F. for 15 minutes, reduce heat to Gas 4, 350°F. for a further 25 to 30 minutes until firm. Turn out on to wire rack to cool. Glaze as for buns as desired.

These freeze very well after they are baked, but do not glaze before freezing.

## CHELSEA BUNS AND SALLY LUNN

*1 oz. fresh yeast or ½ oz. dried yeast.*
*¼ pt. mixed tepid milk and water*
*1 teaspoon salt*
*1 lb. strong plain flour*
*3 oz. margarine*
*3 oz. castor sugar*
*2 eggs*
*2 oz. currants*
**Glaze:**
*2 tablespoons milk boiled with 1 tablespoon sugar.*

1. Mix the yeast with 1 teaspoon of the sugar and dissolve in the milk and water. If using dried yeast follow instructions on packet.
2. Mix salt into flour.
3. Rub in 2 oz. of the margarine.
4. Add 2 oz. of the castor sugar.
5. Whisk eggs.
6. Mix eggs and liquids into flour and knead until smooth. If eggs are small an extra 1 or 2

tablespoons of warm water may be required, as the mixture must not be too stiff.

7. Place to rise in greased bowl, away from draughts. Cover with polythene or clean tea-towel. It should double in size and take about 1 hour.

8. Knead down on a floured board. Divide dough into 2 portions.

9. **For the Sally Lunn:**
Shape 1 portion in a round and put in a deep 5 to 6 inch cake-tin. Cover and place to rise until doubled in size.

10. **For the Chelsea Buns:**
(a) Roll out second piece of dough, approximately 10 by 8 inches.
(b) Spread with the remaining 1 oz. margarine, softened but not melted.
(c) Sprinkle on the remaining castor sugar and the currants.
(d) Roll up lengthways, to make a roll 10 inches long.
(e) Cut into 9 even slices, place—cut sides down—in a 7 inch square, greased, shallow tin.
(f) Cover, rise until puffy.

11. When Sally Lunn has doubled in size bake in centre oven at Gas 6, 375°F. about 45 minutes. Turn out of tin while hot on to cooling wire.

12. Bake Chelsea Buns on top shelf, Gas 6, 375°F. about 30 minutes. As this is a rich mixture the buns may need to be covered with foil towards end of cooking time or they may brown too much. Cool on wire rack.

13. Brush with glaze while still hot.

These freeze very well, unglazed.

## APPLE CAKE
*6 oz. self-raising flour*
*3 oz. margarine, lard or good dripping*
*6 oz. apples, weight when peeled and cored*
*3 oz. sugar*
*Milk*

1. Rub fat into flour.
2. Add the diced apple.
3. Cover well with the sugar and mix together with a little milk into a very firm dough.
4. Roll out if it will or, if a bit sticky, press out to a round about 7 or 8 inches across. Mark into sections.
5. Put on a greased baking sheet and bake at Gas 5, 375°F. for 20 minutes. Then reduce heat to Gas 3, 325°F. for a further 20 to 25 minutes until the apples are cooked.
Split open, butter well and eat hot. Good as a pudding eaten hot with custard or thin cream.

**Mrs. Joan Ireland,
West Suffolk.**

## ASHBOURNE GINGERBREAD
*8 oz. butter*
*5 oz. castor sugar*
*10 oz. plain flour*
*2 level teaspoons ground ginger*
*Pinch of salt*
*Rind of 1 lemon, finely grated or*
*1 oz. candied peel, finely chopped*

1. Cream together butter and sugar until quite soft.
2. Sift in flour, ginger and salt. Add lemon rind or peel.
3. Knead with the hands until a smooth dough is obtained.
4. Roll out with the hands into a long roll about 1 inch thick. Cut into lengths 2 inches long.
5. Put on lightly greased baking tray and flatten each roll a little with three fingers.
6. Bake for about 20 minutes in moderate oven, Gas 4, 350°F.

**Derbyshire.**

## CHOCOLATE LOG CAKE
*2 oz. soft plain flour*
*½ oz. cocoa*
*2 eggs*
*2½ oz. vanilla sugar\**
*1 dessertspoon warm water*

*\*See page 89.*

## Chocolate Butter Cream

*4 oz. plain chocolate*
*4 oz. butter or margarine*
*6 oz. icing sugar*

1. Grease a shallow (Swiss roll) tin approx. 11 by 7 inches and line with greased greaseproof paper.
2. Sieve together flour and cocoa on to a piece of paper and put to warm in warming drawer of oven so that chill is taken off it.
3. Place eggs and sugar in bowl. Place the bowl over a pan of hot water and whisk thick and pale.
4. Remove bowl from pan and whisk until beaters leave a trail in the mixture.
5. Carefully fold in warmed flour and cocoa and the warm water.
6. Spread evenly in tin.
7. Bake above centre of oven at Gas 7, 425°F. for 7 to 8 minutes until lightly golden and springy to the touch.
8. While cake is baking, place a damp (not wet) tea-towel on table, then a piece of greaseproof paper —2 inches all round larger than Swiss roll, dust this with a little flour and dredge with castor sugar.
9. As soon as cake is out of oven turn out upside-down on to paper, trim edges, place a clean piece of greaseproof paper on roll and roll up lightly with paper inside. Leave to cool.
10. Meanwhile, melt chocolate gently in basin over hot water.
11. Beat together butter (or margarine) and sifted icing sugar.
12. Beat in chocolate.
13. Unroll cake. Spread with a layer of butter cream and roll up. Place on cake board or serving dish.
14. Spread the remaining butter cream on cake and then mark it with a fork to resemble bark of tree, or pipe with fine nozzle.

**To freeze:** Place on cake-board and freeze uncovered overnight. When hard, slide into polythene bag, seal and freeze until required. Take out of bag while still hard— the icing may be damaged if allowed to thaw in bag.

## CHRISTMAS CAKE

*8 oz. butter*
*8 oz. soft brown sugar*
*1 tablespoon dark treacle*
*Grated rind and juice of 1 lemon*
*9 oz. plain flour*
*1 level teaspoon baking powder*
*1 level teaspoon mixed spice*
*A little grated nutmeg*
*Pinch salt*
*8 oz. currants*
*8 oz. sultanas*
*8 oz. raisins*
*4 oz. cherries*
*4 oz. candied peel*
*2 oz. chopped whole almonds*
*2 oz. ground almonds*
*5 eggs*

1. Line an 8 inch square or 9 inch diameter round cake tin with a layer of foil and a layer of greaseproof paper lightly greased both sides. Allow both foil and greaseproof paper to extend above sides of tin about 1½ inches. Tie a double thickness of brown paper round outside of tin.
2. Cream together butter, sugar, treacle and lemon rind.
3. Sift flour, baking powder, spice, nutmeg and salt. Add fruit and both chopped and ground almonds.
4. Beat eggs until frothy.
5. Add half of the beaten egg and 4 tablespoons flour and fruit mixture to butter and sugar, beat in.
6. Add remaining egg and rest of dry ingredients, gradually mixing in strained lemon juice. Do not beat, but mix thoroughly.
7. Spoon into tin.
8. Have oven heated to Gas 3, 325°F. Place cake in centre. Turn heat control down immediately to Gas 2, 300°F. and bake 1½ hours. Over next half hour reduce heat by degrees to Gas 1, 275°F. If, at this stage, cake is browning too quickly, cover loosely with foil. Total time,

$3\frac{1}{2}$ to 4 hours until firm. Leave in tin to cool.

9. Next day wrap in foil and store. This cake will keep several months.

## ALMOND PASTE

To cover top of $7\frac{1}{2}$ to 8-inch Christmas Cake:—
**For the paste:**
*8 oz. ground almonds*
*6 oz. castor sugar*
*6 oz. sifted icing sugar*
*1 teaspoon lemon juice*
*Few drops almond essence*
*1 or 2 beaten eggs*
*1 to 2 teaspoons sherry, optional*
**Also:**
*1 tablespoon sieved apricot jam*

1. Mix almonds, castor sugar, icing sugar, lemon juice, almond essence and 1 beaten egg. If very stiff and will not bind, add 1 to 2 teaspoons of sherry or a little more beaten egg. If soft add more almonds and/or sugar. It should roll without cracking.
2. Roll out almond paste to fit top of cake.
3. Spread sieved apricot jam over top of cake.
4. Press paste firmly on top.
5. Colour any trimmings: a little red to make berries and a little green for leaves. Arrange on top of cake, painting undersides with beaten egg if they will not stick.

## MARZIPAN SWEETS

*Almond paste mixture*
*Pink, green colouring*
*Almonds, walnuts*
*Dates, prunes*
*A little sherry*

Half the quantity of almond paste given in previous recipe will make a nice selection of sweets, in which case, 1 egg white may be used instead of beaten egg.

1. Make up almond paste mixture.
2. Colour some of the paste pink, some green.
3. Mould into rounds, placing nuts and cherries on top. Or, use to stuff dates and prunes which have added flavour if soaked in a little sherry for a short time.

## SALTED ALMONDS

*4 oz. whole almonds*
*½ oz. butter*
*Salt*

1. Blanch almonds as follows: Place in small basin, cover with boiling water. Leave 5 to 8 minutes, drain and press away the skin between finger and thumb. Pat the almonds dry.
2. Heat butter in small frying pan until just frothing.
3. Tip in almonds, stir over gentle heat until golden.
4. Drain on kitchen paper and sprinkle liberally with salt.
When cold, store in airtight container.

## GOOSNARGH CAKES

*8 oz. plain flour*
*Pinch salt*
*1 large teaspoon coriander powder (optional)*
*1 small teaspoon carraway seeds (optional)*
*6 oz. butter (fresh farm butter makes the best Goosnargh cakes)*
*Castor sugar to coat*

**Note:** The coriander powder and carraway seeds give the Goosnargh cakes a delicate flavour but they are very good without.

1. Mix together flour, salt, coriander powder and carraway seeds.
2. Rub in butter and knead to smooth dough with hands.
3. Roll out on floured board to about a quarter inch thick.
4. Cut into 2 inch rounds with a plain cutter—a wineglass is ideal.
5. Coat liberally with castor sugar and place on baking sheet.
6. Leave overnight.
7. Bake in slow oven, Gas $\frac{1}{2}$, 250°F. for 30 to 45 minutes until firm but not golden. They should be pale in colour.
8. While still warm sift on a little more sugar.

When cool put in a tin. They will keep for months.

**Mrs. J. Seed,<br>Garstang.**

## OXFORD LARDY CAKE

**Dough:**
½ oz. fresh yeast
½ teaspoon sugar
¼ pint water
8 oz. strong plain flour
1 level teaspoon salt
½ tablespoon lard

**Filling:**
3 oz. lard
3 to 4 oz. brown sugar
3 oz. currants

**To Finish:**
A little cooking oil
Castor sugar

**Note:**
It was usual to make a large lardy cake using
2 lb. risen white bread dough
6 oz. lard
8 oz. brown sugar
6 oz. currants
and some think this turns out better than the small one. For this, having prepared your bread dough follow instructions from paragraphs 8 to 15 using a larger, but shallow, roasting tin, baking 40 to 50 minutes.

1. Cream yeast and sugar in a small basin, pour on the warm water. Stir to dissolve.
2. Add the salt to the flour.
3. Rub in the lard.
4. Mix to a pliable dough with the yeast mixture.
5. Knead until smooth and elastic.
6. Place in warm greased bowl. Cover and rise until doubled in size.
7. Turn on to a floured board, knead a little.
8. Roll out dough ¼ inch thick and three times as long as wide.
9. Spread one third of the lard on.
10. Fold in three, and roll out to oblong again.
11. Repeat twice more using sugar, lard and currants.
12. Fold up finally to form a cushion 1½ inches thick.
13. Place in a small greased roasting tin. Brush top with oil and shake castor sugar over. Leave covered until doubled in size.
14. Uncover and score across with a knife.
15. Bake at Gas 6, 400°F., 30 to 40 minutes. Baste with the fat which escapes during cooking.
Freezes well. Thaw first and then reheat at Gas 3, 300°F.

## LINCOLNSHIRE FARMHOUSE DRIPPING CAKE

8 oz. plain flour
½ level teaspoon salt
6 oz. dripping
2 oz. candied peel
8 oz. raisins
6 oz. sugar
1 tablespoon black treacle
½ pt. milk (approx.)
2 eggs, beaten
1 level teaspoon bicarbonate of soda

1. Grease an 8-inch square cake tin and line with greased greaseproof paper.
2. Sift flour with salt, rub in dripping.
3. Add chopped candied peel, stoned raisins and sugar to the flour.
4. Warm the treacle in half of the milk, mix with the eggs and add to ingredients in bowl.
5. Dissolve bicarbonate of soda in 1 tablespoon of the milk and add.
6. Stir all together using remaining milk as necessary to make a consistency that will just drop from the spoon when it is shaken.
7. Put into prepared cake tin. Level the top with back of a spoon.
8. Bake in moderate oven, Gas 4, 350°F. for 1½ to 2 hours. Reduce temperature to Gas 3, 325°F. after 1 hour.

**Mrs. G. Farrow, Thornton Abbey.<br>Mrs. Howard, Welbourn.**

## MANDARIN GÂTEAU
### Cake Mixture
4 oz. margarine
4 oz. castor sugar
2 eggs
4 oz. self raising flour
### Orange Butter Cream
6 oz. butter or margarine
Grated rind of 1 orange
12 oz. icing sugar
1 tablespoon orange juice
### Decoration
2 to 3 oz. toasted coconut*
1 tin mandarin oranges
Cherries and angelica
### Glaze
1 teaspoon arrowroot
4 tablespoons mandarin juice

1. Grease a shallow tin approx. 11 by 7 inches and line with greased greaseproof paper.
2. Beat margarine and sugar until creamy.
3. Add eggs, one at a time, beating, adding 2 teaspoons of the flour to prevent curdling.
4. Fold in rest of flour.
5. Bake at Gas 5, 375°F. about 20 minutes.
6. Remove to wire to cool.
7. Remove paper, cut away edges and cut cake in half lengthways.
8. Beat orange cream ingredients together. Keep some aside for piping. Use some to sandwich two pieces of cake together. Spread some more round sides and cover with toasted coconut. Cover top with a thin layer of butter cream. (The cake can be frozen at this stage to finish when required.)
9. Drain mandarin oranges. Arrange two lines lengthways of cake, leaving ¼ inch edge.
10. Mix arrowroot and juice for glaze in small pan. Bring to boil and cook until clear. Cool. Brush oranges lightly.
11. Place rest of butter cream in piping bag, using a star nozzle. Pipe a line down centre and then round edges of cake.
12. Decorate with pieces of cherry and angelica.

*Toasted coconut: Put in shallow tin in low oven turning occasionally so that it becomes golden evenly.

## MINCEMEAT CAKE
3 oz. margarine
1 oz. lard
4 oz. soft brown sugar
2 large eggs
12 oz. mincemeat
7 oz. self raising flour
A little milk, if necessary

1. Grease a 7-inch round cake tin and line with greased grease-proof paper.
2. Cream fat and sugar and beat in eggs.
3. Stir in mincemeat and fold in flour. Mixture should be moist, (this depends on how runny mincemeat is). If necessary, add a little milk.
4. Bake at Gas 3, 325°F. for 10 minutes. Turn oven to Gas 2, 300°F. for about 1¼ hours until the top is firm and cake is shrinking slightly from edge of tin.
Keeps well.

**Mrs. Ward,
Warwickshire.**

## NOTTINGHAM GINGERBREAD
8 oz. plain flour
3 to 4 level teaspoons ground ginger
1 level teaspoon bicarbonate of soda
4 oz. butter or margarine
4 oz. brown sugar
8 oz. golden syrup or black treacle (or half of each)
¼ pt. milk
1 egg

1. Grease a 7-inch square cake tin and line with greased grease-proof paper.
2. Sieve the flour, ginger and bicarbonate of soda together into a mixing bowl.
3. Melt the fat with the sugar, syrup and milk over a low heat stirring all the time. Cool a little.
4. Beat the egg.
5. Add the liquid mixture with the

egg to the dry ingredients. Mix well then beat for five minutes.

6. Pour into prepared tin. Spread evenly.

7. Cook in a slow oven Gas 2, 315°F. for about 1 hour until it is springy and leaving the sides of the tin.

8. When cooked turn out carefully, remove the paper and store in an airtight tin for a few days to let it become sticky.

## OLD HANNAH'S POTATO CAKES

*8 oz. self raising flour*
*½ teaspoon salt*
*2 oz. butter or margarine*
*8 oz. left-over mashed or creamed potatoes*
*1 beaten egg*
*A little milk if required*

1. Place flour and salt in a bowl with the fat.

2. Rub the fat into the flour.

3. Rub or fork in the potatoes.

4. Make a well in centre of bowl and drop in beaten egg.

5. Fork egg into mixture using a little milk if necessary to give a soft pliable dough. Finish by kneading until the dough is smooth.

6. Place dough on a floured board and roll out to ½-inch thickness. Cut into rounds about 2 to 3 inches in diameter. If no large cutter is available use the top of a glass or cup.

7. Space out on baking sheet and bake for 30 minutes at Gas 5, 375°F.

8. Take out of oven and wrap in a clean tea towel to keep them soft and warm.

9. Split and butter or fill with jam or syrup. Eat while hot.

Ideal for freezing uncooked. Left over cooked ones can be re-heated but have a crispy surface.

**Mrs. Sybil Norcott,**
**Cheshire.**

## SINGING HINNIE

*4 oz. plain flour*
*½ teaspoon baking powder*
*¼ teaspoon salt*
*1 oz. butter*
*1 oz. lard*
*½ oz. currants*
*Milk and sour cream to mix (sour milk alone can be used)*

1. Sieve together the flour, baking powder and salt.

2. Rub in the fats.

3. Add the currants.

4. Mix to a soft dough with a little milk and sour cream (or sour milk).

5. Roll out on floured board a round 7 to 8 inches across. Cut in half or quarters.

6. Heat a girdle and grease it—a piece of suet is ideal.

7. Bake about 3 minutes each side until pale golden and firm, turning with a spatula.

Best eaten hot.

A real Singing Hinnie would never be cut before it was baked. In order to turn it on the girdle without breaking it into pieces a pair of wooden "hands" is required.

**Miss Peggy Howey,**
**Northumberland.**

## STAFFORDSHIRE OATCAKES

Makes approximately 12 oat-cakes.

*8 oz. fine oatmeal*
*8 oz. plain white flour*
*1 teaspoon salt*
*½ oz. fresh yeast*
*1½ pt. warm milk and water mixed*
*1 teaspoon sugar*

1. Add salt to flour and oatmeal and stir.

2. Dissolve yeast with a little of the warm liquid and add sugar. Set aside in warm place until yeast begins to work (i.e. bubbles appear on surface).

3. Mix dry ingredients with yeast and rest of warm liquid to make a nice batter.

4. Cover with clean cloth and leave in warm place for about 1 hour.
5. Then bake on well greased bakestone, griddle or thick-based frying pan. Turn each oatcake after 2 to 3 minutes when upperside appears dry and underside will be golden brown, and bake for a further 2 to 3 minutes.
To serve: Fry with bacon and eggs for breakfast or tea, or grill and eat hot with butter.
These will keep for several days in a polythene bag in refrigerator.
Freeze well. Put paper or polythene tissue between each oatcake. May be taken straight from freezer into frying pan.

**Miss P. M. Cherry, Penkridge.**

## SWISS ROLL
2½ oz. soft plain flour
2 eggs
2½ oz. vanilla sugar*
1 dessertspoon warm water
A little extra castor sugar
2 tablespoons jam or lemon curd
1. Grease a shallow (Swiss Roll) tin approx. 11 by 7 inches and line with greased greaseproof paper.
2. Sift the flour on to a piece of paper and place to warm in warming drawer of oven so that chill is taken off it.
3. Place eggs and vanilla sugar in bowl. Place the bowl over a pan of hot water and whisk until thick and pale.
4. Remove bowl from pan and whisk until beaters leave a trail in the mixture.
5. Carefully fold in warmed flour and warm water.
6. Spread evenly in tin.
7. Bake above centre of oven at Gas 7, 425°F. for 7 to 8 minutes until lightly golden and springy to the touch.
8. While cake is baking, place a damp (not wet) tea-towel on table, then a piece of greaseproof paper —2 inches all round larger than Swiss roll, dust this with a little flour and dredge with castor sugar.

9. Prepare jam. If it is a little stiff, warm just sufficiently to spread.
10. As soon as Swiss roll is out of oven turn it out upside-down on to paper, trim off edges quickly, spread with jam and roll up.

## ABERDEEN BUTTERIES
⅜ pint (7½ fluid oz.) tepid milk and water, mixed
1 teaspoon sugar
1½ measured teaspoons dried yeast, or ½ oz. fresh yeast
½ teaspoon salt
10 oz. strong plain flour
1 oz. butter or margarine
2 oz. lard
2 oz. hard margarine
1. Take out 1 tablespoon of the tepid milk and water mixture and keep aside for use later.
2. Stir sugar into the remaining bulk of liquid. Sprinkle on dried yeast and leave 5 to 10 minutes to start working. It is ready for use when frothing up well.
**If using fresh yeast,** stir sugar into the liquid, take out half a cupful and mix the fresh yeast into this to liquify it. Mix both liquids together and proceed with recipe. There is no need to wait as with dried yeast.
3. Add salt to flour and roughly rub in the 1 oz. of butter or margarine.
4. Add the yeast liquid and mix to a soft elastic dough, adding the extra tablespoon of liquid if required.
5. Knead firmly for about 5 minutes.
6. Return dough to bowl and put bowl into a polythene bag. Leave in a warm place to rise until doubled in size, about 45 minutes.
7. Work together lard with the 2 oz. margarine and divide equally into 3 portions.
8. Knock back risen dough by kneading on a floured board. Roll out to a strip half an inch thick and 3 times as long as it is wide.
9. Spread one portion of mixed

fats over bottom two-thirds of dough. Fold top third down and then bottom third up. Turn dough so that fold is at left hand side.
10. Roll out, spread fat, fold and turn twice more. Lay dough aside in a cool place for at least 10 minutes.
11. Roll out again to half an inch thick and cut or pull into 8 or 10 pieces. Place on a baking sheet and put baking sheet into polythene bag. Leave in a warm place to rise again, about 15 to 20 minutes.
12. Brush with a little melted butter and bake at Gas 8, 450°F. for 15 to 20 minutes until golden brown and flaky.
These freeze well.

**Mrs. Anne Wallace,
Dunlop, Scotland.**

## OLD-FASHIONED SPICE BREAD

*2 level teaspoons dried yeast, or*
*½ oz. fresh yeast*
*½ teaspoon sugar*
*¼ pint tepid milk*
*12 oz. plain flour*
*½ teaspoon salt*
*½ teaspoon mixed spice*
*½ teaspoon powdered cinnamon*
*½ teaspoon bicarbonate of soda*
*2 oz. margarine*
*2 oz. lard*
*6 oz. soft brown sugar*
*4 oz. currants*
*4 oz. sultanas*
*2 oz. chopped peel*
*1 beaten egg*
*1 dessertspoon dark treacle*
*A little more milk, as required*
1. Grease a 2 lb. loaf tin, line base with greased greaseproof paper.
2. Add dried yeast and sugar to milk, stir and leave until frothy, (note manufacturer's directions on packet).
**Or,** if using fresh yeast, stir into milk with sugar to dissolve.
3. Sieve together flour, salt, spices and bicarbonate of soda.
4. Rub in fats, add soft brown sugar and fruit.
5. Add yeast mixture, egg and

treacle. Mix together adding a little more milk, about 2 to 3 tablespoons, if necessary, to make a dropping consistency.
6. Spoon into tin, level top.
7. Bake at Gas 2, 300°F. for about 1½ hours, until firm on top and leaving sides of tin.
8. Leave in tin about 10 minutes, then remove and cool on a wire rack.
Serve sliced and buttered. It is particularly good with Wensleydale cheese.
Keeps well.

## CHEESE LOAF

*14 oz. strong plain flour*
*1 teaspoon salt*
*1 teaspoon dry mustard*
*Bare ¼ teaspoon cayenne pepper*
*4 oz. finely-grated Cheddar cheese*
*2 teaspoons dried yeast or ½ oz. fresh yeast*
*1 teaspoon sugar*
*Bare ½ pint tepid water*
1. Sieve flour and seasonings into a large bowl, mix in the cheese.
2. Prepare the dried yeast as indicated in manufacturer's instructions. It is important, with dried yeast, that it is frothing up well when used
**If using fresh yeast,** cream it with the sugar, pour in half of the water, mix and use.
3. Pour yeast mixture into dry ingredients using rest of water as necessary to make a soft pliable dough.
4. Knead well until quite smooth and elastic.
5. Place in a large, lightly-greased, warm bowl. Cover, keep away from draughts and leave to prove until doubled in size.
6. Turn out on to floured board, knead until smooth again.
7. Divide into 2 portions, shape and place in two greased 1 lb. tins, or use one 2 lb. loaf tin.
8. Cover and leave to rise to nearly the top of tin.
9. Bake centre oven, Gas 5, 375°F. for 45 to 50 minutes until

golden brown. To test, slip loaf out of tin into a clean cloth and tap the bottom. It will sound hollow when loaf is done.

Serve sliced and buttered. Also good toasted.

Freezes well.

## EGG FINGERS
*1 egg*
*1 tablespoon milk*
*Salt and pepper*
*Fingers of white bread*
*Bacon fat or a little margarine*

1. Beat the egg and milk with a little salt and pepper.

2. Dip bread fingers into the egg mixture.

3. Fry till golden on both sides, best done in the fat after cooking bacon, but add a little margarine if necessary.

Serve with bacon. Eat at once or they go like leather.

Particularly good when made with fingers from a Cheese Loaf, see preceding recipe.

# CHAPTER 9

# PUDDINGS

## CHRISTMAS PUDDING

6 oz. plain flour
½ teaspoon salt
1 teaspoon mixed spice
½ teaspoon powdered cinnamon
¼ teaspoon grated nutmeg
4 oz. fresh white breadcrumbs
4 oz. shredded suet
3 oz. demerara sugar
4 oz. raisins
8 oz. currants
8 oz. sultanas
2 oz. chopped candied peel
1 medium-sized apple, grated
1 medium-sized carrot, grated
Juice and grated rind of 1 lemon
and 1 orange
1 level tablespoon dark treacle
2 beaten eggs
⅓ pint stout*

For cooking the pudding you will need one 2 pt. basin **or** two 1 pt. basins **or** four ½ pt. basins.
1. Pick over the fruit removing stalks and stones.
2. Sieve into a large bowl flour, salt and spices.
3. Add crumbs, suet, sugar and fruit and mix.
4. Add grated apple, carrot, rind and juice of lemon and orange, treacle, eggs and stout. Mix very well together.
5. Leave several hours, or overnight. Stir again. Place in greased basin(s), leaving an inch at top. Cover securely with two layers of greased greaseproof paper and one layer of foil.
6. Stand on a trivet or upturned saucer in a pan with boiling water half way up basin. (Or, use a steamer which will give you a lighter pudding.) Steam as follows:
2 pt. basin—8 hours
1 pt. basins—6 hours
½ pt. basins—4 hours
Keep water on the boil, replenishing when necessary.

### OR

Pressure cook following instructions in your pressure cooker handbook. Cooking time will be reduced considerably.

7. When required, steam 3 hours for 2 pt. pudding, 2 hours for smaller puddings. **OR** Pressure cook 1 hour for 2 pt. pudding, ¾ hour for smaller puddings.
*See page 164 for home brewed stout recipe.

## ECONOMICAL CHRISTMAS PUDDING

1 beaten egg
2 oz. fresh white breadcrumbs
2 oz. self raising flour
1 level teaspoon mixed spice
8 oz. mincemeat (can use up to 12 oz.)
1 tablespoon milk
1 level tablespoon dark treacle

Recipe for mincemeat is given on page 137.
1. Add crumbs to egg in bowl.
2. Sieve flour and spice and add, with mincemeat, milk and treacle. Mix well.
3. Spoon into greased 1 pt. basin, cover with greased greaseproof paper and a layer of foil, tucking edges round rim of basin.
4. Place on trivet or upturned saucer in pan with boiling water half way up basin. (Or, use a steamer, which will give you a lighter pudding). Steam for 4 hours. Keep water on boil, replenishing when necessary. Or, pressure cook following instructions given in your pressure cooker handbook.
The pudding can be eaten now or kept a week or so. If it is to be kept until another day steam it then for 1 hour.
A 1 pt. basin will take a pudding mixture using 12 oz. mincemeat if you prefer a richer pudding.

## BRANDY BUTTER

3 oz. unsalted butter
3 oz. fine castor sugar
2 to 3 tablespoons brandy
1. Cream butter until white.
2. Beat in sugar gradually.

118

3. Add brandy 1 teaspoon at a time, beating in thoroughly. If the mixture shows any signs of curdling, do not use all the brandy.
4. The sauce should be white and foamy. Pile into small serving dish, allow to become firm.
Use with Plum Pudding or mince-pies.

## CUMBERLAND RUM BUTTER
**Using the melted method**
*7½ oz. soft brown sugar*
*½ wine glass (1½ tablespoons) rum*
*4 oz. slightly salted butter*
1. Crush or sieve brown sugar to ensure there are no lumps.
2. Place sugar into bowl and add rum. Stir until smooth.
3. Put butter into a heat-proof basin and allow to soften near cooker—it should not boil or become oily.
4. Pour butter gradually on to the sugar and rum stirring with wooden spoon until well-blended and starting to set.
5. Pour into old fashioned china bowl and allow to set.
6. Serve spread on scones or plain biscuits.
Traditionally served at Christenings—afterwards the empty rum butter bowl is filled with silver coins and given to the baby.
**Mrs. Sadie Wilson,**
**Caldbeck Wigton.**

## RUM SAUCE
*1 oz. cornflour*
*2 level tablespoons sugar*
*1 pt. milk*
*A nut of butter*
*2 to 3 tablespoons rum, to taste*
1. Mix cornflour and sugar with ¼ pint milk.
2. Heat rest of milk in saucepan to nearly boiling, pour over cornflour mixture, mix and return to pan. Cook for 2 minutes, stirring.
3. Stir in butter and add rum to taste.
Serve with Christmas Pudding.

If this sauce is rather rich it can be made with ½ pt. milk and ½ pt. water.

## FEAST PLUM PUDDING
*12 oz. stale white bread, without crusts*
*4 oz. raisins, or chopped dates*
*4 oz. currants*
*1 oz. mixed peel*
*2 oz. sugar*
*1 egg*
*4 oz. grated suet*
*¼ level teaspoon grated nutmeg*
1. Cut bread into cubes. Soak in water for about 10 minutes, squeeze out moisture and mix with other ingredients.
2. Put into a well-greased deep oven-proof dish, cover with foil.
3. Cook in the oven at Gas 4, 350°F. for half an hour. Then reduce heat to Gas 1½, 275°F. for a further two hours. It can then be left in the oven with the heat off. May be reheated or more usually eaten cold.
It was originally cooked in the baker's oven after the day's baking and was left in all night.
**Mrs. M. D. Dickens,**
**Northamptonshire.**

## FRIAR'S OMELETTE
*6 medium cooking apples*
*2 tablespoons cold water*
*3 oz. butter*
*2 oz. castor sugar*
*Grated rind of 1 lemon*
*Pinch of nutmeg or cloves*
*4 oz. fresh breadcrumbs*
*4 egg-yolks*
*Extra butter*
1. Score skin around top of apples and put them in a casserole dish with 2 tablespoons water.
2. Put them to bake in the oven, Gas 6, 400°F. until tender, about ¾ hour.
3. Scrape out pulp and mash.
4. Cream butter and sugar, add rind and pulp with nutmeg or clove.

5. Grease a large pie dish and sprinkle base and sides with about half of the breadcrumbs.
6. Beat egg-yolks and stir into apple mixture and pour into dish.
7. Cover with rest of crumbs and dot with butter.
8. Bake 1 hour approx. at Gas 5, 375°F. until firm and set.
Eat hot with cream or custard sauce.

**Kate Easlea,
Hampshire.**

## NOTTINGHAM PUDDING
The Bramley cooking apple originates from Southwell, Nottinghamshire. The original tree is still flourishing in a garden in the Minster town.
*6 even-sized Bramley apples*
*3 oz. butter*
*3 oz. castor sugar*
*Nutmeg*
*Cinnamon*
*6 tablespoons flour*
*Water*
*3 eggs*
*Salt*
*Milk*
1. Peel and core apples.
2. Cream butter and sugar, add pinch of nutmeg and cinnamon.
3. Fill the centre of each apple with this mixture.
4. Place in a well-buttered oven-proof dish.
5. Blend flour with a little cold water and add the well-beaten eggs to it with a pinch of salt and sufficient milk to make a thick creamy batter.
6. Pour over the apples and bake at Gas 6, 400°F. for 50 minutes.

## RHUBARB STIRABOUT
*4 oz. plain flour*
*2 oz. margarine*
*2 oz. castor sugar*
*1 egg and 5 tablespoons milk*
*8 to 12 oz. rhubarb*
*Golden syrup*
1. Rub fat into flour till like breadcrumbs.

2. Stir in sugar.
3. Add beaten egg and milk to make stiff batter.
4. Cut fruit into 1 inch pieces and stir in.
5. Pour into greased pie dish and bake about ½ hour, Gas 7, 425°F.
6. Cover with syrup while hot and eat at once.
Other fruit, such as gooseberries, cherries or plums can be used instead of rhubarb if desired.

**Kate Easlea,
Hampshire.**

## STONE CREAM
**A very old Buckinghamshire recipe.**
Makes 8 servings
*4 tablespoons cold water*
*½ oz. gelatine*
*Strawberry jam*
*Whites of 2 eggs*
*½ pt. cream*
*1 dessertspoon vanilla sugar**
*½ pt. milk*
1. Put water in small basin, sprinkle in gelatine. Place bowl over pan of hot, not boiling, water. Stir gently until it becomes clear. Remove from pan and allow to cool a little—not cold or it will set.
2. Put jam in bottom of dish or in small glass sundae dishes.
3. Whisk egg whites until they hold the impression of the whisk.
4. Whip the cream to the same consistency as the egg. Stir in the sugar.
5. Add the gelatine to the milk and mix this into the cream.
6. When beginning to thicken fold in egg whites.
7. Pour quickly into dish or glasses on top of jam.
Serve chilled.
Try also using cherry jam or fresh strawberries, raspberries or cherries. Adjust the amount of sugar to taste.

**Mrs. M. E. Smith,
Stoke Mandeville.**

*\*See page 89.*

## APPLE AND ORANGE PUDDING

*12 oz. apples*
*2½ oz. butter*
*Sugar to sweeten*
*6 oz. stale cake-crumbs*
*Rind and juice of 1 orange*

1. Peel, core and slice the apples.
2. Melt 1 oz. of the butter in a pan, add apple, cook until soft but not mushy, stirring a little. Remove from heat and stir in sugar to taste.
3. Melt 1½ oz. butter in another pan, stir in crumbs, half of the orange rind and all the orange juice.
4. Grease a 7-inch sandwich cake tin, put in half the crumbs and spread them over base. Cover with apple to within half an inch of the sides of tin. Cover with rest of crumbs.
5. Bake at Gas 5, 375°F. for 15 minutes.
6. Invert on to warm plate without removing tin. Leave 5 minutes.
7. Lift off tin and sprinkle on the rest of the orange rind.
Serve with custard or cream.
It is nicer hot but can be eaten cold.

## STEAMED PUDDINGS

**The basic recipe**
*4 oz. margarine*
*4 oz. castor sugar*
*6 oz. self-raising flour*
*Pinch of salt*
*2 beaten eggs*
*2 tablespoons milk*

1. Grease a 2-pint, heat-proof basin.
2. Beat margarine until soft and creamy and then beat in sugar.
3. Mix flour and salt and add it a little at a time alternately with the beaten egg.
4. Fold in milk.
5. Spoon into greased basin, smooth top.
6. Cover with greased, grease-proof paper and foil, tucking edges securely round rim.
7. Steam the pudding in a steamer. Or, stand basin on a trivet or upturned saucer in a saucepan with enough boiling water to come halfway up the basin. Steam for 1½ hours. Keep water boiling replenishing as necessary.
If you have a pressure cooker, cook at pressure for 30 minutes. Reduce pressure quickly.
Serve with custard or chocolate sauce (see page 122) or with warmed golden syrup or a jam sauce.

**Try also the following variations based on the Steamed Puddings recipe:**

**Marble Pudding**
When pudding is mixed:
1. Divide mixture into 3 portions.
2. Colour one portion pink with a few drops of red colouring.
3. Mix 2 teaspoons of cocoa with 2 teaspoons of hot water. Fold this into another portion.
4. Spoon into the greased pudding basin alternate spoonfuls of the plain, pink and chocolate mixtures. Smooth top.
Continue from paragraph 6 of the basic recipe.
Serve with custard or chocolate sauce (see next page).

**Sultana Pudding**
Follow the basic recipe adding 3 to 4 oz. sultanas to the flour (paragraph 3).

**Chocolate Pudding**
Omit 1 oz. flour from the basic recipe and replace it with 1 oz. cocoa. Sieve this with the flour and add as instructed in paragraph 3 of basic recipe.

**Coffee Pudding**
Dissolve 2 level teaspoons instant coffee into 2 teaspoons boiling water. Mix this with the milk and fold in as instructed in paragraph 4 of basic recipe.

### Orange or Lemon Pudding

Omit the milk from the basic recipe and add the rind and juice of 1 orange or 1 lemon.

**Jam, Marmalade or Lemon Curd** may be used as a topping for the pudding. Follow the basic recipe but put 2 tablespoons of jam, marmalade or curd into the greased pudding basin before spooning in the pudding mixture.

## CHOCOLATE SAUCE

*1 level dessertspoon cornflour*
*2 oz. sugar*
*½ oz. cocoa*
*½ pint milk*
*½ oz. margarine*
*½ teaspoon vanilla essence*

1. Blend cornflour, sugar and cocoa with a little of the milk.
2. Bring the rest of the milk to the boil and pour it over the cornflour mixture, stirring to combine.
3. Return mixture to pan and simmer for 2 minutes.
4. Remove from heat and stir in margarine and essence.

## ICE CREAM

*3 eggs*
*1 oz. castor sugar*
*½ pint milk*
*Small tin condensed milk*

1. Separate the whites from the yolks of the eggs.
2. Whisk the yolks and sugar together until lighter in colour.
3. Bring the milk almost to the boil, pour a little on to the egg-yolks whisking all the time.
4. Return the mixture to the pan and heat, without boiling, until the mixture coats the back of a wooden spoon.
5. Pour the mixture into the bowl, add the condensed milk and mix well. Leave the mixture to cool.
6. Pour into a shallow rectangular polythene container (or the refrigerator ice tray with divisions removed) and place in the freezing compartment of the refrigerator or in the freezer. Leave it there until ice forms round the edge of the mixture.
7. Then stir the mixture and put it back in the refrigerator or freezer while the egg-whites are whisked.
8. Whisk the egg-whites until stiff and fold into the ice cream.
9. Place back in the refrigerator or freezer until the ice cream sets hard.

**Try also these flavourings:**

**Apricot Ice Cream**
1. Drain the juice from a 15 to 16 oz. tin of apricot halves. Sieve the fruit or liquidise until a purée.
2. Stir in 2 tablespoons of the apricot juice.
3. After folding the egg-whites into the ice cream fold in the apricot purée and freeze.

**Brown Bread Ice Cream**
After folding the stiffly-whisked egg-whites into the ice cream, fold in 2 oz. fresh, brown breadcrumbs and freeze.
1 teaspoon of rum can also be added with the breadcrumbs.

**Chocolate Ice Cream**
1. Melt 4 oz. plain chocolate in a bowl over hot water.
2. Add 1 dessertspoon golden syrup, mix well and add with the condensed milk at paragraph 5 of the basic recipe.

**Sue Nichols,
British Sugar Bureau**

## CARAMEL SAUCE

**A sauce to serve either hot or cold with ice cream. Serves 4.**

*2 tablespoons golden syrup*
*1 oz. butter*
*2 tablespoons water*

1. Measure the golden syrup with a warm tablespoon and place in a saucepan.
2. Bring to the boil and continue boiling for about 1 minute until just turning brown.

3. Remove from heat and add the butter, stir well.
4. Add the water and mix well. When served hot this sauce is very runny. As it cools it becomes thicker. When cold it is fudge-like.

**Sue Nichols,**
**British Sugar Bureau**

## APPLE OR PINEAPPLE FRITTERS
**Batter**
*4 oz. plain flour*
*Pinch of salt*
*1 tablespoon cooking or salad oil*
*¼ pint tepid water*
*1 egg white*
1. Sieve flour and salt into a basin, make a well in the centre, add the oil and half the water.
2. Beat well, then gradually beat in rest of water. Allow to stand 1 hour.
3. Fold in firmly-whisked egg-white just before using.

**The Fritters**
*Cooking apples*
*Castor sugar*
*Cinnamon*
**Or**
*Tinned pineapple rings*
*Castor sugar*
1. Peel and core required number of cooking apples. Cut into rings about ⅜ inch thick. Each apple should cut into 4 rings. Sprinkle on a little sugar.
**Or** thoroughly drain pineapple rings.
2. Dip fruit rings in batter, using a skewer, and deep-fry for 3 to 4 minutes until crisp and golden.
3. Drain on paper. Dust with castor sugar. For the apple fritters mix a little cinnamon with the sugar.

## A FRUIT SAUCE
To serve with hot sponge puddings, pancakes etc. Also delicious served cold with ice-cream.
*4 tablespoons jam*
*4 tablespoons water*
*Squeeze of lemon juice*
*1 teaspoon cornflour mixed with 2 teaspoons water*
Any variety of jam can be used for this sauce, even a mixture of jams, jelly or marmalade left in jars.
1. Heat jam, water and lemon juice—no need to boil. Sieve.
2. Blend cornflour and 2 teaspoons water. Pour on the jam mixture. Return to pan, bring to boil, stirring all the time.
Freezes well.

## APPLE TRIFLE FOR TWO
*2 small buns or pieces of plain cake*
*2 teaspoons raspberry jam*
*1 orange*
*Approx. 8 oz. cooking apples*
*½ oz. butter*
*A squeeze of lemon juice*
*1 to 2 teaspoons sugar*
*4 tablespoons double cream*
1. Cut across buns, sandwich together with jam, place in small serving dish or 2 sundae glasses.
2. Grate rind finely from orange on to a saucer, cover tightly with foil to prevent discoloration.
3. Squeeze juice from orange, pour over cake.
4. Peel and slice apples wafer thin.
5. Melt butter in small pan, add lemon juice and apples. Stir over gentle heat until soft, but not mushy. Sweeten to taste.
6. Spread apple mixture over cake, leave until cold.
7. Whip cream to spreading consistency, cover apples. Sprinkle on orange rind.

## GRANDMA'S 1234 BUNS
Makes a delicious pudding served hot with a fruit sauce, (see this page). Keep the remaining buns for tea.
*1 egg*
*2 oz. margarine*
*3 oz. castor sugar*
*4 oz. self-raising flour*
*A little milk*

1. Beat the egg.
2. Cream margarine and sugar until fluffy.
3. Add half the egg, half the flour, mix well and add remaining egg, flour and 1 tablespoon of milk.
4. Place in greased bun tins. This quantity will make 12 of the shallow type or 9 deeper buns.
5. Bake at Gas 6, 400°F. 15 to 16 minutes until firm.

**Miss K. A. Butterworth,
Leeds.**

## BAKED ALASKA
**For 4 persons**
This delicious pudding is made of ice-cream on a sponge base with a thick coating of meringue mixture which is baked or "flashed" in the oven for a few minutes before it is served. Some preparation can be done in advance but it does take about 10 minutes for the assembly and baking. It must then be eaten at once and is well worth waiting for.
**For the base**
*2 eggs*
*2½ oz. vanilla sugar\**
*(If no vanilla sugar, use castor sugar, but in this case do not add vanilla essence.)*
*2½ oz. soft plain flour*
1. Grease a shallow tin 11 inches by 7 inches. A Swiss roll tin is ideal. Line with greased grease-proof paper.
2. Put eggs and sugar in a bowl. Place the bowl over a pan of hot water and whisk until the mixture is thick and pale.
3. Remove bowl from pan and whisk until beaters leave a trail in the mixture.
4. Sift flour on top and fold in with a spatula or metal spoon.
5. Spread mixture evenly in the tin.
6. Bake at Gas 4, 350°F. near top of oven for 20 to 23 minutes until firm and shrinking slightly from sides of tin.
7. Cool on a wire rack and remove paper.

**To assemble**
*2 tablespoons sherry or fruit juice*
*1 family-sized block of ice-cream, approximately 17 oz. size*
*3 egg whites*
*4½ oz. castor sugar*
1. Trim the sponge so that when the ice-cream is placed on it there is at least half an inch of cake all round the edge. Save the rest of the cake for tea.
2. Place sponge on a heat-proof dish, sprinkle on sherry or fruit juice. Arrange ice-cream on top.
3. Whisk egg whites until very stiff. Fold in the sugar.
4. Spread over ice-cream right to edge of cake, sealing completely.
5. Bake near top of oven Gas 7, 425°F. for about 4 minutes, until tinged with gold.
Serve within a few minutes on cold plates.

## CHOCOLATE CREAM
*2 tablespoons water*
*½ oz. (1 small envelope) gelatine*
*¾ pint of milk*
*3 egg-yolks*
*3 oz. castor sugar*
*½ teaspoon vanilla essence, or use vanilla sugar\**
*4 oz. plain chocolate, coarsely chopped*
*¼ pint whipping cream or 1 small can of evaporated milk plus a good squeeze of lemon juice*
**To decorate**
*Chocolate vermicelli*
1. Measure water into a cup, sprinkle on gelatine. Stir a little, just to mix. Leave to soften.
2. Heat milk in saucepan **but do not boil.**
3. Cream egg-yolks and sugar in a bowl, pour on the hot milk, stir together and strain back into pan.
4. Stir with a wooden spoon over gentle heat until mixture clings to spoon, **but do not boil.**
5. Pour mixture back into bowl, stir in vanilla essence if used, the chocolate and the gelatine. Beat

until both are dissolved.

6. Leave mixture until quite cold and beginning to thicken slightly, 20 to 30 minutes. Stir occasionally.

7. Whip cream until holding shape, or whisk evaporated milk and lemon juice until thickening, and fold in.

8. Pour into serving dish, or 5 to 6 small ones. Sprinkle top with chocolate vermicelli.

## LEMON FLUFF

*¾ pint plus 3 tablespoons water*
*1 good-sized lemon*
*1 heaped tablespoon cornflour*
*4 oz. sugar*
*2 eggs, separated*
**To decorate**
*Chopped walnuts or toasted coconut*

1. Put ¼ pint of water in a saucepan with the finely-pared rind of the lemon. Simmer gently for 5 minutes.

2. Mix cornflour and sugar in a large basin, blend with the 3 tablespoons of water.

3. Remove pan from heat, add juice of the lemon and strain on to cornflour mixture.

4. Return the mixture to the pan, bring to the boil, stirring, and cook 2 minutes.

5. Put egg-yolks in the basin and egg-whites into another clean basin.

6. Pour lemon mixture on to egg-yolks and beat well together. Set aside until quite cold and thickening slightly.

7. Whisk egg-whites until firm but not dry.

8. Using a metal spoon, fold egg-whites gently into lemon mixture.

9. Pour into 1 large or 4 small dishes, sprinkle top with chopped walnuts or toasted coconut.

## MERINGUES

*4 egg whites*
*8 oz. castor sugar*
*An extra 1 oz. castor sugar for sprinkling*

1. Prepare a baking sheet. Cover it with 2 sheets of very lightly-oiled greaseproof paper.

2. Whisk egg whites until stiff. If the bowl is inverted quickly the whites should not fall out.

3. Add 4 teaspoons of the castor sugar and continue whisking until the whites are stiff again.

4. Fold in remaining sugar with a tablespoon or palette knife.

5. Spoon or pipe on to prepared baking sheet.

6. Sprinkle meringues with the 1 oz. of castor sugar.

7. Put on low shelf in the oven at lowest gas setting, 200°F. and leave for about 2 hours until dry. To test, lightly tap with finger nail. If meringues feel crisp and sound hollow they are done.

If any difficulty is experienced in getting meringues to dry out they may be removed from oven after 1½ hours and turned upside down. Using a skewer make a hole in the bottom and return to the oven to dry. Test again before removing from oven.

## RHUBARB WITH ORANGE

*1 lb. rhubarb*
*The zest of half an orange, or peel, thinly-sliced from half an orange*
*Brown sugar to taste, either demerara or soft brown will do*

1. Cut, wash and drain the rhubarb. Put it in a casserole dish. Sprinkle with sugar and orange peel and set aside for 24 hours.

2. Next day cover the casserole and put it in the oven, Gas 2, 300°F. for about half an hour. The rhubarb should be neither hard nor too soft but exact cooking time depends on the age of the fruit.

This method produces a lot of delicious juice without the addition of water.

**Mrs. Marie Holton,**
**Godmanchester,**
**Huntingdonshire.**

See also: Fruit Pie, page 35 and Sherry Chiffon Pie, page 35.

## CHILTERN HILLS PUDDING

*4 level tablespoons seed tapioca*
*⅜ pint (7½ fluid oz.) milk*
*4 oz. raisins*
*1 oz. shredded suet*
*4 oz. sugar*
*4 oz. fresh white breadcrumbs*
*1 level teaspoon bicarbonate of soda*

1. Place tapioca in a mixing bowl, pour over the milk and leave to soak for 2 hours.
2. Strain off the milk and reserve it.
3. Add raisins, suet, sugar and crumbs to tapioca.
4. Dissolve bicarbonate of soda in strained milk, add to other ingredients and mix all well together.
5. Pack into a lightly-greased basin. A 1½ pint basin is just large enough but 2 pint a little safer as mixture rises. Cover with lightly-greased foil, sealing well round edges.
6. Steam for 3 hours, keeping water always boiling and checking when in need of replenishing. If you do not have a steamer stand the pudding on añ upturned saucer in a saucepan of boiling water. This should come half-way up the sides of the pudding basin.

**Mrs. M. E. Smith,**
**Buckinghamshire.**

## LEMON DAINTY

*6 oz. sugar*
*1½ oz. soft plain flour*
*1 oz. butter*
*Grated rind and juice of 1 large lemon*
*2 eggs separated*
*6 fluid oz. (9 brimming tablespoons) milk*

1. Mix together in a bowl sugar, flour, butter shredded in tiny pieces, lemon rind and juice and egg yolks. Beat well to combine thoroughly.
2. Add milk gradually, beating well.
3. Fold in firmly-whisked egg whites.
4. Butter a pie dish or a soufflé dish holding about 2 pints and pour in the mixture.
5. Pour 2 inches of hot water into a small roasting tin and stand dish of pudding mixture in it.
6. Bake at Gas 4, 350°F. 40 to 45 minutes until golden and firm on top.
7. Allow to stand for 5 to 10 minutes before serving.

This pudding has a spongy top and a delicious lemon sauce underneath.

## PINEAPPLE UPSIDE-DOWN PUDDING

**Base:**
*1 oz. butter*
*2 oz. demerara sugar*
*4 pineapple rings*
*6 glacé cherries*

**Pudding:**
*2 oz. soft margarine*
*2 oz. castor sugar*
*1 large egg*
*2½ oz. self-raising flour*
*½ oz. semolina*
*1 to 2 tablespoons milk*

**Glaze:**
*1 teaspoon arrowroot or cornflour*
*¼ pint juice from tin of pineapple (if not sufficient make up with water)*

1. Butter a 7 inch sandwich tin with the 1 oz. butter, spreading it lightly round sides thicker at the bottom. Sprinkle on the demerara sugar.
2. Arrange pineapple rings and cherries in a pattern over base.
3. Place all pudding ingredients except the milk in a mixing bowl and beat until smooth adding enough of the milk to make a soft dropping consistency.
4. Spread carefully into tin on top of fruit smoothing top level.
5. Bake in centre of oven at Gas 5, 375°F. for 30 to 35 minutes until

top is firm and pudding is shrinking from sides of tin.

6. Remove from oven, leave 2 to 3 minutes then invert on to a warm plate leaving tin in position.

7. Mix arrowroot and juice in small pan, stir over gentle heat until boiling and transparent.

8. Remove tin carefully from pudding, spoon over a little of the glaze, serve remainder as a sauce.

## QUEEN OF PUDDINGS

*¾ pint milk*
*1 oz. butter*
*Rind of 1 small lemon*
*4 oz. castor sugar*
*3 oz. fresh white breadcrumbs*
*2 eggs, separated*
*2 oz. (2 tablespoons) jam*

1. Heat milk to nearly boiling point, stir in butter and finely-grated rind of lemon and 1 oz. of the castor sugar.

2. Pour this over the crumbs in a bowl and stir in egg yolks. Leave 15 minutes.

3. Pour into a lightly-greased 1½ to 2 pint pie dish and bake at Gas 4, 350°F. for about 20 to 25 minutes or until set.

4. Remove from oven, lower heat to Gas 1, 275°F.

5. Spread jam over top of pudding.

6. Whisk egg whites stiffly, fold in the remaining 3 oz. castor sugar and spread on top. Sift on a little castor sugar.

7. Return to oven, leave until meringue sets and is just tinged with gold, about 20 minutes.

**See also: Lincolnshire Potato Cheesecake, page 41.**

**Staffordshire Yeomanry Pudding, page 41.**

## CARLINS

Many centuries ago the Scots lay siege to Newcastle and it is said that the people were only saved from starvation when a French ship with a load of grey peas crept up the River Tyne. It was Passion Sunday, two Sundays before Easter, when the peas were distributed and on this day each year, now known as Carlin Sunday, it has been the custom, particularly in public houses to serve carlins free.

"Carlins" is a Geordie name for the peas. They are properly named Maple Peas. Outside the North East of England they are stocked by corn merchants and some pet stores for sale as pigeon feed. They are quite rich in protein, about 25%.

*8 oz. Carlins (Maple Peas)*
*Water*
*Pinch of salt*
*1 oz. butter*
*2 oz. soft brown sugar*
*Dash of rum*

1. Soak carlins overnight in water.

2. Drain and place in a saucepan of boiling water with a pinch of salt. Boil for approximately 20 minutes or until cooked but not overdone.

3. Melt butter in a frying pan, add drained carlins, fry for 2 to 3 minutes.

4. Remove from heat, stir in brown sugar and dash of rum. Serve hot. They are delicious.

**Miss P. Howey,
Northumberland.**

## POACHING FRUIT

Poaching fruit as opposed to stewing gives a much better end result both to eat and to look at, particularly as with a little care it is possible to keep the fruits whole and unbroken.

The syrup is made first and the fruit very gently simmered in it. For a special occasion a little wine, brandy or liqueur may be added. Soft fruits containing a lot of juice, such as plums, cherries and apricots, require a heavy syrup but only a little of it. Hard fruits such as pears, apples and gooseberries, require a lighter syrup but a greater quantity.

**Heavy syrup:**
*4 oz. sugar to ½ pint water*

**Light syrup:**

*3 oz. sugar to ½ pint water*

1. Place water and sugar in a wide, preferably shallow, pan. Stir over gentle heat to dissolve sugar and simmer with lid on pan for 2 to 3 minutes.
2. Wash any fruit not to be peeled.
3. If peeling fruit use a stainless steel knife peeling just the quantity to be poached at one time. Fruit which discolours easily—pears, apples etc. keep a better colour if a teaspoon of lemon juice is added to syrup.
4. Place prepared fruit into syrup in one layer and simmer very gently with lid on pan until tender. Time will vary according to ripeness of fruit.
5. Lift carefully into serving bowl and repeat process until required quantity of fruit is cooked.
6. If several batches are to be cooked, syrup may require replenishing. If only a small amount of fruit is poached and too much syrup is left, boil it rapidly with lid off pan to reduce a little and to thicken slightly.
7. Add the odd teaspoon of wine, brandy or liqueur to syrup and pour over fruit. Serve when cold. For sweet shortcrust pastry flan cases, see page 29.

## BAKED BANANAS

*4 bananas*
*Lemon juice*
*2 oz. dessicated coconut*
*2 oz. demerara sugar*
*Pat of butter*
*A little rum (optional)*

1. Lay peeled bananas in lightly-buttered, shallow, fireproof dish.
2. Sprinkle with lemon juice, then with coconut and sugar mixed.
3. Add shavings of butter and a sprinkling of rum if you wish.
4. Bake at Gas 4, 350°F. about 15 minutes.
Serve with custard or cream.

## BLACKBERRY MOUSSE

*1 lb. blackberries*

*3 level tablespoons sifted icing sugar*
*½ oz. gelatine*
*2 tablespoons water*
*¼ pint whipping cream*
*2 egg whites*

1. Cook blackberries until soft. This is best done without water in a casserole with lid in a slow oven no higher than Gas 4, 350°F. If cooked in a saucepan, 2 to 3 teaspoons water may be required if fruit is dry, but liquid should be kept to a minimum.
2. Sieve the fruit and add icing sugar.
3. Measure puree, there should be ½ pint. Pour into a bowl.
4. Measure water into a small basin, trickle in the powdered gelatine. Stand this in hot water to dissolve gelatine, stirring once to combine.
5. Pour this very gently into fruit, stirring continuously. Allow to become quite cold, and slightly thick.
6. Whip cream until holding its shape. Fold in.
7. Whisk egg whites until firm but not dry. Fold in.
8. Spoon into a large bowl, or 4 to 5 sundae glasses.

## FARMHOUSE CRUMBLE

*1½ lb. cooking apples*
*3 oz. butter*
*Water*
*Squeeze of lemon juice*
*1 to 2 tablespoons white sugar*
*8 oz. fresh white breadcrumbs*
*3 oz. light brown sugar*
*¼ pint whipping cream*
*Grated chocolate*

1. Peel, core and slice apples.
2. Cook gently in 1 oz. of the butter, and 1 tablespoon water, until soft. Some apples may need a little more water, but keep it to a minimum.
3. Sieve or liquidize, adding a squeeze of lemon juice, and the white sugar to taste. As the dish is

quite rich, keep the apple slightly tart. Cool.

4. Mix together crumbs and brown sugar.

5. Heat remaining butter and fry crumbs until crisp and butter is absorbed. Watch carefully to prevent excess browning. Cool.

6. Use a deep, rather than shallow dish, holding approximately 2½ pints. Place a layer of crumbs, then apples, then crumbs, and so on until used, leaving crumbs for top. Leave at least 12 hours as this will improve the flavour.

7. Whip cream lightly, pile on top.

8. Decorate with grated chocolate. Nicer if chilled for about 2 hours before serving.

## GOOSEBERRY FOOL

*1 lb. gooseberries*
*2 tablespoons sugar, or more*
*to taste*
*¼ pint whipping or double cream*

1. Cook gooseberries until soft. This is best done without water in a casserole with lid in a slow oven no higher than Gas 4, 350°F. If cooked in a saucepan add 1 tablespoon water, put on a very low heat and then strain away liquid when berries are cooked.

2. Sieve and then sweeten to taste. The puree should not be too thin.

3. Whip cream lightly, but not too stiff. Best results if puree and cream are same consistency.

4. When puree is cold, carefully fold together. A few drops of green colouring can be added during folding to enhance the colour.

## COMPÔTE OF FRESH ORANGES

*3 large or 4 smaller oranges*
*Water*
*4 oz. sugar*

1. Scrub oranges and score into 4 sections. Cover with boiling water and leave 5 minutes. Peel.

2. Reserve 4 to 5 sections of peel, cut away white pith and discard. Cut the remaining rind into very fine strips.

3. Place strips of rind in small pan of water, bring to boil, drain, and half-fill pan with fresh water. (This is to remove any bitterness). Simmer about 30 minutes, until really tender. Drain, discard water.

4. Place sugar and ¼ pint fresh water in pan, dissolve sugar over a low heat, bring to boil, simmer for 3 to 4 minutes until looking syrupy.

5. Add shredded peel, simmer 2 to 3 minutes.

6. Peel away any white pith from oranges, cut into thin slices, removing pips.

7. Place orange slices in serving dish, pour over syrup and shredded peel when quite cold. Chill a little before serving.

2 tablespoons of sherry or even a tablespoon of Grand Marnier, Orange Curaçao or Brandy can be used to cool syrup, and adds a very special flavour.

130

# CHAPTER 10

# FRUITS, JAMS, PICKLES, PRESERVES, CONFECTIONERY AND THE STORECUPBOARD

## BOTTLING

To achieve good results, it is essential to observe the recommended processing times.

### The Jars

Only proper bottling jars should be used and the discs must be in perfect condition to ensure correct sealing.

Sterilise jars and sealing discs beforehand. Rub the inside of metal rings with a little cooking oil.

### Fruit Preparation

All fruit should be in prime condition.

Most fruits bottle well and should be clean and cut into even-sized pieces. For example: Rhubarb, about 1 inch long. Pears, apricots and peaches skinned and halved. Plums can be bottled whole where small, but larger fruit, like Victoria plums, can be halved and stoned. Tomatoes are classified as fruit for the purpose of preservation and should always be skinned. Large tomatoes are better halved.

### The Syrup

Fruit can be packed in water but a syrup gives a better flavour and colour. A very heavy syrup may cause fruit to rise in jars. The maximum strength syrup is made with 8 ozs. sugar to 1 pint water, first dissolving the sugar over a low heat, then bringing to boiling point. Less sugar can be used according to taste. Syrup is used boiling when bottling by the Pressure Cooker Method but cold for the Slow Water Bath Method.

### Packing the Jars

Pack fruit firmly but without damaging into sterile bottling jars. Pour on the syrup or brine. Be sure that the fruit is covered and top of jar is clear from particles of fruit, seeds especially, before placing on sealing disc.

Screw metal ring on to jar. Give the ring a slight turn backwards to allow for expansion and prevent jars bursting during processing.

### Solid Pack

Tomatoes are best packed into jars with a sprinkling of salt and a very little sugar between each layer.

Apples, particularly windfalls, may also be bottled solid pack and are then ready for use in pies etc. Peel and core apples and remove all damaged parts. Cut into even-sized slices. Pack into jars sprinkling sugar between each layer. 3 teaspoons of sugar for the small bottling jars is sufficient.

### Pressure Cooker Method

Pressure Cooker must be deep enough when rack is in bottom to allow a space between bottling jars and lid.

Pour in about 1½ inches in depth of water and 1 tablespoon vinegar to prevent discolouration of pan. If more than one jar is to be processed at a time, place pieces of firm cardboard between them to prevent them touching each other and cracking.

Place lid on pan, without pressure control, over medium heat, and allow between 5 and 10 minutes for steam to escape through vent. Then place on 5 lb. valve weight, raise heat, bring to pressure and leave for recommended time.

All soft fruits, gooseberries, rhubarb and small plums require 1 minute processing.

Peaches, large plums, apricots and solid pack apples require 3 to 4 minutes depending on size.

Pears and whole tomatoes, 5 minutes.

Solid pack tomatoes, 15 minutes. After this time, remove pan carefully from heat, leave 15 minutes before removing valve weight.

Lift jars from pan and screw down tightly.

Do not touch the jars during the next ½ to 1 hour. The seal is not complete until the sealing disc goes pop and appears concave. Leave overnight before removing ring and testing seal.

Label jars indicating contents, date of processing and method used.

### Slow Water Bath Method

This method is perhaps better than the pressure cooker for preserving the colour and shape of the fruit or tomatoes, but is NOT to be used for vegetables as it does not kill the bacteria present in these.

Use a vessel deep enough to allow bottling jars to be immersed in water. A fish kettle is ideal, but any vessel, providing a rack is fitted in bottom, can be used.

Place jars in pan, cover completely with cold water. Insert thermometer, if used.

Raise from cold to required temperature in 90 minutes.

Soft fruits to 165°F. or until the odd bubble breaks on top of the water, maintain for 10 minutes.

Gooseberries, rhubarb, plums, apples, peaches, apricots: raise temperature to 180°F., maintain 15 minutes.

Pears and whole tomatoes: raise to 190°F. maintain 30 minutes.

Solid pack tomatoes: raise to 190° F. maintain 40 minutes.

After this time, remove jars, screw down, leave to seal.

Do not touch the jars during the next ½ to 1 hour. The seal is not complete until the sealing disc goes pop and appears concave. Leave overnight before removing ring and testing seal.

Label jars indicating contents, date of processing and method used.

### BOTTLING FRENCH OR RUNNER BEANS

1. Wash, slice and blanch beans.
2. Pack tightly into jars.
3. Make a brine by dissolving ½ oz. salt in 2 pints of boiling water. Pour the boiling brine over the beans.
4. Be sure that the beans are covered and that the top of the jar is clean from particles or seeds before placing on sealing disc.
5. Screw metal ring on to jar. Give a slight turn backwards to prevent jars bursting during processing.
6. Process in pressure cooker using 10 lb. valve weight following instructions above. Recommended time 35 minutes.

### BLACKBERRY SYRUP

1. Fruits should be sound but fully ripe.
2. The best method of extracting the juice is to place fruit in a casserole, adding ¼ pt. water to 3 lb fruit. Cover and leave in very slow oven for several hours. OR, fruit can be placed in a large bowl over a pan of simmering water for 2—3 hours.
3. Strain through 3 to 4 thicknesses of muslin. It will require 1 to 2 hours. The fruit can be gently pressed until all liquid is released.
4. Measure juice, allow ¾ lb. sugar to each pint and place in large pan. For flavouring, a few cloves or a piece of cinnamon stick tied in muslin can be added.
5. Heat to dissolve sugar. Do not boil.
6. Pour into sterile bottles to within 1½ inches of top. Place on screw tops, not too tightly.
7. Sterilize in deep vessel with false bottom, filling with cold water up to neck of bottle. Bring to simmering, 180°F. in one hour, maintain for 20 minutes.
8. Remove, screw down tops, label, store in dark, cool place.

### BLACKBERRY AND APPLE JAM

*4 lb. blackberries*
*½ pint water*
*1½ lb. prepared cooking apples*
*6 lb. sugar*

**Note:** The weight of the apples must be 1½ lbs. after peeling and coring.

1. Place the blackberries in a pan over a low heat, adding half the quantity of water and stew until tender.

2. Peel, core and slice the apples, put in another pan, add the remaining water and cook until quite soft.

3. Combine the two pulps in one pan.

4. **Make a Pectin Test.**

(a) Use a glass or china basin, or a clean cream carton will do. Measure into it 3 teaspoons methylated spirits and add 1 teaspoon from pan.

(b) Shake gently, leave 1 minute. If ready for sugar, a firm clot will result. If not, boil fruit pulp a few minutes, and test again.

5. Add the sugar and stir until dissolved and then boil rapidly until setting point is reached.

**Setting point** can be determined either by temperature, 220°F., or by a cold plate test as follows: Place no more than 1 teaspoon of the jam on a plate, allow to cool. The surface will crinkle when pushed with the finger if setting point is reached. Take care while conducting the test not to over-boil the rest of the jam.

6. Pour into hot, dry jars. Fill right to the top. Put on waxed disc immediately. Covers may be put on when jam is either hot or cold.

7. Label and store in a cool dark place.

Yield 10 lb.

## SEVILLE ORANGE MARMALADE
### In the Pressure Cooker

*2 lb. Seville oranges*
*2 lemons*
*Water*
*4 lb. sugar*

1. Scrub the oranges, and cut in half.

2. Remove pips and place these in a square of scalded muslin. Tie securely.

3. Shred oranges, place in pressure cooker without trivet. Add bag of pips.

4. Squeeze juice from lemons, make this up to 2 pints with water. Strain through a nylon strainer into pressure cooker.

5. Place lid on pressure cooker, bring to pressure. Place 10 lb. valve weight on top, and pressure cook for 10 minutes. This ensures that the peel is quite soft.

6. Remove from heat, leave 15 minutes when valve weight will remove easily.

7. Remove bag of pips and squeeze out any liquid. The contents of pressure cooker should measure 2¾ pints. It is advisable to make a pectin test.

8. **Pectin Test**

(a) Use a glass or china basin, or a clean cream carton will do. Measure into it 3 teaspoons methylated spirits and add 1 teaspoon from pressure cooker.

(b) Shake gently, leave 1 minute. If ready for sugar, a firm clot will result. If this is stringy, boil a few minutes without lid, and test again.

9. Add the sugar, stir until completely dissolved.

10. Place over heat, bring to a rolling boil, and boil to setting point 220°F. This will only take a short time, usually 10 to 15 minutes at the most.

If not using a thermometer, setting point can be determined by a cold plate test as follows: Place no more than 1 teaspoon of the marmalade on a plate, allow to cool. The surface will crinkle when pushed with the finger if setting point is reached. Take care while conducting the test not to over-boil the rest of the marmalade.

11. Remove from heat, allow to cool a little (15 to 20 minutes) until peel remains suspended when stirred and does not rise to the top.

12. Pour into dry, clean jars, place waxed disc on top immedi-

ately and then leave until quite cold.

13. Cover, label, and store in a cool, dark place.

Yield 6 lb.

## BUSY WOMAN'S MARMALADE

*4 seville oranges*
*1 large juicy orange*
*1 juicy lemon*
*6 pints water*
*5 lb. sugar*

1. Cut all fruit in halves across. Squeeze out juice and add this to 5 pints of the water.
2. Put pips in a jug with remaining 1 pint cold water and leave till the following day.
3. Cut the halved fruit cases in pieces to fit mincer. Put twice through mincer using finest blades. If you have an electric mincer or like a coarser marmalade you may prefer to put fruit only once through.
4. Put the minced fruit into the juice and water and leave to soak for 24 hours.
5. Then turn soaked fruit, juice and water into a preserving pan adding the strained water from the pips.
6. Bring to the boil and boil gently until peel is soft when pinched between finger and thumb.
7. Add sugar, bring to the boil again and boil rapidly until marmalade sets when tested.

**To test by the cold plate method:** Take out no more than a teaspoonful of the marmalade on to cold plate. Allow to cool. The surface should set and wrinkle when pushed with the finger. Do not allow the marmalade to boil rapidly while making this test or the setting point may be missed.

8. Allow to cool a little in pan but pot while still warm into clean, dry, warmed jars. Place on waxed tissue disc to cover surface completely. Cover jars with a clean cloth and leave till cold.
9. Fasten on jam pot covers, label and store in a cool, dark place.

## LEMON MARMALADE

A marmalade following the same method as Busy Woman's in which the fruit is soaked and minced but which may be made at any time of the year.

*4 lemons*
*1 sweet orange*
*(Total weight of fruit should be 1¼ to 1½ lbs.)*
*2½ lb. sugar*
*3 pints water*

1. Cut all fruit in halves across. Squeeze out juice and add this to 2½ pints of the water.
2. Put pips in a jug with remaining ½ pint of cold water and leave till the following day.
3. Cut the halved fruit cases in pieces to fit mincer. Put twice through mincer using finest blades. If you have an electric mincer or like a coarser marmalade you may prefer to put fruit only once through.
4. Put the minced fruit into the juice and water and leave to soak for 24 hours.
5. Then turn soaked fruit, juice and water into a preserving pan adding the strained water from the pips.
6. Bring to the boil and boil gently until peel is soft when pinched between finger and thumb.
7. Add sugar, bring to the boil again and boil rapidly until marmalade sets when tested.

**To test by the cold plate method:** Take out no more than a teaspoonful of the marmalade on to cold plate. Allow to cool. The surface should set and wrinkle when pushed with the finger. Do not allow the marmalade to boil rapidly while making this test or the setting point may be missed.

8. Allow to cool a little in pan but pot while still warm into clean, dry, warmed jars. Place on waxed tissue disc to cover surface

completely. Cover jars with a clean cloth and leave till cold.
9. Fasten on jam pot covers, label and store in a cool, dark place.

## GRAPEFRUIT MARMALADE

*2 large grapefruit (approximately 2 lb.); 1 lb. lemons; 4 pt. water; 3 lb. sugar.*

1. Wash fruit, peel thinly (a potato peeler helps) and cut peel finely with scissors.
2. Remove pith from fruit, cut up roughly.
3. Cut up flesh, reserving pips. This is best done on a deep plate to prevent loss of juice.
4. Tie pips and pith in scalded muslin, place in pan with water, peel, flesh and juice.
5. Simmer for two hours or until peel is very soft. The contents of the pan should be reduced by half.
6. Remove muslin bag on to a plate, cool, squeeze well to extract juice and add juice to pan. Test for pectin (see previous recipe).
7. Add warmed sugar, dissolve, boil until set is obtained. 220°F. is setting point or else use cold plate test, see previous recipe. Skim.
8. Allow to stand for 15 to 20 minutes to stabilise peel as this rises to top of jars if potted at once. Fill jars to top, place on waxed paper disc. Cover and label when cold.
Yield: Approximately 5½ lbs.

## APRICOT AND ALMOND JAM

*1½ lb. dried apricots; 4½ pt. cold water; 4½ lb. granulated sugar; 4 oz. almonds, blanched and halved; juice of large lemon.*

1. Snip apricot halves in about 4 pieces, soak 24 hours in the cold water.
2. Bring to boiling point and simmer gently for three quarters of an hour, stirring from time to time until apricot skins are soft and tender.
3. Add sugar, almonds and lemon juice, lower heat and stir until sugar has dissolved.
4. Boil rapidly for about half an hour until setting point is reached.
5. Cool until almonds are suspended then pot and place waxed paper disc on jam.
6. Cover when cold.
Yield: 7½ lbs.

## STRAWBERRY JAM

*2 lb. small, firm strawberries*
*2 lb. granulated sugar*
*Juice of 1 large lemon*

1. Hull strawberries, place with sugar, in layers, in a bowl. Pour over juice. Cover and leave for 24 hours.
2. Drain away juice into a large pan (a large sieve is a help.) Scrape in any undissolved sugar but keep strawberries aside.
3. Heat gently to dissolve sugar, bring to a brisk boil and boil to 220°F.
4. Add strawberries and any more drained-away juice. Boil again to 220°F. stirring as little as possible.
5. Pour carefully into a cold bowl and stir once or twice so that fruit mingles in syrup and stops rising to the surface.
6. When cool, pour into sterile jars. Place on waxed paper disc to cover surface of jam completely. Cover with a clean cloth and leave until quite cold.
7. Fasten on jam pot covers, label and store in cool, dark place.
This recipe does not make a firm jam but flavour is excellent.

## LEMON CURD

*4 oz. butter; 6 to 8 oz. castor sugar; 2 large lemons, rind and juice; 2 large eggs, beaten.*

1. Put butter, sugar, lemon rind and half of the strained lemon juice in the top part of a double saucepan with boiling water in the lower part

(or use a basin fitting well over a pan of water).

2. Stir well until butter has melted and sugar has dissolved.

3. Add remainder of strained lemon juice and beaten eggs.

4. Continue cooking over pan of simmering water, stirring frequently until mixture has thickened enough to coat the back of a spoon.

5. Pour into hot small jam jars — glass baby-food jars are ideal. Cover in the usual way.

Yield 1 lb.

Store in refrigerator if possible and use within 6 weeks.

N.B. Use 6 oz. of sugar for the curd if you like a sharp taste or if you prefer a sweeter lemon curd use 8 oz. sugar.

## FIG AND LEMON PRESERVE

*2 lb. figs*
*2 pt. cold water*
*3 lb. sugar*
*Rind and juice of 4 lemons*

1. Wash the figs, removing stalks, and cut into about 6 pieces.

2. Put them into a basin with the water and leave soaking for 24 hours.

3. Turn into a pan, add sugar and cook slowly until dissolved, then bring to the boil and remove the scum.

4. Wipe lemons and grate rind finely, squeeze out juice and strain it.

5. Add rind and juice to the figs and boil all together until a spoonful on a plate will jelly when cold. Keep it stirred and skimmed as required.

6. Cool, pot and, when cold, tie down.

Yield over 5 lb.

**Miss Peggy Mills,**
**Leicestershire.**

## MINCEMEAT

*1 lb. apples*
*½ oz. butter*
*8 oz. currants*
*8 oz. raisins*
*8 oz. sultanas*
*4 oz. candied peel*
*4 oz. dates, chopped small*
*8 oz. soft brown sugar*
*6 oz. grated suet*
*Grated rind and juice of 1 lemon*
*1 teaspoon cinnamon*
*½ teaspoon grated nutmeg*
*4 tablespoons rum*

1. Peel, core and finely chop apples.

2. Melt butter in pan, add apple and cook gently to soften. Allow to become cold.

3. Add rest of ingredients and mix all well together.

4. Leave in bowl, covered, stirring occasionally during next 24 hours.

5. Put in cold but sterile jars, do not fill quite to top. Place on waxed paper disc and cover with jam-pot covers. Label.

6. Store in cool, dry, dark place.

I find that cooking the apple helps mincemeat to keep longer. With raw apple it can ferment after a few weeks.

A cheaper version can be made—substituting chopped dates for raisins and omitting rum.

## APPLE OR CRAB APPLE JELLY

1. Choose crab apples or cooking apples with a decided flavour, or add a flavouring such as ginger, cloves or lemon peel. Windfall apples can be used.

2. Wash and cut up the fruit, removing any bad portions.

3. Put it in a saucepan with ginger, cloves or lemon peel to taste. Add just enough water to cover (2 to 3 pt. water to 4 lb. fruit) and simmer for about 1 hour.

4. Strain through a scalded jelly bag or several thicknesses of scalded muslin. Do not press. Allow to drip.

5. **Test for pectin:** Place 3 tea-spoons methylated spirits in a small container, add 1 teaspoon of juice. Shake gently, leave 1 minute. If a firm clot is obtained the correct amount of pectin is

present. If clot is stringy and broken, boil apple liquid to reduce water content and test again until correct. Discard samples.

6. Measure juice. Place in pan, add 1 lb. granulated sugar for each pint of juice.

7. Stir gently over low heat until sugar is dissolved.

8. Bring to boil and boil rapidly until setting point is reached, 220°F. or when a teaspoon or two will set on a cold plate.

9. Pour into small hot sterile jars, place waxed paper disc on top.

10. Can be covered at once with jam-pot covers or left covered with cloth until quite cold, then covers placed on.

11. Label and store in cool dark place.

## SUFFOLK DAMSON CHEESE

**Note:** Fruit cheese is very rich and should be potted in small quantities. Use small moulds or jars, even old cups, from which it can be turned out whole and served on a plate. The moulds should be warm and preferably smeared with glycerine on the inside so that the cheese will turn out easily.

1. Wash damsons well. Cover with water and stew well.

2. Rub flesh through sieve leaving stones and skins behind.

3. Measure pulp. Allow 1 lb. sugar to 1 lb. pulp.

4. Put pulp and sugar in pan and stir over low heat until sugar is dissolved.

5. Bring to boil and simmer gently until a spoon drawn across the bottom of the pan will leave a clean line.

6. Meanwhile, prepare the moulds or jars. See **Note** above.

7. Pour the cheese into moulds. Cover immediately with waxed paper discs. Cover with a clean cloth until cool and then put on jam covers.

Store at least a year before eating —if you can wait that long.

Turn out to serve. Decorate with blanched almonds to make a hedgehog. Serve whipped cream if desired.

It is also eaten with cold meats.

**Mrs. Nancy Leeson,
Horringer.**

## APPLE BUTTER

*3 lb. apples - crab apples or windfalls can be used.*
*1 pint cider or apple wine* **OR** *if you don't use cider or wine: ½ pt. water will be sufficient*
*Granulated sugar*
*Powdered cinnamon*
*Ground cloves*

1. Wash apples. Remove damaged parts if any, but do not peel or core. Cut into small pieces.

2. Place in pan with liquid. Cover and simmer until soft.

3. Sieve and weigh pulp. If very fluid, simmer in clean pan to thicken a little. Add ¾ lb. of granulated sugar for each 1 lb. of weighed pulp, and ½ a level teaspoon of powdered cinnamon plus ½ teaspoon of ground cloves.

4. Simmer gently until a spoon drawn across the mixture leaves its own impression.

5. Pot at once into sterile, hot jam jars. Place on waxed disc to cover surface completely. Cover with a clean cloth and leave until quite cold.

6. Fasten on jam pot covers, label and store in cool, dark place.

## BLACKBERRY AND APPLE JELLY

*3 lb. blackberries; 2 pt. water;*
*3 lb. sound cooking apples;*
*sugar.*

1. Wash fruit, slice apples thinly but do not peel, core or remove pips.

2. Place in large pan with water, simmer gently until quite soft, approximately 1½ hours.

3. Strain through a jelly bag (several

138

layers of muslin or fine woven cotton cloth will do). Do not press fruit, just allow juice to drip. It is advisable to scald jelly bag with boiling water before use as this speeds up the process of dripping which can take from 1 to 2 hours.

4. **Carry out a pectin test:** Put 3 teaspoons of methylated spirits in a small jar. Add 1 teaspoon of the mixture. Swirl it around. If a good clot is obtained the juice is ready for the next process, if a poor clot, boil to remove excess moisture and test again.

5. Measure juice, weigh out 1 lb. sugar to each pint and place sugar and jars to be used in a warm oven.

6. Heat juice in clean pan, stir in sugar and dissolve before bringing to boil.

7. Have thermometer in a pan of hot water. Boil jelly rapidly without stirring (as stirring causes bubbles to form in jelly). Place thermometer in pan of jelly and when it registers 220°F. remove pan from heat, skim away any scum and pot at once into hot jars. Place waxed paper disc on top.

8. Cool away from draughts. Cover and label when cold.

Do not use large jars for jelly as once opened it does not keep for any length of time.

**Recommended book on all methods of preservation:** "Home Preservation of Fruit and Vegetables", Bulletin 21, produced by Ministry of Agriculture, Fisheries and Food. Obtainable from H.M. Stationery Offices, or their suppliers.

## GENERAL NOTES ON MAKING PICKLES, CHUTNEYS AND SAUCES

**Vinegar:** Use a good quality malt vinegar, with a 5% acetic acid content for a good flavour and keeping quality.

**Pans:** Enamel lined, monel metal, aluminium or stainless steel pans should be used. Iron, brass or copper give an unpleasant taste to vinegar-based pickles and chutneys.

**Spoons:** Always wooden, not metal.

**Sieves:** Nylon, not metal.

**Jars:** Chutneys are better if stored and allowed to mature for a good 3 months. Any type of jar can be utilised providing it can be sealed correctly, as chutneys shrink with storage if air is allowed to penetrate. Waxed paper discs should be used, as for jams, but cellophane covers are not sufficient as an outer seal. Metal screw-tops should be lined with vinegar-resistant discs. Plastic coffee jar lids are ideal. If you have no suitable lids a good seal can also be obtained by pouring a little molten paraffin wax on top of the waxed paper disc. If you cover this with aluminium foil or a cellophane top the wax will remain clean and may be used again.

**Labels:** Should always be used, stating type of chutney, date and whether mild, sweet or hot.

**Fruit and vegetables for chutneys:** Should be chopped finely and, unlike fruit for making jams and jellies, need not always be of top quality. Try mixing different fruits and vegetables and produce your own individual flavours.

## PICCALILLI

*6 lb. prepared vegetables (a mixture of diced cucumber, marrow, beans, small onions, cauliflower florets and, if liked, green tomatoes)*
*1 lb. cooking salt*
*1 gallon water (optional)*

**Note**

(a) When preparing vegetables make sure they are cut to even sizes.

(b) Copper, brass or iron pans should not be used.

1. **Either** spread the prepared vegetables on a large dish and strew with salt between the layers and on top.

**Or** dissolve the salt in the water and place the prepared vegetables in this brine. Keep the vegetables submerged by a weighted plate or board.

2. After 24 hours, drain and rinse the vegetables and finish by one of the following methods:

### For Sharp Hot Piccalilli

*1 to 1½ oz. dry mustard*
*1 to 1½ oz. ground ginger*
*6 oz. white sugar*
*2 pt. vinegar, preferably white*
*¾ oz. flour or cornflour*
*½ oz. turmeric*

### For Sweet Mild Piccalilli

*¾ oz. dry mustard*
*1½ teaspoons ground ginger*
*9 oz. white sugar*
*3 pt. vinegar, preferably white*
*1½ oz. flour or cornflour*
*½ oz. turmeric*

3. Stir mustard, ginger and sugar into most of the vinegar.

4. Add the prepared vegetables and simmer until texture is as liked, either crisp or tender, but not hard or mashed.

5. Blend the flour and turmeric with the rest of the vinegar and then add to the other ingredients in the pan. Bring to the boil, stirring carefully, and boil for 2 to 3 minutes.

6. Pour into hot, dry screw-top jars, taking care that the lids are vinegar-proof. While still hot, place on waxed disc.

7. Cover jars with a clean cloth until quite cold. Screw on lids, label and store in a cool dark place.

If preferred, the vegetables can be strained out of the vinegar before the thickening is added. They are then packed into the jars, the liquid drained off and the piccalilli sauce added. It is difficult to avoid air pockets with this method but it allows more careful packing.

Keep 2 or 3 months before eating to allow to mature.

### PICKLED DAMSONS

*8 lb. damsons*
*4 lb. sugar*
*2 pints vinegar*
*½ oz. whole cloves*
*½ oz. allspice*
*¼ oz. root ginger*
*¼ oz. stick cinnamon*
*Rind of ½ lemon*

1. Wash and stalk the damsons, prick and place in a bowl.

2. Dissolve the sugar in the vinegar.

3. Crush the spices and tie them with the lemon rind loosely in a piece of muslin.

4. Put this into vinegar syrup and bring to the boil.

5. Pour the hot spiced vinegar over the damsons. Cover and leave 5 to 7 days.

6. Drain vinegar off the damsons, reboil it and pour back over the damsons. Cover and leave 5 to 7 days.

7. Once more drain the vinegar off the damsons, reboil and pour back over the damsons. Cover and leave 5 to 7 days.

8. Drain the vinegar off the damsons, reboil—allowing it to reduce and thicken slightly.

9. Pack the damsons into clean dry jars, pour the syrup over the fruit.

10. Cover immediately with vinegar proof lids.

This method ensures damsons remain whole and undamaged in the finished pickle.

This fruit can also be pickled in unsweetened spiced vinegar, the ingredients and method of pickling are as above omitting the sugar.

### Quicker Method

**Note:** With this method the damsons tend to burst and the result is not as good as the first method.

1. Wash and stalk the damsons.

2. Make the spiced vinegar as above.

3. Simmer the fruit in the spiced sweetened vinegar until tender, then drain the liquid from the fruit and pack the damsons neatly into jars.

4. Boil the vinegar gently until slightly thick and fill each jar with enough hot vinegar syrup to cover the fruit.

5. Cover with vinegar proof lid.

## PICKLED EGGS

For this you will need a wide-mouthed jar with a well-fitting vinegar-proof lid.

*6 eggs*
*1 pt. white vinegar, preferably wine or cider vinegar*
*1 oz. pickling spice*
*Small piece of bay leaf*

1. Put eggs into pan of cold water, bring to boil and boil 10 to 11 minutes according to size of eggs. Plunge them into cold water.

2. When cool remove shells and pack eggs loosely into jar.

3. Boil vinegar, spice and bay leaf for 10 minutes. Strain and allow to cool.

4. Pour over eggs in jar.

5. Cover with well-fitting vinegar-proof lid.

6. Leave 3 to 4 weeks before eating. Save the vinegar. It can be used for 2 or 3 batches of pickled eggs before going cloudy.

## SPICED VINEGAR FOR PICKLES

Either brown or white vinegar can be used depending on type of pickle. White vinegar is more expensive, but looks better with onions and cauliflower.

*2 pt. best vinegar (use the bottles for your finished product)*
*¼ oz. cinnamon bark*
*¼ oz. whole cloves*
*1 doz. peppercorns*
*¼ oz. whole mace*
*¼ oz. whole allspice*
*1 or 2 bay leaves*

Tie spices in small piece of muslin, place in vinegar and allow to steep for 1 to 2 months for a good flavour.

**Quick method:**

Place vinegar and spices in a glass or china bowl (not metal or polythene) standing in a pan of water. Cover bowl, bring water slowly to boil, remove from heat. Allow to get quite cold - at least 2 hours.

Spiced vinegar is used for most pickles. Those to be kept crisp should be covered with cold vinegar, softer types with hot vinegar.

## PICKLED ONIONS

1. Select small, even-sized onions. Place without peeling in a brine made from 1 lb. salt to 1 gallon of water. Place a plate on top to keep onions submerged.

2. Leave 12 hours, peel and place in fresh brine for 24 hours.

3. Drain thoroughly, pack into screw-top jars, and cover with cold, spiced vinegar which should be half an inch above onions. Cover securely with vinegar-resistant tops. For best flavour keep about 3 months before eating.

## PICKLED CAULIFLOWER

1. Select sound, firm, white cauliflowers, break heads into small pieces.

2. Place in brine (as for onions) leave 24 hours.

3. Drain well, pack into jars, cover with cold, spiced vinegar and seal as for pickled onions.

## PICKLED RED CABBAGE

1. Choose a firm cabbage of a good colour. Remove any discoloured outer leaves, cut cabbage into 4 portions, remove any very large white pieces. Shred finely.

2. Place on a large dish, layered with a good sprinkling of salt, using approximately 2 oz. coarse salt to each 1 lb. cabbage. Leave for 24 hours.

3. Drain well, rinsing away any surplus salt. Pack loosely into jars - cover with cold spiced vinegar. Tie down securely. (Kilner jars are good for storage.)

Suitable for eating after 1 week, but will lose its crispness after 3 months.

## PICKLED ORANGES

*4 oranges*
*¾ pt. water*
*Pinch of bicarbonate of soda*
*½ pt. white malt vinegar*
*½ lb. granulated sugar*
*1 teaspoon ground cloves*
*⅓ inch stick of cinnamon bark*
*A few whole cloves (optional)*

1. Wash oranges and place in pan with water and soda. Cover and simmer approximately 20 minutes but watch for signs of peel cracking.
2. Remove to plate and allow to cool. Reserve the water.
3. Cut into 8 wedges or 6 rings.
4. Make a syrup as follows: Measure ½ pt. of the orange water, add vinegar, sugar, ground cloves and cinnamon. Stir over gentle heat to dissolve sugar then bring to boil.
5. Add orange, a few pieces at a time, simmer until turning transparent, about 10 minutes.
6. Lift out and allow to drain on to a plate. Simmer remaining oranges and drain.
7. Pack into preserving or honey jars with screw tops (jam jars not recommended) and pour over hot syrup. Cover at once.
Whole cloves may be placed in jars to give added flavour.

## GREEN TOMATO PICKLE

Not a long-keeping pickle.

*3 lb. green tomatoes*
*2 tablespoons salt*
*1 pint vinegar*
*4 tablespoons black treacle*
*1 tablespoon made mustard*
*1 dessertspoon curry powder*
*½ teaspoon mixed spice*
*1 lb. onions*
*½ teaspoon cayenne pepper*

1. Wash tomatoes, slice thinly, layer in a bowl with salt. Allow to stand 24 hours.
2. In a large saucepan place

vinegar, treacle, mustard, curry powder and spice. Bring to boiling point.
3. Drain tomatoes and add to pan with thinly-sliced onions and cayenne pepper. Bring to boil again and simmer 10 minutes or until liquid is evaporated to desired consistency.
4. Pack into screw-top jars, preferably with plastic lids.

## GREEN TOMATO CHUTNEY (1)

*3 lb. green tomatoes*
*1 lb. apples*
*1 lb. marrow*
*1 lb. onions*
*4 oz. dates*
*8 oz. raisins or sultanas*
*2 lb. soft brown sugar*
*½ oz. salt*
*¼ teaspoon cayenne pepper*
*1 oz. root ginger*
*1 oz. mustard seeds*
*1½ pt. malt vinegar*

1. Wipe tomatoes, cut into small pieces.
2. Peel, core and chop apples.
3. Peel marrow, remove seeds, cut flesh into ½ inch cubes.
4. Peel and chop onions finely (or mince).
5. Chop dates finely.
6. Place prepared fruit and vegetables in pan with raisins or sultanas, sugar, salt and pepper.
7. Bruise the ginger, tie in a piece of muslin with mustard seeds and put into pan.
8. Add 1 pt. of the vinegar.
9. Stir over gentle heat to dissolve sugar, bring to boil, cover and simmer gently for approx. 2 hours stirring occasionally, adding more vinegar if mixture thickens before contents are quite soft.
10. To test, draw a wooden spoon across mixture, there will be a mark which should disappear slowly. If mixture is too thick add a little more vinegar and bring to boil. Chutney thickens a little on cooling.
11. Remove muslin bag and press out juices. Mustard seeds can be

added to mixture if you like them.
12. Pour into hot, sterile jars. Cover with waxed paper disc and leave until cold, covered with a cloth.
13. Use vinegar proof lids. If these are not obtainable, pour on 1 to 2 teaspoons of melted paraffin wax, allow to set, then cover with jam-pot covers. If chutney is not sealed, it will shrink on storage. Plain metal tops should not be used, as vinegar will corrode them.
14. Label and then store in a cool, dark place for at least 2 months before eating.

## GREEN TOMATO CHUTNEY (2)

*4 lb. green tomatoes*
*1 lb. apples*
*1¼ lb. shallots, or onions*
*½ lb. stoned or stoneless raisins*
*½ oz. dried whole ginger*
*12 red chillies*
*1 lb. brown sugar*
*½ oz. salt*
*1 pt. vinegar*

**Note:** Copper, brass or iron pans should not be used.
1. Cut up the tomatoes, peel and cut up the apples and shallots or onions and chop the raisins.
2. Bruise the ginger and chillies and tie in muslin bag.
3. Place all ingredients in pan. Bring to boil and simmer until all the vinegar has been absorbed, that is, when a spoon drawn across the mixture leaves its impression. Simmering may take 2 or more hours.
4. Remove the bag of spices and pour chutney into hot dry screw-top jars, taking care that the lids are vinegar proof. While still hot place on waxed disc.
5. Cover jars with a clean cloth until quite cold. Screw on lids, label and store in a cool dark place.
Yield about 7¼ lb.

## PRUNE CHUTNEY

*2 lb. prunes*
*1 lb. onions, sliced*
*1 oz. salt*
*1 teaspoon ground ginger*
*1 teaspoon cayenne pepper*
*2 oz. mustard seed*
*1 oz. mixed pickling spice*
*1 pint vinegar*
*1 lb. soft brown sugar*
1. Soak prunes for 48 hours in just enough water to cover.
2. Drain off water and remove stones.
3. Put prunes and onions through mincer into pan.
4. Add salt, ginger and cayenne pepper, also mustard seeds and pickling spices tied in muslin.
5. Add half the vinegar, bring to boil and simmer until mixture is thick.
6. Add sugar, stir to dissolve.
7. Add remaining vinegar.
8. Simmer until thick again. Chutney is ready if no liquid is visible when a wooden spoon is drawn through the mixture.
9. Pot at once into hot, sterile jars and place on waxed tissue disc. Leave until cold.
10. Cover with vinegar-proof lids or melted wax. Label and store in a cool dark place.

## RHUBARB AND DATE CHUTNEY

*4 lb. rhubarb*
*1 lb. dates*
*1 lb. onions*
*½ oz. ground ginger*
*2 oz. mixed ground spice*
*¼ oz. curry powder*
*½ oz. salt*
*2 lb. sugar (brown or white)*
*1½ pt. malt vinegar*
1. Cut up rhubarb, chop dates finely, mince or finely chop onions.
2. Place in pan, add spices, salt and sugar with ½ pt. of vinegar.
3. Simmer gently for at least 2 hours until tender, add a little more vinegar to prevent mixture sticking to pan.
4. Add most of the vinegar, simmer until mixture is thick and leaves no loose liquid when a spoon is drawn through. Rhubarb may be fairly moist and therefore up to ¼ pt.

vinegar may not be required. Reserve this amount until a final test is made.

5. Pot at once into hot, sterilised, screw-top jars, cover with waxed paper disc.

6. When cold cover with vinegar-proof lids. Label and store in cool dark place.

### SHROPSHIRE APPLE CHUTNEY

*4½ lb. apples, peeled and cored*
*2 lb. soft brown sugar*
*1½ lb. onions, chopped*
*1 quart malt vinegar*
*1½ lb. sultanas or raisins*
*1 oz. ground ginger*
*½ oz. garlic, crushed*
*1 oz. mustard seed*
*¼ oz. cayenne pepper*

1. Cut apples in small pieces, put in large pan with sugar, onions and vinegar.

2. Bring to boiling point, simmer until pulpy.

3. Add all other ingredients, simmer 10 minutes or until thick.

4. Bottle and cover with a waxed paper disc. Leave till cold.

5. Cover with vinegar-proof lids. Label and store in cool dark place. Leave to mature 3 months before using. Yield: 5 to 6 lbs.

### SAUCES    A Tip

These can be made from chutney, which is sieved and thinned down with a little vinegar at the rate of 1 pt. of chutney to ½ pt. vinegar. Spiced vinegar can be used instead of plain to give a more piquante flavour. The sauce is then boiled and poured through a funnel, into hot sterilised jars. Place in a good fitting cork boiled in readiness and dipped in molten paraffin wax to give a good seal. Alternatively vinegar-resistant screw-tops can be used. The Rhubarb and Date Chutney makes a pleasant brown sauce following this method.

### BEETROOT IN JELLY

*2 lb. beetroot*
*½ pint white vinegar*
*6 cloves*
*6 peppercorns*
*A small bay leaf*
*Half a packet of raspberry jelly*

1. Wash beetroot, trim stalks leaving 1 inch. Do not cut away root as beetroot "bleeds" when cooking if skin is pierced.

2. Pressure cook 20 to 25 minutes or boil for 1½ to 2 hours. Exact time depends on size of beetroots.

3. Allow to cool, rub away skin, trimming ends. Cut into half inch dice. Pack into jars.

4. Place vinegar and spices in a pan and cover. Bring to boil and simmer for 10 minutes, strain, discarding spices.

5. Pour on to jelly and dissolve it completely. Cool but do not allow to set.

6. Pour over beetroot covering completely. When set, put on waxed paper disc, screw on top (preferably non-metallic). If lids are not available pour over 2 to 3 teaspoons of melted paraffin wax and cover with jam-pot covers.

### TO MAKE HERB VINEGARS
*Tarragon, Thyme, Mint, Garlic or any mixture of your choice.*

1. Take a good handful of your chosen herb, bruise it well and then put it into a wide-necked glass jar (a bottling jar is suitable).

2. Cover with white vinegar. Put on a vinegar-proof lid.

3. Allow this to stand in full sunlight in a warm room for at least two weeks.

4. Then strain into vinegar bottles. A fresh sprig of the herb inserted into the bottle looks attractive. Label the bottles.

### LONG-KEEPING MINT SAUCE
*Mint leaves*
*For the syrup: ½ pint white vinegar to ½ lb. white sugar and a little green colouring.*

1. Gather a good quantity of mint, when about 18 inches high.
2. Wash and shake as dry as possible
3. Remove leaves from the stems and pass them through a liquidiser, a herb mill or fine plate of mincing machine.
4. Heat the vinegar, sugar and colouring to dissolve sugar and make the syrup.
5. Use a wide-necked jar with a vinegar-proof lid. Pack in a little mint then add a little syrup, which can be either hot or cold, and fill the jar in this manner. Cover. Make sure jar is tightly packed. If it is not packed tightly enough the mint may rise in the jar. Check the next day and top up with more mint if necessary.

This will keep 12 months or more. Use as required adding extra vinegar to taste.

## LONG-KEEPING HORSERADISH SAUCE

*Horseradish*
*For the syrup: ½ pt. white vinegar to ½ pt. white sugar and a little salt.*
1. Dig horseradish root in mid-summer.
2. Wash well and peel under water, (to avoid severe eye-watering).
3. Cut the root up roughly and put through finest cutters of mincer.
4. In meantime make syrup by dissolving the sugar and salt in the vinegar over a low heat. Allow to go cold.
5. Use a wide-necked jar with vinegar-proof lid. Pack in a little horseradish then add a little syrup and fill the jar in this manner. Make sure it is tightly packed and no air spaces are left.

This will keep 12 months or more. To serve: To a tablespoonful of horseradish add same quantity of thick cream and extra vinegar to taste.

Use with roast beef or beef dishes. Also very good with cold ham.

## DRYING HERBS

Most herbs should be gathered for drying just before they flower.
1. Gather in fairly large bunches, wash in clear water and swing to dry.
2. For large-leafed herbs like sage and mint take the leaves off the stem. Small leaved herbs like thyme and winter savory can be left on stem. Put leaves into a large piece of butter muslin.
3. Have ready a large pan of fast boiling water. Holding the four corners of the butter muslin plunge the leaves into water for about 10 seconds.
4. Lift out and lay cloth on cake cooling racks. Spread herbs out evenly.
5. Put racks into a **very** cool oven, leaving the door ajar, for 2 to 3 hours. They should be brittle when cold.
6. Rub large-leafed varieties through a fine mesh sieve and crush small-leafed varieties between your hands discarding the stems. Sieve if necessary. If there is any leatheriness, return to oven or leave in airing cupboard overnight.

Always store dried herbs away from light, preferably in dark bottles with tight lids.

### To Dry Parsley

This method preserves Vitamin C and good green colour.
1. Blanch without thick stems and then put into a baking tin, (without muslin).
2. Dry in a hot oven, 425°F., Gas 7, for about 7 to 10 minutes. Keep turning to prevent burning at the edges.

### To Dry Fennel Stems

Cut stems in Autumn into short lengths and leave in airing cupboard for about 48 hours.

These are used to infuse in milk when making fennel sauce to accompany fish.

## FUDGE

*½ lb. butter; 2 lb. granulated sugar*
*1 large tin evaporated milk; half the*
*milk tin of water.*

1. Place all ingredients in a large heavy saucepan.
2. Stir gently over a low heat until the sugar is quite melted.
3. Bring to boil and boil steadily stirring occasionally, until thermometer reaches 238º–240ºF. or "soft ball" stage. The mixture can be tested by dropping a teaspoon of fudge into half a cup of cold water, and testing with finger and thumb. When ready, it will hold together in a soft ball.
4. Remove from heat, dip base of pan in cold water to check cooking. Leave five minutes. Beat with a wooden spoon until the mixture loses its gloss, looks "grainy", thickens a little and will just pour from pan.
5. Pour into a buttered or oiled shallow tin (12 inch by 7 inch is suitable). Leave until cold and nearly set. Cut into squares.

## TOFFEE

(without a thermometer)
*¼ lb. butter; ½ lb. granulated sugar;*
*2 tablespoons vinegar; 2 level*
*tablespoons golden syrup.*

Use a heavy pan, not too small, as the mixture froths a little.

1. Place butter in pan over heat to begin melting. Add rest of ingredients, stir until sugar is melted.
2. Bring to boil and boil briskly, stirring very occasionally, until mixture turns golden brown.
3. Pour into a greased, shallow tin, (7 inches square is a suitable size).
4. Mark into squares before quite set. It will then break more easily.

## CHOCOLATE TRUFFLES

*4 oz. plain cooking chocolate;*
*½ oz. butter; 4 oz. icing sugar;*
*4 oz. sieved cake crumbs, or plain,*
*semi-sweet biscuits, crumbled and*
*sieved; 1 egg yolk; 2-3 tablespoons*
*rum; chopped walnuts, chocolate*
*vermicelli or sweetened chocolate*
*powder.*

1. Place broken chocolate and butter to melt in a large basin over a pan of hot but not boiling water. Make sure bowl does not touch water.
2. Remove bowl from pan, stir in sifted icing sugar, crumbs and then egg yolk. Add rum to taste. If mixture is a little soft, leave 5–10 minutes to firm up.
3. Roll into balls the size of a small walnut.
4. To finish, roll the balls in finely chopped nuts or chocolate vermicelli or chocolate powder and leave to harden before placing in sweet papers.

## PEPPERMINT CREAMS

*1 egg white; 1 lb. icing sugar;*
*oil of peppermint or peppermint*
*concentrate; plain cooking*
*chocolate, optional*

1. Beat the egg white until frothy but not stiff.
2. Sieve icing sugar, mix with egg white and add peppermint to taste. The exact amount of icing sugar needed depends upon the size of the egg white. Mix and knead to a firm paste.
3. Roll out on a board well dusted with sifted icing sugar. Cut small rounds. Or, make small balls and flatten them with a fork. Place on waxed paper, (use the paper from a cornflakes packet). Leave overnight.
4. The plain round sweets may at this stage be dipped in melted chocolate to give a half coating. Place on waxed paper to allow to set.

## TO CANDY FRUIT

Use fruit of a distinct flavour e.g. pineapples, apricots, plums, dessert pears, crab apples, orange and lemon peel. Angelica stems. Fresh ginger root.

**Using canned or bottled fruit:**

1. Take ½ pint syrup from the can (or bottle). To it add 8 oz. sugar, in a saucepan and bring to the boil. Great care should be taken all through process to stir sugar and dissolve it before boiling point is reached. Pour boiling syrup over the drained fruit in basin. Cover with weight to keep fruit below surface of liquid. As much fruit as possible should be used, but must be submerged in syrup. Leave 24 hours.

2. Strain syrup from fruit into pan and add 2 oz. sugar. Stir and boil and pour over fruit. Cover and leave for 24 hours.

3. Repeat for 2 more days adding 2 oz. sugar daily.

4. On fifth day, drain syrup and add 3 oz. sugar, stir and boil. Then add the fruit to boiling syrup and simmer for 3 or 4 minutes. Return all to basin and leave for 2 days.

5. Then repeat the 3 oz. sugar and re-boil once more. Leave for 3 or 4 days in the heavy syrup.

6. Lift out pieces of fruit and spread separately on a cake cooling rack over a tin to catch drips and dry in a cool oven (not more than 120°F.) with door open for 3 hours, or for a longer period in an airing cupboard. Fruit should feel dry on surface when cool.

**To crystallise candied fruit:**

Dip each piece in boiling water and shake, then roll in sugar. Re-dry.

**To glacé:** Make fresh syrup of 8 oz. sugar to ⅛ pint water. Dissolve sugar then bring to boil and dip each piece of fruit quickly into syrup and spread to dry on cake cooling rack for about 1 hour. This results in a hard coating of sugar on the surface.

**For fresh fruit:** Cook until just tender, but not broken. Take ½ pint of water in which fruit was cooked and add 8 oz. sugar, dissolve and cook fruit for a minute and then allow to stand for 3 days. Then proceed as for canned fruit starting with 8 oz. sugar.

The left over syrup can be used to stew other fruit in season. Can be used in a cake mixture or as a base for sauce for ice cream or pudding.

### HOME-MADE BREAKFAST CEREAL—MUESLI

*1 to 2 oz. dried apricots*
*½ oz. hazelnuts, walnuts, or both*
*2 to 3 oz. soft brown sugar*
*3 oz. sultanas*
*3 oz. raisins*
*12 oz. good quality porridge oats or rolled oats*
*1 to 2 oz. porridge wheatmeal or wheat, rye or barley flakes\**
*½ to 1 oz. bran or millet\**
*(\*optional, but try at least one of them)*

**Note:** It is worth visiting a high class grocer or health food shop or a shop dealing in whole or natural foods for the oats, etc. There is a wide selection of interesting ingredients available.

1. Cut the apricots into small pieces and chop the nuts roughly.

2. Mix all ingredients together adjusting the fruit, nut and sugar content to suit the quantity of cereal ingredients. Don't be mean with the fruit.

3. Keep in a large covered bowl or tin to use when required.

4. **To serve:** The night before, place the quantity required in a bowl and pour on just enough milk to cover.

5. Next morning, add a little top of the milk. It is good to eat like this but even better with grated fresh apple, sliced banana or stewed fruits.

## The essentials in
### DOROTHY SLEIGHTHOLME'S STORECUPBOARD

Plain flour
Self-raising flour
Strong plain flour
Soft plain flour
Wholemeal flour

Baking powder
Bicarbonate of soda
Cream of Tartar

Cornflour
Arrowroot

Granulated sugar
Castor sugar
Vanilla sugar
Soft brown sugar
Demerara sugar
Icing sugar
Golden syrup

Currants
Raisins
Sultanas
Candied peel
Glacé cherries
Dates
Dried fruit salad

Mixed spice
Powdered cinnamon
Cloves
Ground ginger
Whole nutmeg
Plain cooking chocolate

Cooking salt
Savoury salt
Pepper
Peppercorns
Mustard

Curry powder
Mixed herbs
Bay leaves
Sage
Garlic
Stock cubes
Tomato purée

Cooking/salad oil
Vinegars
Plastic lemon
Salad cream
Worcestershire Sauce

Tea
Coffee
Cocoa

Macaroni
Spaghetti
Rice
Semolina

Gelatine
Jelly squares

Oatmeal
Porridge oats

Dried milk powder
Evaporated milk
Cream

Dried peas
Lentils

Shredded suet

Parmesan cheese

Condensed soup
Sardines
Ham
Sweetcorn
Tomatoes
Vegetables

Mandarin oranges
Pineapple rings
Grapefruit segments
Orange juice

Butter
Margarines
Lard
Yeast
Cheese
Eggs
Bacon

### Home-made essentials:
Jams
Jellies
Pickles
Chutneys

Dried breadcrumbs

Dripping

Stock*
Fresh breadcrumbs*
*kept in freezer

148

# CHAPTER 11

# HOME-MADE WINE BEER AND POP

## WINE
## YEAST STARTER

Successful wine-making depends largely upon a successful fermentation. To help achieve this the yeast should already be working actively when it is required.

A yeast starter is prepared as follows:

½ pt. cold boiled water
l level tablespoon light dried malt extract
1 teaspoon sugar
Acid (Tartaric, Malic or Citric) sufficient to cover one New Penny piece
Yeast nutrient, sufficient to cover one New Penny piece
The yeast recommended in recipe.

Mix the ingredients, stir well until completely dissolved. Pour into a small sterilized bottle and plug the top with cotton wool. Leave at a fairly constant temperature, ideally 65º to 70º, until working actively.

## HOCK-TYPE GOOSEBERRY WINE – One Gallon

Water
2 tablespoons light dried malt extract
2 lb. sugar
¼ oz. Tartaric acid
¼ oz. Malic acid
¼ oz. Citric acid
†Yeast energiser or nutrient
†Grape tannin
†Pectin reducing enzyme
†For quantities, follow manufacturer's instructions.

2 lb. green hard gooseberries
Hock, Champagne or General Purpose yeast*
5 Campden tablets

1. 48 hours before you begin to make the wine prepare a yeast starter using one of the yeasts suggested. See method above.
2. Bring to boil 6 pts. or so of cold tap water, then remove from heat and allow to cool. When cool, pour into a sterilized plastic bucket and then dissolve into it all the ingredients except the gooseberries, yeast and Campden tablets. Stir well to ensure that everything has thoroughly dissolved. Allow mixture to become cold, that is, room temperature. Now aerate it well by pouring back and forth into another sterilized container, but finishing in the plastic bucket.
3. Meanwhile, wash the gooseberries well, preferably in sulphited water (3 Campden tablets per gallon), then rinse well to remove any sulphite. Cut the berries in half with stainless steel knife, and drop into the now cold mixture in the plastic bucket. Finally add the yeast starter preparation. It is important that this is working properly before it is added. Stir well, cover closely and set aside to ferment for 24 to 36 hours.
4. After 24 to 36 hours, strain off the pulp into a sterilized one gallon glass fermenting vessel. A fine cotton muslin or a piece of cotton sheeting is ideal, but do not squeeze the liquid through. Top up with cold boiled water to one gallon, fit air-lock and allow fermentation to proceed to dryness at a fairly constant temperature, ideally 65º to 70ºF. This should take from three to four weeks, no longer. The time taken depends upon temperature and care with which the must* has been prepared.
5. When fermentation ceases, carefully rack* from the lees* into another sterilized 1 gallon jar, without introducing air into the wine. Top up jar with similar wine, or if the space is small, with cold boiled water. Add 1 Campden tablet, fit airlock and set aside in cool, dark place to clarify.

6. In 5 to 6 weeks the wine should be quite clear. Rack it off its lees once again, top up jar, add 1 Campden tablet, cork jar well and leave preferably for about a month before drinking. It will improve somewhat with keeping for a few months but no great improvement will occur as the wine will already be fine and good for drinking. Always serve the wine well cooled. It then tastes much better.

**Points to remember**
DON'T at any time use hot water
DON'T use more than 2 lb. sugar
DON'T ferment on the pulp for more than 24 to 36 hours
DON'T squeeze the fruit when straining off
DON'T expect the same results if you alter the recipe
DO make sure all equipment and fermenting vessels have been sterilized and rinsed well with cold tap water before use
DO make sure your yeast starter is active before starting wine making
DO be accurate with the quantities, particularly the acid
**\*Yeast**
It is always recommended that you use a true wine yeast, either liquid, dried or in tablet form. Liquid cultures are best.
**\*Must**
The pulp, juice or combination of basic ingredients from which wine is made.
**\*Rack**
To syphon the wine off the lees.
**\*Lees**
The deposit of yeast and solids formed during and after fermentation.

**BILBERRY WINE**
**as a Dry Red Wine.**

*1 large (2 lb. 2 oz.) jar
Bilberries in Syrup; If using fresh or frozen bilberries 1 lb. is needed. Allow also an extra 5 oz. sugar as a substitute for the syrup in the jar. If using dried bilberries 4 oz. are needed with an extra 5 oz. sugar as syrup substitute.
⅓ kilo (approx. ¾ lb. or 9 fluid oz.) Red Grape Concentrate; 1½ lb. sugar; 1 only 3 mg Vitamin B.I. tablet; yeast nutrient and pectin reducing enzyme (follow manufacturer's instructions for 1 gallon of wine); active yeast starter using General Purpose Wine Yeast\*; Campden Tablets; cold boiled water.*

**As a Sweet Dessert Wine**
**(1 gallon)**
*1 large (2 lb. 2 oz.) jar Bilberries in Syrup; If using fresh or frozen bilberries 1 lb. is needed. Allow also an extra 5 oz. sugar as a substitute for the syrup in the jar. If using dried bilberries 4 oz. are needed with an extra 5 oz. sugar as syrup substitute.
⅔ kilo (approx. 1½ lb. or 18 fluid oz.) Red Grape Concentrate; 2 lb. 6 oz. sugar; 3 only 3 mg Vitamin B.1. tablets; yeast nutrient and pectin reducing enzyme (follow manufacturer's instructions for 1 gallon of wine); active yeast starter using General Purpose Wine Yeast\*; Campden Tablets; cold boiled water.*

1. At least 3—4 days before you begin to make the wine, prepare yeast starter following directions on page 150.
2. Make sure that all the equipment is clean and sterilized. If the fruit is fresh, frozen or dried, wash well in a sulphited solution (3 Campden Tablets to the gallon of water) to kill wild yeasts and clean the fruit. Rinse several times in fresh cold water.

3. Have on hand about 6 pints cold boiled water.

4. Put the fruit in syrup and the grape concentrate into a fermenting bucket. Dilute with about 2 pints of the cold boiled water. (If using fresh, frozen or dried bilberries the additional 5 ozs. sugar should be made into syrup with less than ½ pint water and added with the fruit). Stir well to mix the concentrate. Then add the Vitamin B.1. tablet, yeast nutrient, pectin reducing enzyme and yeast starter. Cover closely and leave in a warm place to ferment for about 36 hours.

5. Strain off through fine mesh, sterilized muslin or cloth, to separate fruit, and pour into a 1 gallon glass fermenting jar.

### 6. (As a dry red wine)
Meanwhile, make a syrup of the sugar using 3 pints of cold boiled water.

### 6.(As a sweet dessert wine)
Meanwhile, make a syrup of 1½ lbs. of the sugar using 3 pints of cold boiled water.

7. Mix this syrup into contents of the glass jar, shake well, and then make up to about seven pints with cold boiled water. Fit airlock, stand jar in warm place, and allow to ferment. The fermenting must will form a thick sticky head, but because the jar is not full, this will not percolate through the airlock.

### 8. (As a dry red wine)
When, after a few days, the froth-ing head has subsided, add the balance of the cold boiled water, making it up to about one gallon. Leave to ferment right out, which should take some three weeks at the most.

### 8. (As a sweet dessert wine)
When, after a few days, the froth-ing head has subsided, gradually make up the contents of the jar to one gallon with syrup made from cold boiled water and the remaining sugar. This syrup must be intro-duced with care to the fermenting must and a little at a time, because there is usually a lot of frothing which can come over the top if too much is put in at once. Leave in a warm place to ferment right out. It will take about three months.

9. When fermentation finishes, allow to stand for a few days so that the majority of the suspended matter falls to the bottom.

10.The new raw wine is now ready for racking. This means taking the reasonably clear wine off the heavy deposit which is on the bottom of the jar. In doing this, be careful to use tubing, and **never, never** pour it from one jar to the other. Syphon the clear wine off leaving the deposit in the original jar, then top up the new jar with, at worst, cold boiled water, and at best, with wine of a similar nature. Add one Campden Tablet, fit airlock, and set aside in a cool dark place to clear.

11.After a few weeks, clarity should have come. You can then rack the wine off again, following exactly the same procedure as before. Don't forget to top the jar up again, cork it and then leave in dark place to mature for as long as you can.

12.When you come to drink the wine carefully syphon the whole lot off into bottles which should be sealed with good fitting corks, and store in a cool dark place.

### Dry Red Wine
After 2 months there will be an appreciable increase in quality. Quality will improve up to a year when the wine will be very good. After this further improvement is not likely. Drink before two years.

### Sweet Dessert Wine
If in the end the wine is not sweet

enough, then add some **invert** sugar just prior to drinking, at the rate of 1 oz. to 4 ozs. per bottle according to taste.

Dessert Wine is likely to take 6 months longer maturing than the table wine to reach the same relative quality. It will be very good if you can wait a year before drinking.

## WASSAIL

*6 cooking apples*
*Soft brown sugar*
*½ oz. ground ginger*
*Half a grated nutmeg*
*Pinch of powdered cinnamon*
*8 oz. Demerara sugar*
*3 pt. ale, mild or brown*
*½ bottle raisin wine, or ¼ bottle*
*sherry*
*1 lemon*
*Lump sugar*

1. Core apples but do not peel them. Fill the holes with soft brown sugar and roast in oven Gas 3, 325°F. for 45 minutes to 1 hour. Take care they do not burst.
2. Mix in a saucepan ginger, nutmeg, cinnamon and Demerara sugar. Add 1 pint of the ale and bring to boil.
3. Stir in the rest of the ale, the wine and 10 lumps of sugar that have been rubbed on the rind of the lemon. Heat the mixture but do not allow it to boil this time.
4. Put the roasted apples in a bowl, pour in the hot ale mixture with half the peeled and sliced lemon.

## MULLED WINE
### Excellent on a cold winter's evening
*Pinch of nutmeg*
*3 tablespoons brown sugar*
*Juice and rind of 1 lemon or orange*
*1 stick of cinnamon*
*3 cloves*
*½ pt. hot water*
*1 bottle of dry red wine—such as elderberry or blackberry, but if*
*you have to buy a bottle a cheap dry red table wine will do*
1. Simmer all the ingredients except wine for 20 minutes, then add wine. Reheat but do not boil.
2. Serve immediately in thick glasses.

## SPARKLING WINES
Sparkling wines are produced by starting a secondary fermentation, in the bottle, in a basic wine which has been made for the purpose. The Elderflower, Gooseberry, White Currant and Apple Wines given here, if prepared strictly according to the instructions, can be made into sparkling wine. They will however make good drinking even if you do not make them into sparkling wines.

**Four important rules** upon which depends success in making sparkling wines:—
1. The basic wine is dry and has finished fermenting.
2. The alcoholic content of the basic wine is not really more than 10% by volume, which is equivalent to a **total** sugar content of about 2 lbs. per gallon including the sugar of the ingredients.
3. The yeast used as a primer in the secondary fermentation is active and will do its job.
4. No more sugar is added to each bottle for the secondary fermentation than is strictly recommended.
**Failure** to observe the first and fourth rules can bring disastrous consequences due to excess pressure, namely exploding bottles.
**Failure** to observe the second and third rules will result in a non-sparkling wine.

### Elderflower
1 gallon
*Champagne yeast culture*
*Cold boiled water*
*1 pint fresh elderflowers*
*2 tablespoons light dried malt extract*
*½ oz. wine acid (a mixture, if*

*possible, of citric, malic, and tartaric) OR juice of 2 good lemons*
*Yeast nutrient, quantity as given by manufacturer*
*2 lb. sugar*
*Campden tablets*

1. 48 hours before you begin to make the wine prepare a yeast starter using the Champagne yeast culture. The best results in wine making are derived from liquid yeast cultures. Instructions to prepare a starter may come with the culture. (If not, see page 150).
2. Choose if possible white, not cream-coloured, flowers.
3. Pick on a dry, fine day. Flowers deteriorate so quickly that this is quite necessary.
4. Lightly dry the flowers in the sun, if possible, to facilitate stripping and shake each head well to remove maximum pollen. (Too much pollen in the wine may make it hazy.)
5. Strip off all the petals into suitable 1 pint measuring vessel. The taste of elderflowers is quite powerful, and overdoing things will not help, unless you particularly like the extra flavour.
6. Having previously boiled some water and allowed it to become cold, pour about six pints of it into a plastic bucket, and into this dissolve the malt extract, wine acid (or lemon juice), yeast nutrient and sugar.
7. Add the actively working yeast starter, then the flowers. Stir well.
8. Cover closely and leave for 36 to 48 hours to ferment. Stir at intervals, about 2 or 3 times a day. Do make sure you don't forget any of the ingredients. Flower wines have no yeast foods or nutrients in them, consequently these must be added. Failure to do this might result in the fermentation not being completely successful, which is most important when making sparkling wines.

9. After 36 to 48 hours strain off through a fine cloth, pour into a 1 gallon glass fermenting vessel, top up with cold boiled water, fit airlock and allow to ferment to dryness. This should be about 3 weeks if the must* has been prepared properly and the fermentation temperature is correct at 65° to 70°F.
10. When fermentation has ceased, carefully rack* the wine off the lees*, into another 1 gallon jar, without introducing air. That is, with rubber tubing, syphon from one jar to another without splashing the wine, leaving the sediment at the bottom of the jar.
11. Top up the new jar with similar wine, right to the top, or in the absence of similar wine and if the space is small, cold boiled water. Add 1 Campden Tablet, and set aside in cool dark place to clarify.
12. In five or six weeks the wine should be quite clear. Rack it off its lees once again, top up the jar, close neck with a cork or well-fitting lid, and set aside.

This wine should now be quite dry to the taste, i.e. without any taste of sweetness, and if tested with a hydrometer, the hydrometer reading should certainly read below 1000.

If the wine does taste sweet, and the hydrometer reading is quite above 1000, or if there has been any sign of slackening of the fermentation at an early stage, then do not proceed with the sparkling wine making, with this batch.

However, if all is well, and there is no reason why it should not be if the wine has been made properly and allowed to ferment in the proper temperature of some 65° to 70°F. then at this stage the wine is ready for converting into sparkling wine. Turn to page 157.

**Gooseberry**
1 gallon

   *See page 151.*

*Champagne yeast culture*
*Cold boiled water*
*2 tablespoons light dried*
*malt extract*
*1 lb. 14 oz. sugar*
*½ oz. wine acid (a mixture, if*
*possible, of tartaric, malic and*
*citric)*
*Grape tannin, enough to cover a*
*Half New Penny piece*
*Yeast nutrient, quantity as given*
*by manufacturer*
*Pectin reducing enzyme, quantity*
*as given by manufacturer*
*2 lb. green hard gooseberries*
*Campden tablets*

1. 48 hours before you begin to make the wine prepare a yeast starter using the Champagne yeast culture. The best results in wine making are derived from liquid yeast cultures. Instructions to prepare a starter may come with the culture. If not, see page 150.

2. Bring to boil 6 pts. or so of cold tap water, then remove from heat and allow to cool. When cool, pour into a sterilized plastic bucket and then dissolve into it all the ingredients except the gooseberries, yeast and Campden tablets. Stir well to ensure that everything has thoroughly dissolved. Allow mixture to become cold, that is, room temperature. Now aerate it well by pouring back and forth into another sterilized container, but finishing in the plastic bucket.

3. Meanwhile, wash the gooseberries well, preferably in sulphited water (3 Campden tablets per gallon), then rinse well to remove any sulphite. Cut the berries in half with stainless steel knife, and drop into the now cold mixture in the plastic bucket. Finally add the yeast starter preparation. It is important that this is working properly before it is added. Stir well, cover closely and set aside to ferment for 24 to 36 hours.

4. After 24 to 36 hours, strain off the pulp into a sterilized one gallon glass fermenting vessel. A fine cotton muslin or a piece of cotton sheeting is ideal, but do not squeeze the liquid through. Top up with cold boiled water to one gallon, fit air-lock and allow fermentation to proceed to dryness at a fairly constant temperature, ideally 65° to 70°F. This should take from three to four weeks, no longer. The time taken depends upon temperature and care with which the must* has been prepared.

5. When fermentation ceases, carefully rack* from the lees* into another sterilized 1 gallon jar, without introducing air into the wine. Top up jar with similar wine, or if the space is small, with cold boiled water. Add 1 Campden tablet, fit airlock and set aside in cool, dark place to clarify.

6. In 5 to 6 weeks the wine should be quite clear. Rack it off its lees once again, top up the jar, close neck with a cork or well-fitting lid. Set aside.

This wine should now be quite dry to the taste, i.e. without any taste of sweetness, and if tested with a hydrometer, the hydrometer reading should certainly be below 1000.

If the wine does taste sweet, and the hydrometer reading is quite above 1000, or if there has been any sign of slackening of the fermentation at an early stage, then do not proceed with the sparkling wine-making, with this batch.

However, if all is well, and there is no reason why it should not be if the wine has been made properly and allowed to ferment in the proper temperature of some 65°-70°F. then at this stage the wine is ready for converting into sparkling wine.

**White Currant**
1 gallon
*Champagne yeast culture*

155

Cold boiled water
1½ lb. sugar
Yeast nutrient (¾ amount
recommended by manufacturer
for 1 gallon)
Pectin-reducing enzyme, quantity
as given by manufacturer
¼ oz. malic acid, optional (for
those who like a high acid
finish)
Campden tablets

The method is the same as for Gooseberry but it is necessary only to remove the stalks from the currants after washing and rinsing and then to squeeze the fruit gently in order to burst the berries. Do not pound them to pulp.

## Apple
1 gallon

The trouble with apple wine is that there are so many varieties of apples, some of which are of general poor quality, particularly "Seedlings", that you have to be more specific about the recipe. Cookers or Eaters on their own tend not to make the best wine. About two thirds eaters for flavour, and one third cookers for crispness and freshness (acidity) are about right, alternatively, **cultivated** crab apples the "John Downie" variety are superb on their own, or perhaps other cultivated crabs, with the same virtues as the John Downie, that is—a good flavour level, neither sweet nor over sharp, and with some tannin in them. Perhaps this is why John Downies make the finest Crab Apple Jelly. However, we want a mixture of flavours and acidity just as these provide.

Champagne yeast culture
Approx. 8 lb. prepared apples
(do not use windfalls, see
paragraph 1)
1¼ lb. sugar
Pectin-reducing enzyme, quantity
as given by manufacturer
Yeast nutrient, quantity as given
by manufacturer
Grape tannin, enough to cover a

Half New Penny piece (not
required if crab-apples are used)
Cold boiled water
Campden tablets

NOTE: The exact quantity of sugar is adjustable according to the sweetness in the apples used. Ideally the hydrometer should read 1080 when the juice and the sugar are added together—however pulp fermentation makes this somewhat difficult so some skill in judgement is required, as all apples contain some sugar. It is better to be on the low side than on the high side.

1. 48 hours before you begin to make the wine prepare a yeast starter using the Champagne yeast culture. See page 150
2. Wash the apples well in sulphited water (3 Campden tablets per gallon), remove all dirt, air pollution, and other foreign substances. Rinse or wash well in clear cold water. Inspect all the apples for badly bruised or torn skins and cut out the affected parts, hence the reason for not using windfalls. Bruised apples with broken skins usually have infections which can lead to poor tasting wine or even vinegar.
3. Put about 4 pints of previously boiled and now cold water into a sterilized plastic bucket. To this add one crushed Campden tablet.
4. Now crush apples, or chop with stainless steel knife, and quickly drop crushed or chopped apple into the cold water, submerging completely. This will help prevent the apple from browning and thus retain good colour and taste.
5. When all the apples are in the bucket, stir in pectin enzyme, nutrient and tannin (if used) and the actively working yeast.
6. Then if possible keep the apple submerged continuously with block of wood or similar. A little difficult, but not impossible. This keeps the apples from the air thus continuing their retention of colour and taste.

156

7. Each day, on two or three occasions, squeeze the apples by hand. After two or three days, they will be quite soft, and are then ready for straining off.

8. Quickly separate the bulk of the apple pulp from the juice by pouring through a plastic or aluminium colander. Then re-strain through finely meshed cloth, sheeting being ideal. Be sure to remove the maximum of solids from the juice.

9. To this add the sugar, already dissolved in about 2 pints of cold boiled water to make a syrup, stir well to mix, pour into a one gallon glass fermenting vessel, top up with cold boiled water, fit an airlock and allow to ferment to dryness at a fairly constant temperature, ideally 65° to 75°F. This should take no longer than 3 weeks. The time taken depends upon temperature and care with which must* has been prepared. Proceed now as for Gooseberry wine, from Paragraph 5.

## TO MAKE SPARKLING WINE FROM BASIC WINE
NOTES

1. The wine **must** be quite dry, finished working and clear before proceeding.

For maximum safeguard, new-comers might invest in a Sugar Test Kit, obtainable from chemists and some home wine-making stockists. This will indicate the presence of inverted sugar in the finished basic wine, which is a guide additional to the hydrometer and your sense of taste. As this test will not indicate the presence of ordinary white sugar, care should be taken that none has been added to the basic wine after fermentation has finished. This should not normally apply as the sugar is added at the beginning of the fermentation, and this will automatically "invert" in the course of fermentation.

2. You **must** use proper Champagne-type bottles, in good con-dition without scratches or defects. All scratches and defects weaken the bottle, as will the scratch of a glass cutter on sheet glass. Thus great care should be taken in removing the label, and other decorations, and plastic tools are recommended for doing this as opposed to any metal scrapers. Champagne bottles are originally made to withstand about 80 lbs. per square inch pressure from within. It is not advisable to go to this pressure with second-hand bottles, or with "home-made" expertise. Consequently the syrup used in the secondary fermentation process gives some 40 to 43 lbs. pressure per square inch and this should not be exceeded.

3. You **must** use the proper form of closing the bottle. Get plastic Champagne-type stoppers and the wires from home wine-making stockists.

4. **Do not** attempt to make the wine stronger alcoholically. Either it will not "sparkle" in the bottle, or probably sparkle too much, causing the bottle to explode.

5. Before you start, it is as well to decide where the bottles will be stored for the duration of the secondary fermentation and mat-uration. If you are prepared to drink the wine without removing the sediment, store the bottles upright for the period of second-ary fermentation and maturation. If you prefer the sediment re-moved obtain a bottle carton in which wine merchants normally receive their bottles and put the filled bottles in upside-down. (See page 159†).

When basic wines requiring long maturation are used for sparkling wine it may be preferable to store the bottles on their sides. This can in fact be done for all wines. When they are ready to drink stand them upright—or upside-down, as des-cribed above, but allow time for the sediment to re-settle before opening the bottles.

*See page 150.

157

**For 1 gallon**

6 Champagne-type bottles
6 plastic Champagne-type stoppers
6 or 7 Champagne-type wires to secure stoppers
*1 gallon suitable wine, already tested for residual sugar and found to be satisfactory*
*6 fl. oz. sugar syrup made with 1½ oz. sugar dissolved in boiling water and allowed to cool*
*6 fl. oz. active yeast starter, using for preference a liquid Champagne yeast culture*
*Campden tablets*

1. 48 hours in advance make the yeast starter. Follow the instructions provided with the culture or those on page 150 but use only sufficient water to bring total quantity of starter up to 6 fl. oz.
2. Soak the bottles overnight in a detergent solution, remove all the labels etc. then rinse the inside of the bottle in a sulphite solution (2 Campden tablets per gallon) then rinse the bottle very well to remove all traces of sulphite.
3. Now, assemble the six bottles on the floor beneath the one gallon jar of selected wine. Carefully syphon the clear wine into the bottles, filling each to a level not only to leave sufficient room in each for the syrup and yeast (2 fl. oz.) but also to leave about an inch of air space. (A test run with ordinary water beforehand will establish this level quite easily.)
4. Now add to each bottle 1 fl. oz. of the syrup and 1 fl. oz. of the active yeast starter. These measurements must be exact.
5. Drive home the plastic stopper and seal in with the Champagne wires, making sure that the wires engage in the grooves provided in the stoppers. Tighten each wire securely, making sure that it has engaged under the lip of the bottle.
6. Shake the bottle well so as to distribute the syrup uniformly throughout the contents. Now set aside ideally in a temperature of say 65°F., either standing upright or upside down in a carton. or lying down. (See note 5, page 112). If space at this temperature is not available either one can leave the making of such wine until the warmer weather, or make allowances for the fact that little is likely to happen in the bottle whilst the temperature is much below this. Thus the wine can be bottled, syruped and yeasted during the cooler months, but no fermentation will take place in bottle until milder temperatures prevail which will allow the yeast in the bottle to work.

Having satisfactorily fulfilled these conditions, that the yeast has done, or is doing its work can be seen from the fact that the wire retaining the stopper has become strained, and the stopper tends to protrude under the force, and/or, on carefully lifting the bottle a deposit, perhaps quite slight, can be seen. Should this be so, then all is proceeding well. It is difficult to say how long this will be, but easier to say that if after 6 months no such developments look as though they have taken place, then a test bottle can be opened to find out. (How to open bottles is described later.) A failure can develop through there being too much alcohol in the basic wine, or the yeast not being properly active.

7. When it can be seen that the progress described above has taken place, the bottles should be transferred to a cooler place for maturation. Long maturation is not necessarily desirable, and the lighter the wine, the quicker it can be drunk, even to the point of no maturation at all. Sparkling wine based on the Elderflower, Gooseberry, White Currant and Apple recipes given here will be delicious if drunk as soon as the secondary fermentation is complete.

It must be understood that each bottle if well made now has a sparkling interior together with an undesirable sediment, consisting mostly of dead yeast cells. A decision has therefore to be made as to whether you want to drink the wine without first removing the sediment and risk any cloudiness, or whether first to disgorge the sediment and be sure of drinking the wine bright.

At this point it is useful too, to know that the colder the wine is then the less the pressure at the time of opening the bottle.

**To drink without removing the sediment**

The bottles should have been standing in an upright position. Thus all the sediment will have formed around the punt at the base of the bottle.

To get the best from this:

(a) Lift the bottle without tipping into the refrigerator and cool it down to the lowest temperature you can. (Not in a home freezer).

(b) Then with one hand carefully tip the bottle to the horizontal position without disturbing the sediment. Point the stopper to the interior of a plastic bucket previously laid in a semi-horizontal position.

(c) Deftly undo or cut the wires. In all probability, the stopper will blow out gently into the bucket, with slight frothing of the contents.

(d) With slight manual dexterity, pour the whole of the bottle into the waiting glasses, without ever tipping the bottle back which would disturb the sediment.

If the glasses are also cool, there will be little frothing in the glasses, which aids for a straight pour. You should get some 5 to 7 glasses from each bottle.

†**To drink after removing the sediment**

The bottles have stood upside-down. In this way the sediment will have accumulated in the hollow of the stopper.

(a) Without tipping the bottle from its upside-down position, put it in the refrigerator and cool it down to the lowest temperature you can. This can be a little difficult. It will be easier if you have a home freezer. Place the inverted bottle in the freezer propped up in some suitable manner. Leave it there for half an hour. During this time, the sediment in the stopper will freeze up with the liquid in the stopper, and thus facilitate easy removal.

(b) Withdraw the bottle from the freezer (using gloves as the bottle will be very cold), slowly turn it to the horizontal, pointing the stopper to a bucket previously laid in a semi-horizontal position.

(c) Cut or remove the wire cage. The stopper will blow out or may be eased out gently and the sediment with it.

(d) The contents can then be poured without worry one or two glasses at a time.

Always keep sparkling wine in a cool place when it has finished working in the bottle, and always serve it cool.

Red wine can be made sparkling, but it seems less desirable than white or rosé. This is possibly due to the extra tannin content of the wine.

**Further reading**

Making Sparkling Wines, by Cyril Lucus. Published by Mills and Boon.

How To Make Wines With A Sparkle, by J. Restall & D. Hebbs. Published by Amateur Winemaker.

**YEAST STARTER**

**Suitable for the 2 wines and the mead recipes which follow.**

**Should be made at least 48 hours before you start the wine or mead.**
*6 fluid oz. water*

1 dessertspoon malt extract
1 dessertspoon sugar
¼ teaspoon citric acid
Yeast

**Note:** Use the type of yeast recommended in the recipe.

1. Put water, malt extract, sugar and citric acid in a pan, bring to boil and boil 15 minutes.

2. Cool this solution as rapidly as possible, then pour into a clean sterile 10 oz. (½ pint) bottle. Plug the neck of the bottle with cotton wool and cool to below 70°F.

3. If using a liquid yeast culture, shake the phial containing the yeast, then add to the cool malt solution. Tablets are added straight to the cool malt solution. Replace plug of cotton wool and leave in a warm place.

4. The yeast will be fermenting vigorously in 48 hours. Then the wine may be made.

## DRY SHERRY-TYPE WINE
### To be made in early Spring
### For 1 gallon
*Sherry yeast in starter form, see page 159*
*1 gallon birch sap*
*1 lb. sultanas, washed and cut or minced*
*6 oz. dried bananas, washed and cut or minced*
*2 lb. 10 oz. sugar*
*1 teaspoon tartaric acid*
*1 level teaspoon grape tannin*
*1 teaspoon yeast nutrient*
*¼ teaspoon yeast energiser*
*Polish spirit or vodka to fortify the wine after fermentation*
*A few drops per bottle of sherry essence when bottling*

**Birch sap** is collected in early Spring when the sap is rising in the trees and the buds have not yet burst into leaf. It is obtained by drilling a small hole inclined upwards into the tree for about 1½ inches. It is best to drill the hole about 2 feet from ground level. A rubber tube, the same size as the drill used, is then inserted in the tree and the sap is allowed to drip into a gallon jar. Only mature trees of at least 10 inches girth should be tapped and care should be taken to knock a wood plug into the drilled hole after tapping is finished to prevent further bleeding and damage to the tree.

1. When 1 gallon of birch sap has been collected it should be brought slowly to the boil and simmered for 15 minutes, to ensure sterility.

2. Then pour on to the washed and minced sultanas and bananas in a clean sterile bin. Stir in sugar.

3. When cold add acid, tannin, nutrient, energiser and actively-working yeast.

4. Ferment on the pulp for 4 to 5 days, then carefully strain into a clean sterile gallon jar and fit airlock.

5. Allow all ferment to complete. Then rack* into another jar, avoiding disturbance of the lees*. Re-fit airlock.

6. After 3 months the wine should be clear. Rack it once again and fortify to taste with Polish Spirit and sherry essence.

7. The wine may now be bottled and will mature in bottle for a number of years, but will be fit to drink within 12 months.

**By courtesy of
Mr. Alan Greenwood,
Bradford.**

## BLACKBERRY AND APPLE WINE
### Red Table Wine
### For 1 gallon
*Burgundy or Bordeaux yeast in starter form, see page 159*
*5 lb. apples*
*3 lb. blackberries*
*1 lb. elderberries*
*8 oz. sultanas or raisins*
*4 oz. dried bananas*
*Water to 1 gallon*
*Sugar to adjust to gravity of 1.080*
*Pectic enzyme, use quantity*

*See page 151.

*indicated by manufacturer*
*1 teaspoon yeast nutrient*
*¼ teaspoon yeast energiser*
1. Wash apples, pulp them and press out juice. Place juice only in a clean sterile bin.
2. Wash blackberries and elderberries, pulp or squash them and add both pulp and juice to apple juice.
3. Wash and mince sultanas and dried bananas and add to bulk in bin.
4. Make volume in bin up to 1 gallon with boiling water.
5. When cold, strain out sufficient juice to take specific gravity and adjust bulk with sugar to a specific gravity of 1.080.
A useful tip is that 1 lb. sugar dissolved in 1 gallon water will raise gravity by 37°.
For example: if the sample of juice reads 1.025 this means that it is desired to raise the gravity by 55° to 1.080, so 1½ lb. sugar would have to be added.
6. Now stir in all other ingredients including active yeast starter and ferment on the pulp for 3 to 4 days.
7. Strain carefully, without squeezing pulp, into a gallon jar, top up with cold boiled water, fit airlock and ferment out to dryness. The final gravity should be .990 or below.
8. Rack* into a clean sterile jar, avoiding lees*, add 1 Campden tablet, re-fit airlock.
9. Leave to mature for at least 12 months, racking every 4 months if a deposit forms.
10. The wine should now be bottled and allowed to mature at least a further 6 months in bottle.
**Alan Briggs,**
**Batley, Yorkshire.**

## SWEET MEAD
**For 1 gallon**
*Mead yeast in starter form see page 159*
*2 lb. heather honey*
*1 lb. clover honey*
*Water to 1 gallon*
*1 teaspoon yeast nutrient*
*¼ teaspoon yeast energiser*
*1 vitamin B1 tablet, 3 mgm size*
*½ oz. malic acid*
*¼ oz. tartaric acid*
*½ teaspoon grape tannin*
**For sweetening after fermentation**
*8 oz. demerara sugar*
1. Dissolve the honies in about 2 pints of water and bring up to a temperature of 140°F. Hold at this temperature for half an hour to pasteurise the honies.
All honies are high in their content of wild yeasts, bacterias, moulds etc. which must be destroyed before fermentation begins otherwise strange off-flavours may develop in the mead.
2. After pasteurisation, pour honey into clean sterile bin, making up to 1 gallon with cold boiled water. Cover the bin with towels or fit lid.
3. When cold add all the other ingredients, except demerara sugar, and ferment in bin for 4 to 5 days.
4. Transfer into gallon jar, fit airlock, keep at a temperature of about 75°F. until all ferment ceases.
5. Then dissolve the demerara sugar in as small a volume of water as possible, bring to the boil and boil for 10 minutes.
6. Cool this sugar-solution as quickly as possible, pour into a clean, sterile jar and rack the mead on to this sugar syrup. Avoid disturbing lees* at bottom of jar. If the now-racked mead does not fill gallon jar, top up with cold boiled water, re-fit airlock.
Further fermentation may take place, but this can only increase the alcoholic strength.
7. The mead should be racked every 4 months if a heavy deposit forms on bottom of jar, then again topped up with cold boiled water. It may take up to 2 years for the mead to become star-bright, but mead should be matured for a

long period—up to 4 years when using heather honey.

Other flower honies may be used but it is recommended not to use Australian honies which may contain eucalyptus honey.

**By courtesy of**
**Mr. Alfred Francis Buckley,**
**Dewsbury, Yorkshire.**

## SWEET ORANGE WINE
1 gallon

**First make a yeast starter** at least 48 hours before you make the wine.

**Yeast Starter:**
*6 fluid oz. water*
*1 dessertspoon malt extract*
*1 dessertspoon sugar*
*¼ teaspoon citric acid*
*Sauterne yeast*

1. Put water, malt extract, sugar and citric acid in a pan, bring to boil and boil 15 minutes.
2. Cool this solution as rapidly as possible, then pour into a clean sterile 10 oz. (½ pint) bottle. Plug the neck of the bottle with cotton wool and cool to below 70°F.
3. If using a liquid yeast culture, shake the phial containing the yeast, then add to the cool malt solution. Tablets are added straight to the cool malt solution. Replace plug of cotton wool and leave in a warm place.
4. The yeast will be fermenting vigorously in 48 hours. Then the wine may be made.

**The Wine:**
*4 lb. oranges*
*1 lb. raisins*
*3 lb. sugar*
*1 teaspoon yeast nutrient*
*½ teaspoon yeast energiser*
*Pinch of grape tannin*
*2 Weetabix or Shredded Wheat*
*Cold boiled water*
*1 Campden tablet*

1. Wash the oranges, squeeze them and place juice in a sterilized fermenting vessel, a 2 gallon plastic bucket is ideal.
2. Take the skins of half the number of oranges used, remove all the white pith, then roast the skins in the oven at Gas 3, 325°F. until they are crisp and brown, about 25 to 30 minutes.
3. Meanwhile, wash and mince the raisins.
4. Add the roasted orange skins to the fermenting vessel with the raisins, sugar, yeast nutrient and energiser, tannin, Weetabix or Shredded Wheat and the yeast starter, adding cold boiled water until the volume reaches 1 gallon.
5. Cover the fermenting vessel loosely and ferment on the pulp for 48 hours at room temperature (maximum 75°F.), stirring twice daily.
6. Strain carefully into a sterilised 1 gallon jar, fit airlock and leave at room temperature (maximum 75°F.) to allow fermentation to complete, topping up jar with cold boiled water after 7 days if necessary. Fermentation will take 6 to 8 weeks but this depends on temperature.
7. When all fermentation has finished, rack, i.e. syphon, wine into another sterile jar, avoiding disturbing the lees, which is the dead yeast and debris at bottom of jar.
8. Add 1 crushed Campden tablet and top up jar again with either cold, boiled water or sugar syrup if wine is not sweet enough.
9. Leave until brilliantly clear, racking again within 4 months if a heavy deposit forms.
10. Leave to mature at least 9 months when the wine will be ready for drinking.

## BEER
**Sterilisation** of all brewing equipment before use is essential. If articles cannot be boiled, wash first with detergent or household bleach and rinse in cold tap water. Then rinse in a solution of sodium metabisulphite. Finally rinse well

in cold tap water. If your water supply is chlorinated it should be well boiled before the final rinse.

## MILD BEER – (4 gallons)

*2½ lb. malt extract; 1 lb. dark, dried malt extract; ½ lb. crystal malt; 4 oz. roasted barley or black malt; 1 lb. soft brown sugar; 2 oz. hops, recommend Fuggles; water to 4 gallons; top fermenting beer yeast. Castor sugar for priming. Original gravity 1.038.*

## LIGHT BITTER BEER –
(4 gallons)

*3 lb. malt extract; 1 lb. crystal malt; 1 lb. glucose chippings; 3 oz. hops, recommend 2 oz. Golding type, 1 oz. Fuggles; water to 4 gallons; top fermenting beer yeast. Castor sugar for priming. Original gravity 1.032.*

**The method for brewing the above beers is the same.**

1. Boil all ingredients, except the yeast and priming sugar, in 2 gallons water for at least 1 hour. If a 2 gallon container is not available use a minimum of 1 gallon water but take care that the sugar or glucose chips do not stick.
2. Strain into fermenting vessel through fine muslin or similar.
3. Wash the grains and hops by pouring cold water through, preferably boiled first, until volume in fermenting vessel reaches 4 gallons.
4. When cold, below 70°F, pitch with a top fermenting beer yeast and cover brew with lid or towels to exclude dust, flies, bacterias, etc.
5. Ferment 4 or 5 days, at room temperature, skimming froth from surface after first 24 hours.

6. Skim again then rack (i.e. syphon off leaving sediment behind) into closed container (gallon jars may be used), fit airlock. Leave further 7 days to allow ferment to finish and to allow yeast to settle.
7. Bottle into beer bottles priming each 1 pint with ½ teaspoon castor sugar. Screw stoppers in tightly or fit crown corks to ensure bottles are thoroughly sealed.
8. Leave at room temperature for 7 days, then leave to mature for at least 14 days.

## EXPORT PALE ALE

*Water treatment, if required:
either proprietory brand,
or,    1 teaspoon Gypsum
          1 teaspoon Epsom Salts
          1 teaspoon salt
4 gallons water; 6 lb. crushed pale malt; 4 oz. crushed crystal malt; 4 oz. flaked maize; 4 oz. wheat flour.
2½ to 3 oz. Goldings hops; 9 oz. glucose chips; 4 oz. soft brown sugar; Carragheen Irish Moss (use quantity indicated on packet); top fermenting beer yeast; castor sugar for priming bottles*

1. Heat 2½ gallons water to 165°F.
2. Dissolve in this the water treatment, if used.
3. Add crushed pale malt, crushed crystal malt, flaked maize, and wheat flour. It is best to cream the wheat flour with cold water before adding, to avoid lumps.
4. The temperature will now have dropped to 150°F., and this temperature should now be maintained, as near as possible, for two hours during which time saccharification of the starch takes place.
5. At the end of two hours strain sweet liquid (wort) off the grain and sparge* with water at 170°F until volume reaches four gallons.

*See page 164.

6. Return all liquid to boiler or pan and bring to the boil. Boil until frothing ceases and then add the hops, glucose chips and soft brown sugar. Boil for 1½ hours, adding Carragheen Irish Moss 10 minutes from end of boil. Switch off heat. The volume will now be about three gallons.

7. Allow hops to sink to bottom of boiler, or remove bag of hops if they have been boiled in a muslin bag. Cool to about 180°F then drain off into fermenting vessel.

8. Make up volume of wort in fermenting vessel to 4 gallons with cold water. Cool as rapidly as possible to 70°F.

9. Pitch yeast. Skim after 12 hours. Stir. Leave at room temperature for about 5 days or until a hydrometer reading reaches a gravity of 1.010. Then skim off yeast head. Syphon into containers such as one gallon jars fitted with corks and airlocks. Leave seven days, then bottle, priming with ½ teaspoon castor sugar to each pint bottle.

10. Leave in a warm place for seven days. Then store in a cool place for at least six weeks.

**\*Sparge.**
**To spray or wash with water at a given temperature.**


**BARLEY WINE**
**(2 gallons)**
*2½ lb. malt extract; 1 lb. crystal malt; 1½ oz. roasted barley or chocolate malt; 1 lb. glucose chipping; 1½ lb. soft brown sugar; 4 oz. soluble dextrin (or glucose polymer); 2½ oz. hops, recommend 2 oz. Fuggles, ½ oz. Northern Brewers; water to 2 gallons; top fermenting beer yeast AND general purpose yeast.*
*Original Gravity 1,085*

1. Boil all ingredients, except the yeasts, in 2 gallons water for at least 1 hour. If a 2 gallon container is not available use a minimum of 1 gallon water but take care that the sugar or glucose chips do not stick.

2. Strain into fermenting vessel through muslin or similar.

3. Wash the grains and hops with cold boiled water until volume reaches 2 gallons.

4. When cold, below 70°F, take out ½ gallon and pitch with general purpose yeast and add the top fermenting beer yeast to the other 1½ gallons, cover both brews.

5. Ferment for 5 days, at room temperature. Skim froth from surface after first 24 hours and again after 5 days.

6. Now blend both fermenting brews together, rack into two 1 gallon jars, fit airlocks. Keep at room temperature, allow ferment to continue until finished. This may take as long as 6 weeks.

DO NOT bottle whilst the beer is still fermenting.

7. When all ferment has finished, bottle in ½ pint or nip bottles, adding NO priming sugar.

8. Store for at least 6 months and drink with caution. It is very potent.


**DRY STOUT**
2 gallons.
**First make a yeast starter** at least 48 hours before you start the main brew.
**Yeast Starter**
*6 fluid oz. water*
*1 dessertspoon malt extract*
*1 dessertspoon sugar*
*¼ teaspoon citric acid*
*Stout yeast*

1. To the water add malt extract, sugar and citric acid. Then bring to the boil and boil for 15 minutes.

2. Cool this solution as rapidly as possible, then pour into a clean

sterile 10 oz. (½ pint) bottle. Plug the neck of the bottle with cotton wool and cool to below a temperature of 70°F.

3. If using a liquid yeast culture, shake the phial containing the yeast, then add to the cool malt solution. Tablets are added straight to the cool malt solution. Replace plug of cotton wool and leave in a warm place.

4. The yeast will be fermenting vigorously in 48 hours. Then the stout may be made.

### The Stout
*1½ lb. dried malt extract*
*8 oz. barley syrup*
*5 oz. roasted barley*
*3 oz. soluble dextrin (glucose polymer)*
*2 oz. Fuggle hops*
*Water to 2 gallons*

### For priming bottles
*Castor sugar*
1. Boil all stout ingredients in water for at least 1 hour.
2. Strain into sterilised* fermenting vessel (a 2½ gallon plastic bucket is ideal) through muslin or similar.
3. Make up to 2 gallons with cold boiled water and allow to cool to below 70°F.
4. Then add activated yeast, cover brew loosely to keep out dust and bacteria and ferment 5 days at room temperature, skimming froth from top as necessary.
6. Rack or syphon into sterilised gallon jars, fit airlocks and allow to ferment out (about 5 to 10 days).
7. Rack or syphon into beer bottles, adding ½ teaspoon castor sugar per 1 pint bottle.
8. Leave at room temperature for 7 days, then store in a cool place for at least 4 weeks.
This stout can be used for Christmas puddings 2 or 3 weeks before it is ready to drink.

***Sterilising** agents may be bought from home-brewing and wine making shops and from chemists. Household bleach is effective.

Always rinse articles well after using sterilising solution.

## HOME-BREWED LAGER
2 gallons
**First make a Yeast Starter** at least 48 hours before you start the main brew.
### Yeast Starter
*6 fluid oz. water*
*1 dessertspoon malt extract*
*1 dessertspoon sugar*
*¼ teaspoon citric acid*
*A lager yeast, either liquid culture, tablets or granules*
1. To the water add malt extract, sugar and citric acid. Then bring to the boil and boil for 15 minutes.
2. Cool this solution as rapidly as possible, then pour into a clean sterile 10 oz. (½ pint) bottle. Plug the neck of the bottle with cotton wool and cool to below a temperature of 70°F.
3. If using a liquid yeast culture, shake the phial containing the yeast, then add to the sterile malt solution. Replace plug of cotton wool and leave in a warm place. Tablets or granular yeast are added straight to the cool malt solution.
4. The yeast will be fermenting vigorously in 48 hours. Then the main brew may be made.
### The Main Brew
*1½ lb. light dried malt extract*
*1 lb. brewing sugar or white invert sugar*
*1 oz. Hallertauer hops*
*½ teaspoon ground Irish Moss*
*Lager yeast starter*
*Water*
*Campden powder (for sterilisation)*
*Castor sugar (for priming)*

### Note:
(i) Sterilisation of all brewing equipment before use is essential. If articles cannot be boiled, wash first with detergent or household bleach and rinse with cold water. Then rinse in a solution of meta-

bisulphite (Campden powder) finally rinsing with cold boiled water. A Campden solution can be kept in a stoppered bottle and used repeatedly for quite some time:— Dissolve 1½ oz. Campden powder in 1 quart water.

(ii) The water for brewing should be soft and not chlorinated. To correct this it should be preboiled.

1. Boil malt extract, brewing sugar and hops in 1½ gallons water for 1 hour. If a 1½ gallon container is not available use a minimum of 1 gallon but take care the sugar and malt used do not stick. Add the Irish Moss for the last 15 minutes of the boil.

2. Strain into a sterile fermenting vessel through muslin or similar.

3. "Wash" the hops etc. by pouring through them cold water (preferably previously boiled). In this way, bring volume in fermenting vessel up to 2 gallons.

4. Allow to cool to below 70°F. and then add the active lager yeast and stir. Then cover the brew with a lid or towel to exclude dust, bacterias etc.

5. Ferment in this vessel for 4 or 5 days at room temperature. Skim the froth from the surface after the first 24 hours.

6. After 5 days skim the surface again if necessary, then syphon the brew into 2 one gallon jars. Fit airlocks. Leave for a further 7 to 10 days to allow ferment to finish and yeast to settle.

7. Bottle into beer bottles, priming each bottle with half a teaspoon of castor sugar per 1 pint bottle. OR: If you can get a 2 gallon plastic barrel the beer may be stored in bulk.
(a) Dissolve 2¼ oz. castor sugar in a very little water.
(b) Put this priming solution into the barrel.
(c) Syphon in the beer and fix the bung securely.

8. Leave at room temperature for 7 days then remove to a cool place to clear and condition. This will take approximately 4 to 6 weeks.

Lager can be used with good results in cooking. See Lager Loaf on page 104 and Lager Pancakes on page 22.

## STRONG OR OLD ALE
### To be drunk in small quantities
### For 3 gallons
*Water to 3 gallons*
*6 lb. crushed pale malt*
*6 oz. crystal malt (crushed)*
*1 lb. flaked barley*
*1 lb. barley syrup (or maize or wheat syrup)*
*1 lb. glucose chips*
*9 oz. soluble dextrin*
*12 oz. soft brown sugar*
*1 oz. Kent Golding hops*
*1 oz. Northern Brewer hops*
*½ oz. Bullion hops*
*General purpose yeast*

### For priming bottles
*Castor sugar*

1. Heat 2 gallons water to 165°F.

2. Stir in pale malt, crystal malt and flaked barley. The temperature will now have dropped to 150°F. and this temperature should be kept steady for 1½ hours.

3. Now strain out the sweet wort and wash grains with water at 170°F. until volume collected is 3 gallons.

4. Bring this 3 gallons to the boil and boil vigorously for half an hour. Then add all other ingredients, except yeast, and boil vigorously for a further 1 hour.

5. Strain out the hops, make up to 3 gallons with boiled water and cool as quickly as possible.

6. When below 70°F. add yeast and ferment 7 days in fermenting bin which should be kept covered at all times.

7. Then transfer to gallon jars, fit airlocks, and leave till all fermentation ceases.

8. Then bottle, adding priming sugar at the rate of ½ teaspoon per pint bottle.
9. Mature in bottle for at least 3 months before drinking.
The starting gravity will be 1.076 to 1.080, giving about 9° alcohol so the beer should be sipped rather than quaffed.

**Alan Briggs,
Batley, Yorkshire.**

## HONEY BEER FOR HARVEST
*½ oz. or 1 cup hops*
*8 oz. honey or sugar*
*1 gallon water*
*1 teaspoon granulated yeast*
*(baker's will do) or*
*1 tablespoon fresh brewer's yeast*
1. Boil hops and honey or sugar for 1 hour in a large pan with as much of the water as possible.
2. Strain into a plastic bucket and make up to 1 gallon with cold water. Allow to cool to 70°F.
3. Add granulated yeast, or float a slice of toast spread with brewer's yeast.
4. Cover closely and leave in a warm place for 48 hours.
5. Syphon off, without disturbing yeast deposit, into a 1 gallon jar or flagons.
6. Stand in a cool place for a week when it will be ready to drink. Tie the corks down if keeping it longer than a week.

**Mrs. H. Lawson,
West Suffolk.**

## POP
## GINGER BEER
*18 oz. sugar; 2 level tablespoons ground ginger; 2 level tablespoons dried baking yeast; juice of 2 lemons; 16 pints water.*
1. Dissolve (but do not boil) the sugar in a saucepan containing a little of the water.
2. Meanwhile clean a plastic bucket thoroughly, sterilise it with household bleach and rinse thoroughly. Put the rest of the water in the bucket.
3. Add the ginger, yeast, lemon juice and sugar solution and stir.
4. Cover bucket and let it stand in a warm place to ferment for one week.
5. After one week prepare bottles and stoppers (preferably beer, cider or pop bottles with inserted screw stoppers), sterilise with household bleach and rinse well.
6. Bottle the ginger beer with a jug or syphon tubing leaving as much of the scum and sediment behind as possible.
7. Add ½ teaspoon sugar to each pint bottle or 1 teaspoon sugar to each quart.
8. Screw stoppers tightly into bottles and leave for one more week. The ginger beer will then be ready to drink.

## GINGER BEER
Two drinks from a ginger beer plant.
**Ginger beer plant**
*½ oz. general purpose dried yeast*
*½ pt. water*
*Sugar*
*Ground ginger*
*Juice of 2 lemons*
1. Put yeast into a jar, add water, 2 level teaspoons sugar, 2 level teaspoons ginger and mix together.
2. Cover jar with a sheet of polythene kept in place with a rubber band.
3. Each day, for 7 days, add 1 level teaspoon sugar and 1 level teaspoon ginger.
4. Now strain the mixture through a piece of fine muslin and add the lemon juice to the liquid.
The ginger beer may now be made, either as a sweet, still drink or dry and sparkling. **It is important,** however, to follow the instructions carefully so that there is no risk of bursting bottles and flying glass.

## Sweet still ginger beer

*Prepared ginger beer plant*
*1 lb. sugar*
*1 pt. boiling water*

1. Put all in a saucepan. Stir until sugar is dissolved
2. Bring to boil and simmer 5 minutes to ensure that yeast is killed.
3. Make up to 1 gallon with cold water.
4. Bottle the ginger beer, cork tightly. Keep for a few days before drinking.

## Dry sparkling ginger beer

*Prepared ginger beer plant*
*2 oz. sugar*
*Water*

1. Add sugar to ginger beer plant and make up to 1 gallon with cold water, stirring to dissolve sugar.
2. Bottle into screw-stoppered cider, beer or pop bottles. Screw in stoppers tightly. Keep for 7 to 10 days when the ginger beer is sparkling and ready for drinking.
**Note:** Keep the sediment you have left after straining the ginger beer plant. Divide it into 2 jars and give 1 plant away to a friend. To the sediment add $\frac{1}{2}$ pt. water, 2 level teaspoons sugar, 2 level teaspoons ginger and carry on as before.

## LEMONADE

*8 large lemons; 8 oz. castor sugar;*
*4 pts. boiling water.*

1. Wash and dry lemons.
2. Peel off lemon peel very thinly with potato peeler.
3. Squeeze juice from lemons and put in covered plastic container in refrigerator.
4. Put peel in large bowl or jug with sugar.
5. Pour over boiling water, stir briskly, cover and leave overnight in cool place.
6. Next day add reserved lemon juice. Strain into jugs and chill.
Makes about 16 glasses.

# INDEX

172

## W

Warwickshire Chocolate
  Biscuits 98
Wassail 153
Watercress & Orange Salad
  with Soused Herrings 12
Welsh Rarebit 17
White Bread 88
White Currant Wine 155
Whole meal Bread, Janet's
  Quick 90
Wholemeal Bread Quick 92
Wholemeal Scones 97
Wholewheat Gingerbread 95

**Wine**
  Apple, for Sparkling Wine 156
  Barley, see Beer 164
  Bilberry, Dry Red 151
  Bilberry, Sweet Dessert 151
  Blackberry & Apple 160
  Dry Sherry Type 160
  Elderflower, for Sparkling
    Wine 153
  Gooseberry, for Sparkling
    Wine 154
  Hock-Type Gooseberry 150
  Mulled 153
  Sparkling 153
  Sweet Mead 161
  Sweet Orange 162
  White Currant, for
    Sparkling Wine 155
Wood Pigeon Casserole 51
Wood Pigeon Thatched House
  Pie 37

## Y

**Yeast Cookery**
  Aberdeen Butteries 114
  Apricot & Walnut Twist 89

  Bread Buns 88
  Bread Sticks 88
  Bun Loaf 107
  Cheese Loaf 115
  Chelsea Buns 107
  Cottage Loaf 88
  Devonshire Splits 88
  Doughnuts 100
  Hot Cross Buns 107
  Janet's Quick Wholemeal
    Bread 90
  Lardy Cake 89, 111
  Mary Berry's Savoury Tart 89
  Muffins 88
  Oatcakes 89
  Old Fashioned Spice Bread 115
  Oxford Lardy Cake 111
  Quick Wholemeal Bread 92
  Rhum Baba 92
  Rich Bread Dough 91
  Sally Lunn 107
  Savarin 92
  Staffordshire Oatcakes 113
  Sultana Loaf 89
  Swiss Buns 88
  Tea Cakes 89
  White Bread 88
  Wholemeal Bread 90, 92
Yeast Starters 150, 159
Yeast Starter for Beer 165
Yeomanry Pudding
  Staffordshire 41
Yorkshire Cheese Cake or
  Curd Tart 31
Yorkshire Parkin 94
Yorkshire Puddings 65
Yorkshire Salad 12

# NOTES

# NOTES

# NOTES

**NOTES**

# NOTES

**NOTES**

# NOTES

**NOTES**

**NOTES**